"*Baja Camping* should rank as the top priority source of information for those who are going to Baja for the first time as well as those travelers who are veterans of the Baja traveling society. The book is a 'must' buy for anyone planning to tent, car camp, or RV through Baja."

—*The Fish Sniffer*

"If you think you'll ever journey off into Baja for the camping trip of a lifetime, you'll want to take along a copy of this thorough guide that's filled with user-friendly information."

—*Family Travel Log*

"*Baja Camping* not only lives up to the claim of 'going the extra mile,' it exceeds it by leaps and bounds."

—*Gazette-Enterprize* (Seguin, TX)

"Whether looking for bustling coastal towns like La Paz and Cabo San Lucas, or your own private beach cove, *Baja Camping* has the ideal campsite for you. For anyone planning to visit Baja, *Baja Camping* is indispensable. An impressive and highly recommended publication."

—*Motorhome Magazine*

"*Baja Camping* is a great book . . . read this book long before you take off for Baja."

—*Santa Barbara News*

"*Baja Camping* deserves a place on your bookshelf if you're at all interested in Baja California and like camping."

—*Victor Valley* (CA) *Daily Press*

To order individual books, visit the Foghorn Press Web site at www.foghorn.com, or call 1-800-FOGHORN (364-4676) or (707) 773-4260. Foghorn Press titles are distributed to the book trade by Publishers Group West, based in Emeryville, California. To contact your local sales representative, call 1-800-788-3123.

Library of Congress ISSN Data:
November 1997

Baja Camping
The Complete Guide to More Than 6,300 Campsites from the Border to Cabo San Lucas, Including 1,000 Miles of Beaches
Second Edition
ISSN: 1089-0939

Leave No Trace, Inc., is a program dedicated to maintaining the integrity of outdoor recreation areas through education and public awareness. Foghorn Press is a proud supporter of this program and its ethics.

The Foghorn Press Commitment

Foghorn Press is committed to the preservation of the environment. We promote Leave No Trace principles in our guidebooks.

Printed in the United States of America

BAJA CAMPING

The Complete Guide to More Than 6,300
Campsites from the Border to Cabo San Lucas,
Including 1,000 Miles of Beaches

Fred and Gloria Jones

Foghorn
Press

BOOKS BUILDING COMMUNITY™

ISBN 1-57354-013-7

9 781573 540131

5 1495

Editor in Chief Donna Leverenz

Editor Karin Mullen

Production Coordinator Kyle Morgan

Production Assistant Mark Aver

All interior photos were provided by Fred and Gloria Jones.

BAJA CAMPING

The Complete Guide to More Than 6,300
Campsites from the Border to Cabo San Lucas,
Including 1,000 Miles of Beaches

Fred and Gloria Jones

Foghorn
Press
BOOKS BUILDING COMMUNITY™

This book is dedicated to the Vagabundos del Mar Boat and Travel Club. Our involvement in the management of club affairs has given us access to thousands of Baja aficionados who fan out over the entire peninsula every year. With its sense of camaraderie and esprit de corps, the club has afforded all of us an opportunity to form lifelong and enriching relationships with great people who share a special common bond. The previously untapped body of knowledge that we gleaned from this group, along with our own extensive travels, has made this book possible. We also wish to recognize the continuing assistance of one particular Vagabundo—Richard Seleine. Each year, Richard contacts every campground in Baja. His frequent communiqués on changes are invaluable.

—*Fred and Gloria Jones*

Baja Chapter Reference Map

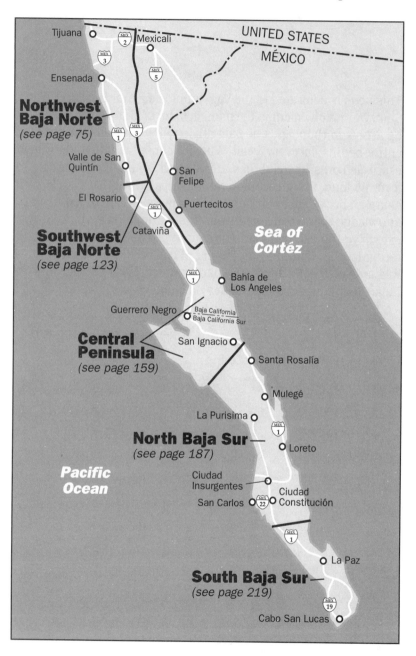

Tijuana

Mexicali

UNITED STATES

MÉXICO

Ensenada

Northwest Baja Norte
(see page 75)

Valle de San Quintín

San Felipe

El Rosario

Puertecitos

Southwest Baja Norte
(see page 123)

Cataviña

Bahía de Los Angeles

Sea of Cortéz

Guerrero Negro

Baja California
Baja California Sur

Central Peninsula
(see page 159)

San Ignacio

Santa Rosalía

Mulegé

La Purisima

North Baja Sur
(see page 187)

Loreto

Pacific Ocean

Ciudad Insurgentes

San Carlos

Ciudad Constitución

La Paz

South Baja Sur
(see page 219)

Cabo San Lucas

Baja Camping
The Complete Guide to More Than 6,300
Campsites from the Border to Cabo San Lucas,
Including 1,000 Miles of Beaches

Contents

Introduction

During our many years spent traveling up and down the Baja California Peninsula, living in tents and campers, we have paid close attention to available camping spots, as well as other aspects of road travel. Writing assignments from various magazines and our responsibilities in helping manage the Vagabundos del Mar Boat and Travel Club—particularly preparing the club's monthly newsletter, *Chubasco,* since 1988—have required it. We have had a continuing obligation to keep the thousands of members of Baja's oldest and largest travel club, and the multitude of people who read the magazines for which we have written, informed of all things related to Baja travel.

We have found the unbroken flow of written and verbal communications from individual Vagabundos, popularly known as "Vags," to be an extremely rich font of information. This, coupled with our personal inspection of campgrounds and beaches and our experiences on the road, constitutes the source of material for this book. We wish to share the knowledge we have gained ourselves, and that distilled from such a huge number of other Baja campers, with the wide audience this book will reach.

Camping on the beach is one of the great attractions for Baja travelers. The fascination with surf washing onto mile after mile of lovely white sand, the call of seabirds and the splashing of pelicans, the spicy salt-tinged ocean air, cool breezes, seclusion, and many other special attributes draw people from all over the world to these beaches. Many are accessible only to four-wheel-drive vehicles, while others may be reached by boat alone. Getting to some constitutes high adventure. We have included spots that are popular for camping and normally accessible by highway vehicles, including midsize motor homes and trailers. We also have listed the 10 best beaches for each of the five regional chapters, including some that are accessible only by off-road vehicle, boat, or foot. Information on backpacking and horsepacking trips into the mountains has been included as well.

Campgrounds for recreational vehicles in Baja come in all shapes and sizes. Some are dedicated solely to annual lessees (commonly referred to as "permanents") who have installed trailers or constructed other housing. Others have some permanents but cater to overnight travelers as well. Still others have no permanents and are geared entirely toward travelers. We have included only the campgrounds that are willing and able to accommodate transients in some way.

These campgrounds are in a continuing state of flux. New ones pop up and existing ones disappear as they are taken over for other types of development. Sometimes, the owners will fill their transient spaces with permanents or simply close the park altogether. Since tourist travel is seasonal, park owners are motivated to generate the dependable income that annual leases provide.

Keep in mind that road conditions in Baja change frequently. Heavy rainfall may wipe out a road temporarily or even permanently. Never go off the beaten path without checking locally on whether your particular vehicle is suitable for driving at that particular time. Nothing is more miserable than getting stuck or breaking down in a remote spot.

Be sure your maps and source materials are reliable and current. We have helped many weary, stuck travelers out of a jam, some due to navigating with bad maps. The most frazzled were a Canadian couple with the wheels of their motor home buried and its rear end hung up on the bank of an arroyo on the rough coast road between San José del Cabo and Los Frailes. The map they had brought from Canada showed that road as paved, which it possibly may be some day.

In Baja, there has always been an unwritten code—among locals and tourists alike—that you aid anyone in trouble. We have benefited from others' helping hands on several occasions. We hope in some way this book helps to keep the process going.

How to Use This Book

The Baja California Peninsula consists of two states. The northern state is officially known as Baja California, but since that is easily confused with the entire peninsula, it is commonly referred to by visitors and locals alike as Baja Norte. The southern state is Baja California Sur, a name shortened to Baja Sur by one and all. For greater detail, we have divided Baja Camping into five chapters: Northwest Baja Norte, Northeast Baja Norte, the Central Peninsula, North Baja Sur, and South Baja Sur. Maps at the beginning of each chapter show where the camping spots in that particular region are located.

For Northwest Baja Norte campgrounds:
see pages 75–122

For Northeast Baja Norte campgrounds:
see pages 123–158

For Central Peninsula campgrounds:
see pages 159–186

For North Baja Sur campgrounds:
see pages 187–218

For South Baja Sur campgrounds:
see pages 219–256

The chapters are further divided into areas that constitute natural clusters of campgrounds. At the beginning of each chapter there's a general description of these areas followed by the outdoor activities and points of historic and cultural interest that can be enjoyed there.

You can search for your ideal camping spot in two ways:

1. If you know the name of the specific campsite where you'd like to stay or the name of the surrounding geographical area or nearby feature (town, beach, bahía, punta, river, national park, etc.), look it up in the index beginning on page 271 and turn to the corresponding page. Page numbers for campgrounds featured in this book are listed in the index in boldface type.

2. To find a campground in a particular region of the peninsula, turn to the maps at the beginning of the appropriate chapter. You can identify entry numbers in the area where you would like to camp, then

refer to the chapter table of contents to find the page numbers for those campgrounds. For a list of map page numbers, refer to the Baja map on page 8 and at the end of the book.

See the bottom of every page for a reference to corresponding maps.

10 Best Beaches

At the end of each chapter, we have highlighted the 10 best beaches in the region. Some of these overlap with the general campground listings, while others are open solely for day use or are accessible only to hardy adventurers driving ATVs or motorcycles. You can easily locate these beaches on the map and within the chapter by looking for the sun symbol ⚓.

Distance Markers

In the directions to campgrounds and beaches, we often mention Kilometer such and such, referring to the numbered markers located along most stretches of highway in Baja. Some are white, round concrete posts, while others are narrow metal signs. All have black numbers painted vertically on them, with "Km." appearing at the top of most. Some are missing or difficult to see, but don't worry—you will spot another before long. These kilometer posts run sequentially between certain cities, from north to south in Baja Norte and from south to north in Baja Sur. Just keep track of whether the numbers are increasing or decreasing as you move along so you can determine if you are approaching your destination or have already passed it.

Ejidos

Some campground names are followed by the word "ejido" in parentheses. These were built by the federal government many years ago to accommodate tourists on the recently paved Highway 1. All were constructed on the same plan and were turned over to the local ejido (a government-supported agricultural cooperative) to operate and maintain as income-producing facilities. However, since nearly all of these parks are in remote areas, the people were unable to keep the electrical, water, and sewer systems in dependable operating condition. Several are currently open for camping, but they often lack services and facilities.

Security

Many campers are as concerned about security as they are about drinking water in Mexico. We have tried to ease their minds about both. In each campground description, we indentify those elements that discourage non-campers from wandering among the campsites[em dash]gates, fences, guards, and resident managers.

About Maps

The maps in this book are designed to show the general location of campgrounds and beaches, and are not meant to substitute for more detailed road maps. Readers are advised to carry additional maps on their travels, particularly when venturing into remote areas.

Campground Fees

Campground fee categories (moderate, high, etc.) are in a range based on fees in Baja.

Every effort has been made to ensure that the information in *Baja Camping* is as up-to-date as possible. However some details, especially prices, are subject to change.

Loreto is the home of Baja's oldest mission, "The Head and Mother of the Missions of Baja and Alta California."

Baja History

Baja History

The border between San Ysidro, California, and Tijuana, Baja California Norte, is the most frequently crossed in the world, with more than 100 million people passing through each year. It seems so much like an extension of California and the United States that visitors at first may not realize they have arrived in a foreign country. Indeed, at one time it all was part of one country, México. What follows is a brief history of the peninsula.

The Name

In a popular Spanish novel published in 1500, "California" was the name of an island of women warriors who armed themselves with gold weapons. Since the Baja Peninsula was originally thought to be an island full of gold, the use of the name California appears to have been inspired by the novel in a spasm of wishful thinking.

The Indians

Huge multicolored murals of Indians and animals exist in shallow caves in and above the deep, rugged canyons of Central Baja California. Their beauty, artistry, and mystery excite the imagination. The greatest concentration of cave murals is in the Sierra de San Francisco, north of San Ignacio. They also occur south through the Sierra San Pedro and in other small, jumbled mountain ranges to the southern end of Bahía Concepción—a total spread of about 125 airline miles.

The earliest known eyewitness report of these magnificent paintings comes from a missionary who was at San Ignacio from 1759 to 1768. There, and at the missions of Guadalupe and Santa Rosalía, the oldest Indians preserved an oral tradition about the Painters (a name coined by Harry Crosby in his definitive work *The Cave Paintings of Baja California*) that had been passed down through generations from fathers to sons. According to the story, in very ancient times a group of men and women of extraordinary physical stature (possibly an assumption based on giant figures painted high on cave walls) had come from the north fleeing one another. Some died at the hands of the others, and some were killed by ancestors of the tellers who would not tolerate such strange newcomers in their land. Obviously, the Painters had plenty of time to create their murals over a large geographical area. Research recently conducted by the Barcelona Group has placed the works at somewhere between 3,500 and 5,000 years old, ending about 350 A.D.

An interesting report by Bernard M. Jones Jr., *Shamanistic Elements in Sierra de San Francisco Rock Art* (published in *Rock Art Papers,* Volume 7, by the San Diego Museum of Man in 1990), hints at a clue to the possible origin of the Painters. Mr. Jones comments on the striking resemblance between a group of three huge human figures in Cueva Pintada (in the Sierra de San Francisco) and a trio of dancers used in the Hopi snake dance ceremony, then describes what he terms "fascinating parallels." He stops short, however, of hypothesizing a Hopi origin for the Painters. (Personally, we are very intrigued by the possibility that these hitherto "mystery" people might be linked to the Hopis.)

We have Erle Stanley Gardner, the prolific mystery writer, to thank for bringing these great art works into the public consciousness. In 1962, *Life* magazine ran a story of Gardner's, "A Legendary Treasure Left by a Long Lost Tribe," and he published a book, *The Hidden Heart of Baja,* later that year. In 1967, he published another book, *Off the Beaten Track in Baja.* Having made several expeditions into the heart of the cave painting country by Jeep and helicopter, Gardner passed on his entrancement with what he saw to a legion of avid readers. His graphic descriptions alone fired the public's imagination.

At the time Spanish explorers arrived in Baja in 1534, the peninsula was populated by several groups of Indians. The Pericús occupied the Cape region, the Guaycuras north to about Loreto, the Cochimís north to about San Felipe, and the Yumanos, with several subgroups, on north to the border.

The Spaniards estimated there were perhaps 50,000 Indians in Baja when they arrived. Successive estimates seen at the Anthropological Museum in La Paz show a steady decline:

1697:	41,500	1768:	7,149
1728:	30,500	1772:	5,094
1742:	25,000	1775:	3,972
1762:	10,000	1777:	5,424

The 1790 census estimated 4,076 Indians, 235 Spaniards, six other Europeans, 183 mulattoes, and 418 Indian mestizos.

The report *Lower California and Its Natural Resources* by Edward

W. Nelson, published by the National Academy of Sciences in 1922, shows 104 Indians in Baja California in 1857. According to various reports, there are still a few hundred in Baja Norte today. European diseases and casualties in various uprisings essentially wiped out the Indians.

The Discovery

It all began with Hernán Cortéz, an adventurous plunderer who took México by storm beginning in 1519. His men worked their way to La Paz in Baja California in 1534 for a short-lived stay, ending when all but one were killed by Indians. Cortéz came a year later, but the land and the Indians were too tough for even the Spaniards, who stuck it out a mere two years. Others explored the coasts and futilely tried to found colonies in order to exploit pearl oysters, which have since all but disappeared.

The Pirates

Spain was also spreading her influence across the Pacific Ocean, conquering the Philippines in 1565. Every year, several Spanish galleons would set off together from Manila on a round-trip voyage across the North Pacific to Acapulco, on to Spain, and back. These ships carried the riches of the Far East—spices, silks, gold coins, and artifacts. It was necessary for them to follow the coast of North America south along the Baja Peninsula. After their long voyage from Manila, many needed to stop in Cabo San Lucas or La Paz for water and other provisions.

The valuable cargoes being transported to Spain attracted Dutch and English pirates who had been raiding Spanish settlements on both sides of the Pacific Ocean. At Cabo San Lucas, it was possible to place a lookout with a spyglass on a high point of land to scan the horizon until sails were sighted, then intercept the galleon with cannon fire. The galleons that anchored in Bahía de La Paz were vulnerable to attack when the regular daytime winds blew from the north into the bay. The pirate vessels would sail in on the wind, while the galleons could not escape against it. In the evening and at night, these winds reverse, coming up from the Pacific Ocean over low hills. Called "Coromuels," these winds—which provide natural air-conditioning for La Paz during hot summers—allowed the pirates to return to their hiding spots.

Many galleons were plundered and much wealth was confiscated over a period of about 150 years until Spanish padres colonized the area in the 1700s and Spain finally gained control over Baja waters.

The Padres

No settlements took hold until the Jesuits came along. The most cherished mission in all the Californias was founded in Loreto in 1697—163 years after the first landing. Being the first, the Loreto mission is properly titled "The Head and Mother of the Missions of Baja and Alta California," and so says the inscription over the front door. The Jesuits worked their way north founding mission after mission for 70 years, until they fell out of favor with the king of Spain and were replaced by Franciscans.

Franciscan missionary Junípero Serra, a prominent figure in California's history, established only one mission in Baja, then moved on to San Diego to fulfill his destiny by creating California's mission system.

The Dominicans were handed Baja California in 1773 and set about establishing and operating more missions in Baja Norte for the next 73 years. At that point, in 1846, the reign of Spain in México came to an end and the last of the Spaniards, including the padres, were expelled.

The Mexican-American War

In 1845, contentious relations between the United States and México culminated into full-scale war. Displays in the Anthropological Museum in La Paz document how the U.S. Navy blockaded Mulegé, Loreto, La Paz, and San José del Cabo. In 1847, the year the war ended, troops landed at La Paz and marched to San Antonio, Todos Santos, Santiago, and San José del Cabo, opposed by guerrillas all the way.

The United States was given Baja California, along with a good chunk of México, but handed it back, not considering the land to be worth much. And that's a good thing, too. Otherwise, all the beaches would have long since been blocked by concrete and asphalt and the Baja we love escaping to wouldn't exist.

The Modern Era

Known in México as *La Frontera* (The Frontier), the Baja Peninsula was considered until recently a remote outpost. Mexico made Baja Norte a state only in 1952 and Baja Sur in 1974. With the completion of the Transpeninsular Highway from Tijuana to Cabo San Lucas in 1973, Baja initiated in earnest a new era of tourism. Currently, the country is devoting great attention nationally to developing tourism in both states. Modern transportation and communications are bringing the region into the fold.

It is difficult to determine who has conquered whom in the past 150 years. The United States has impacted Baja's economy with tourist dollars, while Baja has captivated Americans with its beauty, charm, and hospitality. We have created a marvelous symbiotic relationship—each needing the other—and we've become so assimilated the U.S.-Mexico border is like Swiss cheese. Gringos (Americans) live in Rosarito and commute to jobs in San Diego. San Ysidro has become a Mexican city in all appearances. Mexicans have repopulated California, and tourists outnumber locals in many areas of Baja.

Even the Spanish language is succumbing. In many instances, it is easier to accommodate tourists than struggle with them. Mail is an example. Tourists receiving mail in Baja automatically use the familiar "P.O. Box" terminology, as at home. The term in México is *Apartado Postal,* abbreviated to "Apdo." or "A.P." The mail goes through either way in Baja. Each year, "P.O. Box" becomes more common in advertisements by Mexican businesses.

Whither next?

Camping Tips

Camping Tips

When to Go

Every camper with Baja in his or her sights has to decide when to go. The answer swings on several considerations: why you are heading south, what you plan to do, and where you hope to do it.

Many frequent visitors to Baja are "snowbirds," northerners who head south annually for the winter season. The hint of frost in their nostrils and the promise of bone-cracking, subzero temperatures and multiple feet of snow falling on any given night simplifies the planning—get out of town before it's too late. The old-timers return year after year to their favorite havens and lead the way for new migrants.

With nothing snapping at our heels, the rest of us campers have the luxury of examining all the pros and cons of seacoast versus mountains, Pacific coast versus the Sea of Cortéz, northern Baja versus southern Baja, and beach camping versus full hookups.

The most common notion is that winter is the time to go, but we are convinced this isn't always the case if you have a choice. We have bundled up in heavy jackets, knit caps, and gloves in Cabo San Lucas while singing yuletide carols around Baja Christmas trees (dried flowering stalks of century plants called "chiotes"—pronounced key-*oh*-tays) decorated with handmade wicker ornaments.

We have hunkered down indoors for days on end in January, watching our trailer boat bounce around at anchor under strong East Cape winds, which kept us from the marlin frolicking around out there. We watched the tour promos for great East Cape winter fishing change to tour promos for winter windsurfing, as the travel industry realized that the winter winds had always been there, just waiting for the clientele that desired them.

After reading scads of charts showing when each game fish is most common in each area, a common denominator became apparent: Game fish follow warm water, and that means summer. There are exceptions, though, many of them. The most important one is that striped marlin can be off the tip of Baja all year, making this the greatest big game fishing spot anywhere, no matter what time of the year you come. But if you want marlin, sailfish, dorado, yellowfin tuna, or roosterfish up in the Sea of Cortéz, the warmer the better.

So, if fishing is your thing—and it is the single most popular activity in Baja—summer is the time to go. "Wait a minute," you say. "It's *hot* down there then!" Unfortunately, that's true. However, hot is relative and everyone can tolerate different temperatures. Also, various places do not have the same kind of heat.

San Felipe, in the northern Sea of Cortéz, is in the hottest and driest zone since it's behind the big windbreak of the Sierra San Pedro Mártir, which keeps cool, wet Pacific air away. La Paz, on the other hand, is east of a low dip in the central mountain chain and enjoys daily air-conditioning from the Pacific thanks to the so-called Coromuel winds. One July, we had Sonoran thunderstorms and high humidity in San Lucas Cove just south of Santa Rosalía and sweltered all night—but the lightning over the Sea of Cortéz was spectacular.

The Pacific coast is the place to be in summer if you like it cool and want to be on the water. San Quintín in the north and Bahía Magdalena in the south offer great fishing, fog, and ocean breezes.

If you prefer to find cooler weather in the mountains and have a small vehicle, try the Sierra de Juárez between the border and Highway 3. Laguna Hanson in the pine forest of Parque Nacional Constitución de 1857 is a pleasant spot on a dirt road, or try Parque Nacional Sierra San Pedro Mártir with the highest elevation in Baja California— El Picacho del Diablo at 10,154 feet. Nearby is Baja's only observatory, accessible by a rather steep dirt road. Tired of camping? There are accommodations below at the historic Meling Ranch (see page 115 for more on the park). Places to go in the mountains are limited and are suitable only for smaller vehicles, but the pine forests and trout streams make the trip worthwhile.

Another inland destination for small vehicles is Guadalupe Canyon Hot Springs and Campground, 27 miles south of Highway 2 at the bottom of the Rumorosa Grade. (For details, see the listing on page 132.)

Southern Baja can experience big winds *(chubascos)* in summer. From June to October, sometimes even from May to November, is hurricane season. A late hurricane in December of 1982 tossed several large cruising boats onto the beach at Cabo San Lucas. But hurricanes are not all that common in any particular spot and usually do no more than bring gales and deluges of rain along the coast. The threat of one should not be enough to keep campers away if summer is when they want to travel to Baja.

Winter storms bring rain to northern Baja and summer thunderstorms bring it to the south. The winter storms also blow all along the Sea of Cortéz, making windsurfers happy but giving anglers fits. So what's left? You guessed it—spring and fall. The nice thing about spring is that the weather is warming up and by Easter the winter crowds have left. Incidentally, Easter week is a great time *not* to be on the road in Baja. Everyone is out having fun and boosting sales of *cerveza* (beer). Police conduct safe driving campaigns and erect impressive arrays of wrecked vehicles along Highway 1 to make everyone think twice. Be even more alert if you drive during Easter week.

What is not so nice about spring is that the Sea of Cortéz is still in the grip of winter chill. Swimming, snorkeling, and scuba diving are uncomfortable without a wet suit. Also, most migratory game fish have not yet arrived.

This leaves fall. The water is still warm from heating up all summer, the air temperature has cooled off, *chubasco* season is winding down, game fish are still likely to be around, and winter tourists have not yet arrived. Take your pick.

Water

The question most commonly asked about Baja is "Can you drink the water?" The simplest answer is yes, if you stick to the purified water *(agua purificada)* available in plastic jugs in all grocery stores. Beyond that, it's a maybe. It isn't that the water is necessarily contaminated, it's that your body may not be adjusted to the local flora and fauna. Mexicans may experience distress when visiting our side of the border and sometimes we require an adjustment when returning home after camping in México for several months. Should you get caught, Pepto Bismol is helpful, as is Lomotil and Imodium A-D. You can buy Kaopectate ("kah-oh-peck-*tah*-tay" in Spanish) in pharmacies *(farmacias)* if you write it out or pronounce the name right; otherwise, they won't know what you are talking about.

Upon arriving at Pamul RV Park on the Yucatán Peninsula of México's mainland, we inquired about the water and were told that the locals had no problem but it might not be good for us. The water source was a *cenote* (an open pool in the limestone bedrock) into which anything could fall. Interestingly enough, a jaguar also drank there. So, what do you do to resolve the maybe?

The old standard for purifying water is to boil it for at least 30 minutes at sea level, or longer at higher altitudes. For good measure, throw a quarter ounce or so of bleach into your dish rinse water.

A compact, lightweight, inexpensive water filter that we have used in Baja is Coghlan's. It filters out Giardia lamblia, a microscopic parasite, and other organisms and particles of similar size. It can be used as a pump to take water out of a source or as a straw to drink directly from a container. We paid $20 for one a few years ago.

If you're in an RV, there are all sorts of filters that can be installed in your water system. However, to be certain you are screening out bacteria, the filtering element must be extremely fine. Some RVers chlorinate their water tank at the rate of 8 to 16 drops of liquid bleach per gallon, then use a filter to remove the taste. Campers using jugs allow 10 drops of bleach per quart of water, then let the solution sit for at least 30 minutes so the bleach can do its work and allow the chlorine taste to dissipate.

We like Microdyn, a nontoxic product available in the produce section of Mexican supermarkets such as Gigante and in pharmacies. It destroys bacteria in water and disinfects fruits and vegetables. One drop treats two liters of water, and 10 drops treats 18 liters. A 30-milliliter squeeze bottle sold for about $2.50 on a recent trip. Yodo is a similar product.

As a practical matter, we ask people staying in a campground if they drink the water there without further treatment. If we find several who do and appear to be reasonably healthy, then we will, too. If we're uneasy about taking a chance, we simply keep several jugs of purified water available for drinking and cooking and use the park water for washing up. When we're confident that the water is all right, we'll top off our water tank. We prefer the purified water for making coffee and iced tea and for brushing teeth, in any event—it just tastes better.

There are different schools of thought on purifying produce. Many people just rinse fruits and vegetables in plain water, but our Mexican friends advise purifying, especially foods that come from Guadalajara, we were told. One Mexican friend said she would not purify the many varieties of beautiful fresh lettuce and herbs that come from Todos Santos in Baja Sur.

If you don't have Microdyn or Yodo, use a bleach solution for 30 minutes. For items like tomatoes, soak them for 20 minutes in one position, then turn them over for another 20 minutes. If you have room to pack a salad spinner, lettuce will last much longer. Another way to dry lettuce is to wrap it in layers of paper towels or in dish towels. When living on a boat or camping on the beach, we wash dishes in salt water. Rinse the dishes lightly in freshwater and soak any metal utensils to avoid rust. Melamine or plastic dishes hold up well with this treatment.

We also take saltwater baths. Joy liquid dish soap lathers well and does not produce a salt feeling on your skin, but leaves it soft. It is, joyfully, biodegradable. Another product for saltwater bathing is Sea Savon, a light green liquid that also is biodegradable. It is found in scuba shops in the United States. Coconut bar soap obtained in México lathers in salt water, too.

Ice

Hielo (pronounced *yea*-low), or ice, is sold in cube form *(cubitos)* and small blocks at most grocery stores, liquor stores, beer agencies, and some RV parks. Cubes and small blocks bagged up by companies like Diamonte are made from purified water. The plastic bag will usually say *purificada,* but if it doesn't, ask. If the cubes or blocks are made in the store where they are being sold, which often is the case in out-of-the-way places, the water used is very likely not purified.

Block ice from an ice plant *(planta de fabrica de hielo)* is not made from purified water either, and it gets dirty from being dragged around on the floor and the loading platform. A good practice is to use these big blocks only for keeping food cold (without direct contact with the food) and get bagged ice for all other purposes.

Place your food in double Ziplock freezer bags to keep it from getting wet. Change the outer bag occasionally as it will leak after repeated use. We put a little bleach in the water as the block ice melts. If you are on a boat or in a remote area where freshwater is scarce, save the water off the ice for rinsing or bathing out of a Sun Shower. Another way to keep food from getting wet is to put water in big plastic bottles like the two-liter ones that Coke comes in, leaving some headroom, and freeze it. These make handy ice blocks that last awhile, and then you have the water to drink if it's purified. One will fit in our small RV freezer over the refrigerator.

In remote areas where ice is scarce, keep it longer by wrapping the ice chest or at least placing a silver-colored quilted windshield dash saver on top. This reflects the heat and provides a little insulation. On a boat trip out of La Paz, we placed a big block of ice in an extra ice chest, taped the gap between the lid and the chest, wrapped it, and didn't open the thing for three or four days. When ice was needed, there was still a sizable chunk left.

Sustenance

The Baja travel organization to which we belong and help manage, Vagabundos del Mar Boat and Travel Club, sprang from the desire of travelers to meet Baja and the Sea of Cortéz on their own terms. To us, it made much more sense to bring our friends along from a purely practical standpoint—we'd have more spare parts and more mechanical know-how and ingenuity, not to mention much more fun in sharing experiences.

On our first trip with a Vagabundo group many years ago, we carried enough provisions to supply a unit of the National Guard. It just seemed that this strange and wondrous remote land of mountains, deserts, and beaches wouldn't have enough food to sustain us for a whole month. The camper was packed so tight with canned goods, including canned bacon and butter, that it was difficult to determine what we had and where to find it. Much of it came home with us. Now, though, if there is extra, it's left behind with a longtime or new Mexican friend from a smaller village.

Although canned goods are necessary sometimes, especially if you are planning to be in a remote area for a period of time, they are inherently full of salt and not the healthiest for you. A trick to reduce the salt is to hold the item (particularly meats like corned beef and bacon) under hot running water. Another method is to place the meat in cheesecloth to keep it from coming apart and boil it in hot water for 10 minutes or so. This greatly cuts the salt taste and makes the food more palatable.

For backpacking and horseback pack trips where weight is a factor, dehydrated food found in groceries and most sporting goods stores comes in handy. A brand we like and have used extensively is Mountain Home. Be sure you have ample purified water to rehydrate these foods.

Half the fun of traveling in México is learning to exist on food found in the local markets. Of course, if you like fish, you're liable to supplement your diet with all kinds of fresh seafood that you can catch or gather. Even if you don't fish, there is a bounty of fresh and frozen seafood available. You don't want to miss the fresh fruits and vegetables, either, both familiar and exotic. Agriculture is big business in Baja, and the United States imports much of Baja's produce—tomatoes, melons, and much more. The saladette tomatoes with the best tomato flavor you can find in winter come from México.

Be prudent in your provisioning and be assured that you will be able to find most of what you need in the local market. There also are many good restaurants, should you need a break from shopping and cooking.

There are supermarkets, many that carry much more than just food items, in all the major cities of Baja, and *tiendas* (small food stores) in most villages. When shopping at the *tiendas,* try to have small bills and change with you. Also take a shopping bag. The Mexican bags made of plastic mesh come in a variety of sizes and are most helpful for shopping and for many other uses, such as carrying wet bathing suits or storing garlic and onions.

Another rewarding and colorful experience is shopping at the municipal markets in larger cities like La Paz and San José del Cabo. These markets have everything. Just practice your Spanish a little and learn about their metric weights and measures. (For a conversion chart, see Metric Conversions, page 265.)

The fish displays will offer a full array of choices for fresh seafood and give you an idea of what fish are being caught at the time. If you are lucky, you might even see a behemoth being dragged in whole before it is cut up. You can bargain with the vendors. Take a first walk-through and check prices in different stalls for a particular item. The second walk-through is the time to buy. Be careful when buying shellfish—your nose is the best indicator of freshness. Seafood in the markets comes from all over Baja and is usually very fresh, but you should always be careful with shellfish, no matter where you are.

If shrimp is your fancy, keep a sharp eye for vendors. Once on a street corner in Rosarito, a young girl with a covered basket was selling delectable shrimp. She wouldn't come down on her price, but we bought some anyway. As it turned out, her price was close to the going rate elsewhere.

In larger campgrounds, usually once a week or so, a produce truck will come through with fresh vegetables and fruits and sometimes shrimp. Don't be surprised if the shrimp market is the trunk of a car or the bed of a pickup. Just make certain the catch is fresh and negotiate a price.

For regular supplies, a good stop is a Gigante grocery store. These are found in shopping centers with plenty of parking and easy access. Gigante is a "superstore"—it has a pharmacy and carries clothes, sundries, prepared food for takeout, and baked goods (at its *panadería*, or bakery). Stock up on fresh produce, lettuce, eggs, milk, and meat. Don't pass up the *bolillos*, a delicious bread that comes in large loaves or smaller rolls, and *orejas*, a flaky pastry from the *panadería*.

In these superstores that sell prepared foods, and in certain shops and restaurants in larger towns, a quick and easy meal is roast chicken *(pollo rostizado)* that's been cooked slowly on a rotisserie over charcoal. This makes a very good on-the-spot meal, or you can pop it in the ice chest for lunch or dinner later.

Prices for United States' goods are higher throughout Baja. You can find most anything in the larger supermarkets, but some of the specialty items such as low-fat, low-calorie foods will be quite a bit more. One item we priced, Lipton's decaffeinated iced tea mix with artificial sweetener, cost 25 percent more. It was a pleasant surprise to find it available at the big Centro Comercial Californiano (CCC) supermarkets in La Paz—one at Isabel La Católica and Bravo, the other at Abasolo and Colima. The CCC store in town at Isabel La Católica and Bravo right now is better stocked and has more variety, although the parking lot is smaller and tighter.

If your taste buds have been longing for something familiar, you most likely will find it at CCC. There is a large freezer section with pizza and frozen cakes, as well as most any other frozen food you would find north of the border. We do our major provisioning here. If you need liquor, prices in the grocery stores are generally lower than in the liquor stores.

Aramburo's at Madero and Hidalgo in La Paz also stocks United States' items and has great meat, but their prices are higher than at CCC. The Aramburo's in Cabo San Lucas is a larger store with a greater selection. On each successive trip, we find a wider variety of foods available in CCC and Aramburo's.

It's best to pack things that are difficult to find everywhere—special diet items such as Nutrasweet, light or low-cholesterol mayonnaise and margarine, and favorite salad dressings and dressing mixes. Diet sodas and other diet drinks are available, but not everywhere. There is even nonalcoholic beer—a big surprise in beer-drinking México.

Another invaluable item is the dry Mexican sauce packet with spices and herbs made by French's, Lawry, and Schilling for tacos, taco salad, burritos, fajitas, enchiladas, Spanish rice, and more. Just cook up ground beef, meat strips, or whatever you like, then add the sauce packet, mix and stir, and you're done. Dried spices that add flavor and take up precious little space are helpful in adding varied tastes— you might bring dill, thyme, minced onion, parsley, garlic powder, or paprika, among others. A friend of ours who loves to cook and travels by boat and RV to various places of abode takes along a box-shaped plastic container filled with his favorite spices.

Ziplock freezer bags are very handy for storing or freezing fish and other foods, but are not readily available. Bring them with you.

Small fruit and vegetable stores *(fruiterias)* have fresh fruits and vegetables, usually a small supply of canned goods and juices, and sometimes flour tortillas. Pick up corn tortillas at special shops *(tortillerias)* where they are cranked out by the thousands and sold by the kilo for next to nothing.

Don't be afraid to try new and different fruits. *Guayabas* (small, round yellow guavas, pronounced guay-*yah*-bahs) are very sweet. *Chayote* (pronounced kay-*oh*-tay), a hard, light-green vegetable that becomes tender and opaque when cooked, is delicious. *Jícama* (pronounced *he*-cah-mah) is a round, hard brown root with a firm white interior that is sweet and crunchy. The small, round *limones* (limes, pronounced lee-*mo*-naise) are found everywhere. They are great for *ceviche* (pickled fish, pronounced say-*vee*-chay), salsa, and iced drinks like margaritas, or just sprinkled over seafood. Limes are said to have medicinal properties and taken along with garlic ward off some intestinal problems before they begin. Mexicans use limes in numerous other ways, and the fruit is kept on the table beside the salsa in many restaurants.

Fresh cuts of meat are sold in supermarkets, municipal markets, and meat shops *(carnicerías)*. The beef is leaner than that found in the United States because cattle are allowed to roam on open range and are rarely put in feedlots for fattening. The meat is also not aged in the same way. Mexican beef is tasty and, being leaner, is better for you. Just learn the different cuts and weights so it will be easy to prepare. With ground beef, use the sauce packets designed for tacos, burritos, fajitas, and enchiladas to make an easy meal. Adolph's Meat Tenderizer or your favorite marinade helps with the steak cuts.

Meat Market Talk

We have Jack Poole to thank for this lexicon, most of which doesn't show up in dictionaries. He submitted it a few years ago for use in the Vagabundos del Mar Boat and Travel Club's monthly newsletter, *Chubasco*.

- *Res de Sonora*: Sonora beef—the best
- *Carne molida*: ground meat; *hamburguesa* when in a bun
- *Pulpa*: round. To get it ground, say *"Lo muele, por favor."*
- *Pulpa steak* (pronounced more like "stek"): full round
- *Pulpa cuete*: eye of round
- *Pulpa negra*: top round
- *Pulpa bola*: tip roast
- *Pulpa larga*: rolled roast—you roll it yourself. (Note: *Pulpo* is octopus, so watch your tongue.)
- *Schuck steak*: chuck (seven-bone) steak and blade steak
- *Asado de paleta*: arm roast, also chuck
- *Chuleta costado*: club or top loin steak
- *T-bone*: Porterhouse or T-bone steak
- *Chamorro*: shank crosscuts
- *Costillas*: short ribs
- *Pecho*: brisket
- *Flank steak*: flank steak
- *Chuleta entera*: rib roast
- *Filete de res*: filet mignon

For pork, try the following:

- *Chuletas ahumadas*: smoked pork chops
- *Tocino*: bacon
- *Pierna ahumada*: smoked ham, either sliced *(rebanada)* or whole *(entero)*

- *Costillos de puerco*: spare ribs—you may have to help by showing where to cut.
- *Chuleta de puerco entero*: pork loin
- *Chuletas de puerco*: pork chops—specify thickness.
- *Rebanadas de paleta*: shoulder steaks

For variety, try these:

- *Conejo*: rabbit
- *Cabra*: goat, or *cabrito* (kid)—cook like lamb.
- *Higado*: liver—beef *(de res)* or pork *(de puerco)*
- *Rinon*: kidney
- *Chorizo*: sausage
- *Pollo*: chicken

A Note on Conserving Provisions

After crossing the border, the special necessities you bring with you become more precious. In the cities of Baja, you can find almost anything if you have the time to shop, but asking and searching can be time-consuming. We find it easier to bring items that are hard to find, then save and conserve them by using greater care than we might at home. Would that we could bring this frame of mind back with us.

It's not so much the money involved when supplies of special necessities are depleted or a piece of equipment breaks or is lost—more important is the feeling of deprivation over not having it while you are there and the time and energy it takes to replace something. Space is limited, so choose carefully which items you'll carry, keeping in mind where your travels will take you. When packing our 20-foot Born Free camper, which has two large storage pods on the roof, we know that having an inventory list of what was packed in each pod and in other nooks and crannies will save nerves and time later on. Large plastic covered containers (Sterlite and Rubbermaid make some) are good for storing extra food items. Number the boxes, stow them in a storage pod or wherever, add to your inventory list, and note the location. It's best to keep the list up to date and to delete items as you use them.

After being on the road for a few days, everything seems to shake down and is easier to find.

Viewing Wildlife

Whales

By far the stars of the wild animal scene, gray whales fascinate nearly everyone. Endangered after decades of unrestricted slaughter, they have been restored to healthy population status, thanks to the laws that protect them. The dedication of the Mexican government to protecting the whales' all-important breeding and calving grounds has been critical to their recovery, as has the cessation of hunting. Scammon's Lagoon (Laguna Ojo de Liebre), Laguna San Ignacio, and Bahía Magdalena have become prime whale-watching spots in the winter months, from January through March. Arrange for guided *panga* trips in Guerrero Negro, San Ignacio, Puerto López Mateos, or San Carlos for the wildlife experience of a lifetime. If you are moderately lucky, a "friendly" will come alongside and you may be able to touch it. Beach campers can expect to see gray whales broaching and spouting close to shore as they swim south from the Arctic in the fall and north in the spring.

In the midriff area of the Sea of Cortéz, you can see resident fin whales—second in size only to the monstrous blue whale. With luck, any number of different kinds of whales can be seen in Baja's waters: blues, sperms, minkes, killers, Bryde's, humpbacks, and perhaps others.

During a Vagabundo fishing tournament at Bahía de Los Angeles, a whale leaped out of the water and crashed onto the bow of a fast-moving boat. The bow rail was broken, and the captain broke a finger as he was bashed about. The whale went on its way. We surmised that either the boat had come between a mother and her calf or else the whale had been on loco weed.

Dolphins

Several species of dolphins are commonly seen in Baja—common, bottle-nosed, long-snouted, and spotted—some frolicking in the surf and others in huge pods in the open ocean (often with yellowfin tuna). They enjoy playing around the bow waves of boats. With their grace, speed, and great beauty, these creatures are always an uplifting sight.

Big fish

The largest fish of all, the whale shark, is sometimes seen in Baja waters. We have not been lucky enough to view one, but people we've traveled with have.

The huge 20-foot manta rays have become quite scarce. Most of them, and the smaller ones as well, have wound up as dried, shredded manta raya *machaca*. What a shame.

Billfish (marlin and sailfish) sometimes will be seen jumping or snoozing on the surface. It's always a thrill to watch one of these well-crafted swimming machines come clear out of the water, often in a long series of leaps.

Sharks are not seen as often as they once were, due to heavy fishing by those who ship their fins off to Asia to be cooked up in soup. It is exciting to see one of those distinctive fins cleaving the water, however. While cruising from Bahía de Los Angeles to Bahía Kino with a group of Vagabundos, we suddenly saw a fin sticking three feet out of the water just off our starboard bow and heading across our path. There was no time to pull the throttle back and slow down. We were sure we were going to hit the shark's back, but we didn't. We passed over the fish without a bump. It had to be a whopper with a very tall dorsal fin, for our stern drive extended three feet below the surface. We wished we could have seen the entire creature.

A real oddball that we have seen just once is the sunfish or *mola-mola*. These goofy fish grow to about 1,000 pounds or so and flop around weakly on their sides, creatures of the currents with little or no movement control.

Birds

By far the most engaging wild camping companions are birds. Brown pelicans give endless entertainment, their lumbering flight instantly transformed into precise dive bombing attacks on schools of baitfish. Underwater photography discloses that they hit the water with their beaks open, ballooning out their pouches to unbelievable dimensions—which also stops them dead in their tracks. They close their beaks and squeeze the water out, swallowing the fish. They have a very solemn look when they perch with their long beaks tucked down against their breasts. With their red upper throat, bright white and glossy black stripes, and pale yellow patches on the head, the males are quite handsome.

In the southern part of the peninsula, frigate, or man-o'-war, birds circle endlessly on long wings, adroitly riding thermals. When they begin to gather over a spot in the ocean, that is the signal for fishermen to put the boat on plane and head on over, for game fish are working bait. They are great thieves, outmaneuvering gulls and boobies in the air to force them to drop fish they have picked up, then gracefully snatching their booty as it falls.

On the beach, sandpipers and other shorebirds put on a constant show of feeding activity as they race to follow a receding wave, then reverse to keep just ahead of the next one. With a bird identification book in hand, you can readily identify the varied species you'll encounter. Once in awhile, you find a stray from somewhere far away who doesn't belong in Baja. It's like looking for a pearl in every oyster, for the thrill is in the seeking.

Gulls, of course, are always entertaining with their boldness, well-groomed coiffures, and constant mewing. They are fun to identify, too, as are the terns.

In the southern reaches of Baja, you might spy a very handsome hawk with white chest, pale patches on dark wings, black crest, and red face sitting on *cardón* cacti. This eye-catching fellow of the south is the *caracara* or Mexican eagle.

Ospreys, or fish hawks, are common and are often seen carrying a fish with the head pointed forward as it is tightly gripped with both talons. A pair has nested on a pole near the steel eagle monument at the state line north of Guerrero Negro for years. They have created a huge pile of sticks, adding to it each year.

Exotic animals

A remnant population of 100 or so pronghorn antelope hang on in the Vizcaíno Desert south of Guerrero Negro. It is a vast area, and they are seldom seen except by biologists making aerial surveys. Once populating Baja's flatlands north into California and over to Sonora and Arizona, now they are nearly gone from Baja. There are severe penalties for killing a pronghorn antelope, which are well known among the local population, and there is hope for their survival. The antelope drink no free water, getting what they need from nightly condensation on plants and from the plants themselves, which is most unusual for an animal of their size.

Desert bighorn sheep inhabit the rougher, more remote mountains from the border south to about 40 miles north of La Paz. It has always been impossible to police the hunting of these animals, and the population is way down from its original numbers. There have been no legal hunting seasons for desert bighorn for several years, since there has been insufficient knowledge on which to base the number of permits to be sold. Tourists will not encounter bighorn sheep unless they go out of their way to arrange for a guide. The curious can do so in San Felipe, Bahía de Los Angeles, Santa Rosalía, or Loreto.

Primitive Camping

Camping Outside of Established Campgrounds

Baja is a desert bordering on the tropics. The sun is intense and both air and ground temperatures can be hot. The air is usually very dry, but it can also be very wet when storms set in. The Pacific coast is subject to periodic fog and frequent dew.

A basic rule for desert camping is to be wary of camping in arroyos, or streambeds. Infrequently a cloudburst occurs in the mountains, out of sight and hearing. A good night's sleep can be ruined by a wall of water rolling big boulders down the arroyo to scour out your campsite and you along with it. Keep in mind that these are the very forces that carved out the arroyo in the first place and they do occur periodically.

Beach Camping

When you set up camp on a beach in Baja, whether in a tent or an RV, be prepared for a primitive experience. Camping alone is not advised. You may find yourself on one of the few beaches with improvements or in one of the handful of RV parks situated on a beach. Elsewhere, you won't find picnic tables, rest rooms, parking areas, trails, signs, or water spigots. You may find trash barrels.

What you certainly will find are privacy and beauty—mile after mile of pristine sand beaches, white enough to blind you, where you can walk and walk until you drop and never see another soul, except your traveling companions. What looks to be a mile away will prove to be four miles. When you set off walking down a beach, it pays to bring something to drink and to go only so far that you won't be too tired to return to camp.

It also pays to plan ahead on what to do with your trash and human waste. A firm commitment to carrying out what you carried in will keep camping spots attractive and safe for all. It's worth the effort. Burn paper, cardboard, and toilet tissue. Crush the rest, bag it up, and take it to the next town dump *(basurera)*.

Bring a shovel—the small folding ones take up little space. Emulate the cat by burying your personal deposits well back from the high tide line. If you settle in with an RV, drive it away when you have to dump your holding tanks. Don't put paper in the sewage tank and use discretion in selecting a spot in which to dump it, preferably the sewer system of the nearest RV park. Offer to pay for the privilege.

People who settle into a beach spot for the winter in an RV are accustomed to digging a hole, covering it with a piece of plywood, and running their sewer hose into it. Some popular spots with a high density of such campers have become noxious and badly polluted, adversely affecting adjacent beaches.

Accordingly, some beaches have been fenced off to prevent vehicular access and overnight camping. Usually a pedestrian walkway is provided for day use. All of the former camping beaches between Cabo San Lucas and San José del Cabo have been restricted in this way. Hotels and condominiums now dominate that coast, with more on the way.

The right of public access to beaches in México has its limitations. There is a federal zone *(Zona Federale)* extending 20 meters back from the mean high tide line around the entire coastline of the country that is open to public access. However, adjoining landowners can be held responsible for the cleanliness of the beach in front of their property. Abuse leads to fences.

We have done considerable camping in both tents and campers on Baja's beaches over the years and have found a few security precautions to be well advised. There is nothing so effective as camping with other people to establish a comforting peace of mind. That way, there can always be someone in camp to deter those who may consider appropriating your equipment and belongings. Do everyone a favor and don't create temptation.

We lost a clam fork many years ago from alongside our tent, which undoubtedly better served a local youngster. However, we weren't through chasing clams and missed it. Other campers have mentioned ice chests and other easily portable items walking off, including small boats and motors. The worst offenders are other campers, particularly those who have established semipermanent quarters on a shoestring and can use just about anything that comes their way. Your unattended campsite will look like an open bazaar to someone seeking acquisitions.

The local fishermen and ranchers are hospitable folk who work for what they have and respect the property of others, but kids will be kids—like the little shavers who peeled a magnetic sign off one of our truck doors while we were sitting inside the camper having lunch. They apparently told their mother we gave it to them. We should have caught on when she came over and politely asked if she could have the other one.

A sound practice is to completely avoid sharing alcohol with strangers. What starts out as jovial conviviality can quickly turn unpleasant and unmanageable—the more remote and isolated the area, the less inhibited people feel.

Getting Stuck in the Sand

One of the little chores you learn how to do when getting off the beaten path in Baja is how to get unstuck. Years ago we used to tent camp on Playa Santa María south of San Quintín behind the dunes, just about where the La Pinta Hotel now sits. We had a standard two-wheel-drive station wagon and loved to drive it on the beach. The drill was to reduce tire pressure to about 15 pounds, determine a path through the dunes, then make a mad dash to the beach. Once there, we drove on the hard sand below the high tide line and had about eight miles of beach for a playground.

One day, full of confidence, we tried coming off the beach in a new spot and dug in. Most of the afternoon was spent jacking up the rear wheels, packing brush, driftwood, and whatever else we could find under the wheels, then surging ahead a few feet to repeat the process. It was definitely not fun.

More recently, our one-ton Ford truck (the worst vehicle to get stuck we've ever had)—with nothing behind or on it, just the naked truck—buried itself in the middle of the Villa Vitta RV Park at Bahía de Los Angeles.

In another instance, while towing a 5,000-pound, 21-foot boat behind our 20-foot Born Free camper, we turned off Highway 1 near Puerto Escondido onto what looked to be hard-sand wheel tracks. They weren't. Everything got totally buried. We had to unhook the trailer, tow the truck and camper out, then pull the boat and trailer out with a long cable. That qualified as one of the dumbest moves of all time, for which we earned the label of "Sand Crabs" from a sneaky Vagabundo who happened by and ratted on us.

Some people carry two long pieces of canvas or carpet to put under the drive wheels. Others find wetting the sand makes a difference. Nylon tow straps can apparently be used to slingshot the stuck vehicle out of its hole by a second vehicle. Have that vehicle run out to the limit of stretch (about another one-fifth the length of the strap), then slam on the brakes. As the brake lights come on, pour the gas to the stuck vehicle. We haven't seen this done, but we've been told of the technique. It presents a pleasant mental image of the stuck vehicle simply shooting forward like a rocket. When you're stuck, you'll try anything, right? We'll just keep on with the old jack-it-up-and-stuff-it method.

One more stuck story. Once, during the year we spent in Iran, we ventured out on a dry lake bed in our standard station wagon, decided we had gone far enough as the bushes were petering out, stopped, and tried to back up. We dug in. We jacked up the rear wheels, stuffed thornbrush under them, went back a couple of feet, got stuck, and repeated the process numerous times. A sheepherder steered his flock over our way to see what these goofy foreigners were up to, gave us an enormous toothless grin, put one finger on the top of his six-foot-long staff, and gently pushed it all the way down. When he pulled it out, wet muck was clinging to it. Goggle-eyed, we realized the station wagon was resting on a very thin crust over mushy goop. With renewed vigor and a sense of the whole shebang slowly sinking out of sight, we jacked and stuffed in a frenzy to the limit of our endurance. Once we had traction, the pedal went to the floor, the wagon shot up and over a six-foot-tall thornbush in reverse, and finally reached solid ground.

Moral: Getting stuck isn't such a big deal. It's what you do next that counts.

Backpacking

Unless you have a great deal of experience backpacking in the desert, we do not recommend backpacking in Baja. If you get too far away from the car, even in the mountains, you can encounter a water problem. It is easy to forget that this is an arid peninsula that has very limited water sources and finding them may take local knowledge. It is also dry and can be numbingly hot.

Read *Into a Desert Place* by Graham Mackintosh before you think about backpacking in Baja. Mackintosh walked the entire coastline on both sides of the peninsula, carried all the water he could, including a gallon plastic jug in each hand, and tried several types of water distillation devices. He still had some close calls. It is an unforgiving, harsh environment and not to be approached lightly.

Having said that, the mountains do offer some challenging backpacking opportunities. The Sierra San Pedro Mártir in Baja Norte is a massive mountain range with a high forested plateau some 40 miles long and 10 miles wide between roughly 6,000 and 8,000 feet in elevation. Jeffrey pine is the dominant forest tree, alongside some sugar pine and incense cedar. At higher elevations, you will find lodgepole pine and white fir. There also are huge meadows on whichcattle graze.

Off to the east is the highest peak in Baja—El Picacho del Diablo at 10,154 feet elevation. Climbing it is a major event and is usually done from the eastern base of the steep escarpment of the Sierra San Pedro Mártir because of the 3,000-foot-deep Cañon del Diablo separating the plateau of the main range from El Picacho. This canyon is a rather weird geological quirk—as if extra effort was expended to isolate El Picacho from mankind.

Trails were established long ago by Indians and have been further delineated by *vaqueros* (cowherds). Unlike what we are accustomed to in the United States, there are no signs, no trail markers, and no good maps. Trails peter out. You can get lost. You can fail to find water.

Before setting out, drive to the Meling Ranch and talk to the people there about where to go, how to find your way, and other lifesaving advice you can't leave without. Hire a guide if you feel the slightest bit doubtful about your outdoors expertise. We packed out of there on horseback many years ago with a guide and packer and had a great experience. You can, too, on foot or horseback, if you go about it right.

If you're an angler, you can enjoy fishing for Nelson rainbow trout, native to Arroyo San Antonio and later introduced into Arroyos San Rafael and La Zanja. They are not big—up to a foot long—but catching one in such an unlikely place is fun. There is also a scenic waterfall in Arroyo San Antonio.

To get to the Meling Ranch, drive about 6.5 miles south of Colonet or about eight miles north of Camalu on Highway 1. Turn east toward San Telmo and continue beyond it to the ranch—a total distance of about 31 miles. The road is dusty and has some fairly steep grades, which were all we wanted to handle with our big camper.

At the other end of the peninsula, the Sierra de La Laguna rises high in the sky above the desert. Surrounded by the tourist centers of La Paz, Los Cabos, and the East Cape, its isolated lushness is unsuspected by visitors in the popular resorts fronting the ocean. The heart of the sierra can be reached only by arduous effort over rugged, steep, centuries-old trails that are unsigned and difficult to find. They have been beaten two to three feet into the rock by thousands of hooves and feet over the past 200 years or more.

The sierra's rugged peaks can be seen from the surrounding circle of Highways 1 and 19. An especially striking vista is from Highway 1 between Buena Vista and San José del Cabo, from which jagged peaks loom to nearly 7,000 feet.

The area's most startling feature is the dense forest of 60-foot pine and oak trees with trunks up to three feet in diameter, a scattering of huge red-trunked *madroños* with large, glossy, bright-green leaves, and the bizarre *sotol* with clusters of long, slender yucca-like leaves atop tall thin trunks.

The pines are Mexican *piñón,* others of which are found far away in northern México and adjoining Arizona and Texas. The massive black oaks and *madroños* are species unique to the Sierra de La Laguna. The *sotol* occurs elsewhere only in a few widely scattered groups farther north in Baja. In a moister, cooler climate in the far distant past, the progenitors of all these species found their way out of northern México and down the Baja Peninsula. When the climate grew drier and warmer, they became isolated in the higher, moister reaches of the Sierra de La Laguna. As time went on, most were supplanted by new species.

Up in the sierra, level land is hard to find. The one sizable meadow, about one mile by a half mile, is known as La Laguna. Local lore has it that originally there was a lake here, which broke out of its confines 100 years or so ago.

The shortest route to it is from Rancho La Burrera at a 1,600-foot elevation out of Todos Santos. Some maps show this as San Juan del Asserradero. Start at the microwave dish on the south side of Todos Santos on Highway 19. Drive 1.3 miles south just past Kilometer 54 and turn left on a sandy road across a cattle guard at the top of a hill. Starting from zero on the odometer, ignore a road to the left at 2.2 miles. Continue straight ahead toward the fire lookout tower. At 4.0 miles, take the left fork. Cross a cattle guard at 5.4 miles, pass a dam on the left at 6.4 miles, and cross another cattle guard at 7.2 miles. At 8.8 miles, continue straight past a signed road on the left to San Martín, then pass another road to the right. At 12.3 miles, marked by a gate, the road makes a steep descent down the north bank of an arroyo to the ranch at 13.3 miles. Find a place to park and start walking. At the ranch you may be able to arrange for horses and to have the gate opened. If you are able to drive in, remember to build momentum to traverse the drifted humps of sandy soil on the return out of the arroyo. Our conventional one-ton pickup, which has a propensity for digging in, handled it easily. Motor homes and trailers should not make the drive in from the highway, however.

The trail heads easterly from La Burrera up the big wash coming out of the mountains, then climbs up the north slope. The 4,000-foot ascent of seven miles to La Laguna took us about four hours on horseback. A shaded water source about midway affords refreshment.

At La Laguna, a two-room *casita* (house) in the trees at the meadow's edge is used by "forest guards" who keep an eye on things and gauge rainfall in the meadow. Another little two-room casita in the open can be used for shelter and cooking. Cattle and pigs forage over the land, watering in the stream that runs east into Cañon San Dionisio. The trail continues down that canyon to a ranch of the same name.

Backpackers have used two other trans-sierra routes with hard-to-find ancient trails. South of Rancho La Burrera, the next trail goes from Rancho Santo Domingo on the west to Rancho Boca de La Sierra on the east. Another trail farther south goes from Rancho El Guerigo on the west to Rancho El Salto on the east. Farther south yet, the iffy Naranjas Road crosses from its junction with Highway 19 at a sign to El Saltito de Los Garcia to Highway 1 at a point 9.5 miles south of the turnoff to Miraflores.

What to Bring

Horseback pack trips

We've taken horses into the Sierra San Pedro Mártir, Sierra de San Francisco, and Sierra de La Laguna. Here is what we bring on horseback pack trips:

- Two-person mountain tent with an anteroom that can be closed and a sun fly

- Nylon or plastic ground cloth to go under the tent and to serve as an apron for wiping your feet before entering the tent
- Rubber air mattresses with box sides and built-in pillows
- Sleeping bags that zip together so we can snuggle
- Small folding table
- Coleman propane three-burner stove and folding aluminum stand
- Several disposable propane bottles
- Coleman two-lamp fluorescent lantern with a new battery
- Cooking kit with pots, frying pan, plates, cups, and utensils
- Small plastic squeeze bottle of dishwashing liquid
- Dish rag, scrub brush, and dish towel
- Food, including dehydrated meals, canned chicken and shredded beef for tacos, etc., eggs in a plastic egg carrier, powdered iced tea mix with sweetener and lemon, cheese, salami, crackers, cookies, tortillas, and other goodies our taste buds require (several planned meals, for us *and* our guide, plus a little extra)
- Clothes, including jeans, hiking boots, lightweight tennis shoes and sandals for around camp, hats, light jackets, lightweight long-sleeved cotton shirts, T-shirts, underwear, socks, swimsuits, plastic ponchos (good for ground cloths and rain, too), and shorts
- Swiss army knife, ever present on the belt
- Pair of binoculars
- Cameras and ample slide and print film (we're photographers)
- Notebook (we're writers)
- First-aid kit in an easy-to-pack container off the shelf, prepared for the usual cuts, punctures, and abrasions
- Bug spray and squeeze bottle
- Sunglasses
- Medications and personal hygiene items
- Lip balm
- Sunscreen
- Flashlights with spare bulbs and batteries
- Nylon cord

- Small water filter and collapsible five-gallon plastic water jug with a spigot
- Quart canteens
- Ziplock bags for trail snacks and other unforeseen uses
- Plastic garbage bags—what goes in, goes out

Backpacking equipment

We would pare down our horseback pack-trip list and substitute more lightweight items:

- Sleeping pads instead of rubber air mattresses
- No table
- Small single-burner stove
- No lantern
- No canned goods
- Fewer clothes

Camping out of a vehicle

In addition to what we'd bring on a horseback pack trip, we add:

- Water in two five-gallon collapsible plastic containers
- Ice chest
- Small propane grill
- Small folding shovel
- Tow cable
- Sun Shower
- Rope
- Bungee cords—a bag full
- Duct tape, a great fixer-upper
- Field guides for birds, plants, and fish
- Fishing tackle essentials—fillet knife, spinning rods and reels, hooks, swivels, swivel snaps, sinkers, and several lures of the Rapala, Scampi, tuna feather, and jig types (if we charter a boat, we take marlin rods and Penn International 50W reels; the rods and reels take the most room, while the rest fits in a small cosmetics case)

Boat camping

Camping either in a boat or in a tent on shore has a great deal of potential in several sections of the Sea of Cortéz. The many islands around Bahía de Los Angeles, Puerto Escondido, and La Paz have attractive coves and beaches. Since stretches of open ocean must be crossed, small open boats like inflatables and cartop aluminum models are not suitable. Strong winds can whip up on short notice, churning the ocean into a maelstrom. Trailer boats of 20 feet or so in length can handle rough seas, although the open-cockpit, center-console designs can get awfully wet. Cuddy cabins give protection and are adequate for sleeping. Camper canvas to the stern makes a cozy home for living on board.

We have lived aboard our old 21-footer for several weeks at a time, though our present 27-footer is far more comfortable with its aft-cabin layout. We have lived in it for four months while on the road to and from Florida and cruising in the Bahamas as comfortably as in our big camper. We have spread mosquito netting across the deck and slept peacefully under the stars in a double sleeping bag.

We once set up a tent camp on the beach on Isla Partida north of La Paz for a week with some dive buddies who had a small compressor. We had a great time exploring the underwater world there.

Boats require special equipment. It is much tougher to get help having broken down on the water than having broken down on the highway. You must be more self-sufficient with tools and parts. Having a buddy boat may mean the difference between getting back to shore or being stranded. There are times when being towed is unavoidable. Necessary items in addition to those listed for vehicles and for primitive camping are:

- Towing bridle
- Propeller
- Water pump impeller
- Hoses
- Belts
- Marine alternator
- Distributor parts
- Spare gas

Fending Off Critters

Mosquitoes and gnats can make your life miserable. Sooner or later you will run into both of them, so have plenty of bug spray on hand at all times. Read on for tips on how to deal with these and other annoying creatures and plants.

Mosquitoes

These ubiquitous pests can be controlled with any of the commercial compounds containing DEET (N, N-diethyl-metatoluamide), the one chemical that can be counted on to do the job. We have a squirt bottle of U.S. Army-type repellent with 71 percent DEET and found that it works. The only thing about DEET is the recommendation that it be washed off. We haven't been able to find the Army type lately, but there are various brands of DEET out—Muskol is effective and comes in 100 percent strength and lesser amounts, too, like 40 percent. After Bite, a different type of product, helps relieve the itch and pain from mosquito and gnat bites. Be sure to read the labels.

Keep covered up and spray or rub the repellent on exposed skin. Also spray clothing. There's one other thing about DEET: It melts certain kinds of plastic, like watchbands and eyeglass frames, so be careful with the stuff. We know that a lot of people don't like using strong doses of DEET on their skin because it is so potent, but when the bugs are biting, it works.

Gnats

The most vicious biting bug in Baja is the *jejene* (pronounced hay-*hay*-nay). Everyone likes to call this teeny-weeny gnat a no-see-um, but you can see um, though barely. They walk right through mosquito netting. The first thing you'll notice is that something is biting you and you are beginning to sting and itch all over. Soon you'll have scads of little welts that itch even more. There's a photo of one of our friends in which he looks like he has a bad case of measles. Talk about an unhappy camper.

In our experience, DEET repellents aren't as effective on *jejenes* as on mosquitoes, but if you keep slathering on the stuff it helps a lot. People are usually happier when they depart the *jejene* encampment. If you can find a breezy spot, the winds should blow them away. Fortunately, they are not troublesome in many places, but when you are among them they will drive you crazy.

Many people swear by Avon Skin-So-Soft as a bug repellent. We haven't found that to be so, but it may be just the right combination for you. Avon won't say what is in their product and doesn't market it as something that will chase away bugs, but your friendly Avon lady may be happy to sell you some with no questions asked.

Stingrays

This fish can whack you with its whiplike tail if you wade around carelessly in salt water. Stingrays are common off Baja and should be kept in mind, for their barb can inflict a painful wound. The best thing to do is shuffle your feet or keep thrashing a stick ahead of you. They bury themselves in the sand and can't be seen, but as they don't relish being stepped on they will swim away if alerted. Be particularly cautious when stepping down off a surfboard or sailboard or out of a boat.

If you are unlucky enough to get hit, the standard advice is to cleanse the wound with cold salt water and extract all pieces of the barb or its sheath. Soak the injury in hot water at as high a temperature as can be tolerated for 30 to 90 minutes. Disinfect and bandage it as you would any other puncture.

Some people swear that the pain can be relieved by zapping the spot with a stun gun or a live spark plug. We have no experience with these stunning techniques, which reportedly also neutralize the effects of snakebite and other venoms.

Sea urchins

Some sea urchins with long, slender spines are present in both the Pacific Ocean and the Sea of Cortéz. These types of spines penetrate booties, sneakers, or bare skin like needles and are difficult to remove because they are barbed. It is important to try to extract all pieces of broken spines. Local remedies may involve frequently dousing the skin with citrus juice to help eliminate any unremovable bits. Disinfect the punctures and keep them clean.

Jellyfish

Tiny jellyfish, whose stings encourage you to leave the water, are found in Baja. Rub in meat tenderizer—Adolph's is considered good. Other recommended treatments are ammonia and urea. After Bite, in a pen form, is mainly ammonia. Tentacles on the skin can be covered with dry sand, then scraped off after a few minutes.

Cactus

It was an exciting moment. Fred was assisting other biologists in Arizona on a desert bighorn sheep project. While hiking up an arroyo, he spotted a big ram climbing out on one side. He plunked down to a restful sitting position for a steady look with the binoculars and nailed his Levi's to his butt by landing on a jumping cholla cactus ball. The ram was forgotten, so that total attention could be devoted to getting unstuck. A wadded-up handkerchief held around the spiny ball gave sufficient leverage to pry it loose without impaling his fingers. These little devils are barbed and resist being pulled out.

On a similar expedition in Baja, Gloria brushed too close to a cactus alongside a steep, rough trail and collected a cactus spine in her leg. One of the Mexican biologists whipped a pair of tweezers out of his shirt pocket and removed that rascal in an instant.

If you walk around where cacti live, it is best to be fully clothed, pay them serious respect, and carry a pair of tweezers. Carelessness can be painful.

Cactus spines are also disrespectful of automobile tires. We have received flats in big truck tires after four-wheeling on desert roads and have had to endure the big grin of the tire guy (the shop is a *llantera,* pronounced yawn-*tear*-uh) as he holds up a little spine in his pliers and says, "Espina!" We now watch out for chunks of cactus branches across the road and get out and remove them. That takes less time than changing a tire.

Problems with Sun, Heat, and Cold

Sunburn

People are a lot wiser today than they used to be about taking it easy in the sun. If you want to avoid getting burned when you hit Baja, give yourself only a half hour of exposure the first day, then a half hour more for each of the four or five days it takes to start tanning. Use sunscreen or sunblock ointments all the time. Sun protection factors (SPFs) range from 2 to 45 or higher, meaning you can stay out in the sun without burning two to 45 times longer than you would with no protection. An SPF of 15 or higher will block most of the sun's harmful rays. Put it on about one-half hour before becoming exposed, rub it in, and be sure it's absorbed. Reapply often, especially if you get wet or sweat a lot.

Exposure may occur anyway, and you can develop some bright red spots. For instance, switching to a smaller swimsuit can uncover white skin that needs extra protection. Light-skinned people burn very quickly and are better off completely covered. At the other end of the spectrum are those who tan readily but will burn if they push it too fast. Everyone should determine how they react and protect themselves accordingly.

If you become sunburned, get out of the sun, cover yourself up, and apply a soothing ointment such as Solarcaine or Noxema. Suffer as silently as possible and be wiser the next time.

Heat exhaustion

We were having a great time fishing in a friend's *panga* off of Isla San José north of La Paz. It was hot, but Fred was comfortable in a swimsuit and cap. After several hours, we headed back to San Evaristo, where he became a little nauseous and couldn't eat the delicious *tacitos* our friend's wife had prepared. During the long drive back to La Paz, Fred became more uncomfortable. He climbed right into bed, feeling disoriented and woozy.

Some years before, while hiking strenuously on a July day for a desert bighorn sheep survey in Death Valley National Monument, Fred became overheated from the exertion. His legs ceased to function, and drinking copious amounts of water and pouring it over his head had no effect. He was able to move to a nearby spring by lifting each leg by hand from behind the knee, swinging the leg forward, then doing the same thing with the other leg. Finally at the spring, he fell headlong into a pool. The rising steam blotted out the sun and he was soon able to stagger to the car.

Both of these events were cases of heat exhaustion, which is caused by loss of fluids and salt. Hot, dry desert air sucks moisture out of the body at a high rate. One may experience muscle cramps and headaches, pale and clammy skin, and dizziness and fainting.

Here's what the *American Medical Association (AMA) Family Medical Guide* says to do: Lay the person down in a cool, quiet place with feet raised a little. Loosen any tight clothing and give the victim water to drink, adding a teaspoon of salt to each quart.

In order to avoid heat exhaustion, it is important to maintain adequate moisture in your body and to limit your activity level. We have learned from United States Army studies (made when General Patton's tank corps was undergoing training in the California desert) that people performing strenuous activity in the desert require at least two gallons of liquid a day to offset fluid losses. It was also demonstrated that water by itself is not sufficiently palatable to consume in such quantities. You can guzzle it every time you have the slightest desire and still not take in enough. It is necessary to improve it by adding flavoring—citrus juice, chocolate, powdered tea, whatever you can do to make it more interesting. We have adopted the attitude that it is foolish to carry water around with you when you could be drinking it. It only has value in your stomach, not in a canteen. Just be sure you have enough.

Fred took two college students into the Santa Rosa Mountains of California one July to make bighorn counts at water holes. When it's hot, desert bighorn stay close to water, so it's a good time to count them. Prospectors warned Fred that they couldn't survive in those hot, hot canyons at that time of year. However, armed with the findings of Patton's troops, they guzzled water like it was going out of style and had no problems. The prospectors were right about one thing: Those canyons were like ovens, with rocks so hot they blistered the skin.

Heatstroke/Sunstroke

Heat exhaustion can lead to heatstroke under prolonged exposure to very hot conditions. Body temperature can become very high, the skin can turn flushed, hot, and dry, and the pulse can grow strong and rapid. The *AMA Family Medical Guide* says to remove clothing and wrap the sufferer in a cold, wet sheet or sponge them with cold or lukewarm water. Fan the person by hand or with a fan until the body temperature comes down, then turn them face down in a comfortable sleeping position with upper arms and one leg at right angles to the body, bent at the elbows and knee. Cover the person with a dry sheet and continue to fan. If the body temperature starts to rise, repeat the cooling process.

Hypothermia

Baja really does have everything. If you work it right, you can freeze and fry in the same place on the same day.

After a hypnotic night sleeping to the rhythmic slosh of waves on the beach at San Pedrito RV Park south of Todos Santos, Fred decided the surf must be full of a great many fish. At dawn, he donned his swimsuit, firmly grasped his surf-casting rod and plunged in waist deep for a couple hours of fruitless casting. Deciding it was time for breakfast, he gave it up to return to the camper.

Funny thing! He was shaking so badly he could barely navigate up the slope of the beach. Inside the camper, he went into a frenzy of shivering and shuddering and felt like an ice cube through and through. Gloria whipped up hot chocolate, wrapped him in a blanket, and sweetly told him what a horse's patootie he was. There was nothing he could say, as it was true.

For such cold Pacific Ocean water all the way south to Cabo San Lucas, you can blame the Japanese current, which sweeps north past Japan, across the frigid North Pacific, then south along the North American coast without warming up a whole lot.

Even in the Sea of Cortéz the water can be too cold for long immersion, except in the shallows where it warms up nicely. When we dive in the Cortéz, we always wear a wet suit or jeans and a long-sleeved cotton shirt, depending on the water temperature. It's true that we have never won any awards for sartorial elegance among the diving crowd, but it's also true that we enjoy our dives. One thing about wet clothes is you need to get them off as soon as you're back in the boat. Nothing robs heat from the body faster than wet Levi's.

On an early spring raft trip on the Yampa River in Utah, Fred nearly did it again with the hypothermia by wearing wet Levi's. A few rapids soused his trousers, clouds blocked the sun, and he went into that deep shivering mode. Gloria forcibly pulled his pants off, to the delight of our Vagabundo friends, and with dry legs he warmed right up. We had wondered why all the oarsmen wore nothing but shorts and sandals—they got wet all the time but dried off quickly.

When prolonged exposure to cold drops the body temperature more than four degrees below normal, hypothermia has hit. Our source, the *AMA Family Medical Guide*, says to get the person into warm, dry clothes and administer warm drinks. Hey, that's just what Gloria did at San Pedrito! Hypothermia can become very serious if it's allowed to progress, so catch it at the first shiver.

Medical Care

Gloria once developed an infected finger while in La Paz, so we asked our Mexican friends where to go. There are several hospitals to choose from. We went to the closest one, displayed the finger, and were ushered right into a doctor's office. He specified an antibiotic (no prescription needed), which we obtained at a pharmacy.

Clinics are available in small communities and will handle minor scrapes and cuts. The cities have hospitals where treatment for more serious ailments can be obtained. Prices are minimal compared to what we are accustomed to.

Travel Tips

Travel Tips

México has a different legal system, different customs, a different culture and is, well, different. That is why we all go there—to get away from the treadmill at home and have fun. Here are the most important things to do and become accustomed to before your trip.

Licenses and Permits

Permits and documents are essential for traveling in Baja California, even more so when you'll be entering the mainland of México from Baja.

Tourist cards

The first thing to think about is a tourist card. Most tourists call it a visa or visitor permit. The formal identification is Form FMT. It is a two-piece, 5.5-by-7.5-inch form with a carbon insert. Everyone who will be in Baja for more than three days needs one—no matter what anyone says to the contrary. If you can't obtain one from a Mexican consulate or a Mexican tourism office, phone the Vagabundos del Mar Boat and Travel Club at (800) 474-2252.

Once you fill out the form, it must be endorsed in México at an immigration *(migración)* office. The easiest to locate, as well as the easiest to deal with, is in Ensenada on the waterfront on the north side of town. It's just south of the shipyards (near all the big speed bumps) and just before the arterial stop sign, where you turn right onto the four-lane divided street along the bay in the main shopping district. A sign in the median of the divided road points to the immigration office on the left side of the road next to the Port Captain's office. You will have to go beyond, find a parking place, and walk back. Bring a passport or copy of your birth certificate for identification and your vehicle registration slip just in case they want it. It is a good idea for one person to carry the documents for the others and leave one person behind with the vehicle. Hours are from 8 A.M. to 8 P.M. every day. The phone is 011-52-617-4-0164.

Keep in mind that immigration officials are fining people some $15 per day if they are in the country longer than 72 hours without having their tourist card validated. In the past some officials insisted the form wasn't necessary unless you were traveling to the mainland, but there is no longer any question about the need for having one. In addition, in case of an accident, even a minor one, it is wise to have your papers in order. Also, should you need to fly home in an emergency (commercial airports are in Ensenada at the military base south of town, Loreto, La Paz, and San José del Cabo), you would need to show a validated visitor card.

Vehicle permits

If you are taking a vehicle to the mainland by ferry from Santa Rosalía (to Guaymas) or La Paz (to Topolobampo or Mazatlán), a Temporary Vehicle Importation Permit is necessary. Do not count on obtaining one in Santa Rosalía. Either procure it at a customs *(aduana)* office at the border, in La Paz at the customs office in the Treasury *(Hacienda)* building across from the city dock *(Muelle Fiscal)* in the center of town, or at the vehicle control booth at the customs office at the Pichilingue Port, where the ferry dock is located.

To obtain the permit, you'll need: a tourist card; vehicle registration; a leasing contract (if the car is leased or rented) in the name of the individual importing the car; if it's a company car, a document certifying that you work for the company; and an international credit card (American Express, Diner's Club, MasterCard, or Visa) in the name of the owner or driver of the vehicle.

You must pay an $11 fee, by credit card only, for three items: 1) a six-month Temporary Vehicle Importation Permit; 2) a form on which you promise to take the vehicle back out of the country; and 3) a windshield sticker. Cash is not accepted. If you don't have a credit card, you must go to the nearby Mexican bonding agency, which is the Bank of the Army *(Banjército)*. The bond will cost between 1 and 2 percent of the Blue Book value of the vehicle, plus tax and processing costs.

When you leave the Mexican mainland with the vehicle, you must return the permit, form, and sticker to Customs, unless you are positive the vehicle will be driven back into the Mexican mainland within the permit period. If you have any doubt, turn everything in. It is much simpler to pay the small fee again than to let the permit expire while you are at home. Customs will have no way to determine that you did not illegally leave the vehicle in México. You may be fined or confronted with other bureaucratic problems. For the current official word on this, call the Surface Tourism section of the Mexican Department of Tourism *(Turismo)* office in Houston, Texas, at (713) 892-5353 or (800) 662-6394. If you are going only to Baja and will not be on the Mexican mainland, you will not need the vehicle permit.

If you will be leaving your house trailer, boat, or boat trailer behind when you exit Baja, you must obtain a free 20-year Temporary Vehicle Importation Permit from a customs office. Bring all documents that will establish who you are, that you own the vehicle, and that it is currently registered somewhere other than Mexico.

Fishing licenses and boat permits

These are much simpler to deal with than those for vehicles. Regulations state that in order to operate a boat in Mexican waters, it is necessary to hold a boat permit and personal fishing licenses for everybody aboard the boat, regardless of age and whether or not they're fishing. We were informed that boat permits and fishing licenses are needed only if there is fishing tackle on board (a single hook or a speargun is enough). These can be obtained from the Mexican Department of Fisheries *(Pesca)*. You can get one in México, but locating a Pesca office can be a chore. Contact the U.S. office at 2550 Fifth Avenue, Suite 101, San Diego, CA 92103; phone (619) 233-4324. For faster service, phone the Vagabundos del Mar Boat and Travel Club at (800) 474-2252.

One good reason to have a license on our side of the border is the recent practice of U.S. Fish and Wildlife Service agents confiscating fish being brought into the country by people who don't possess Mexican fishing licenses. Don't trust *panga* or charter boat operators to have a license to cover you, and instead get your own by the week, month, or year.

Pets

If you have a pet, obtain an International Health Certificate from your veterinarian as close to your departure date as possible and bring it with you. We were never questioned about this matter in México when we brought our cat, but we have been asked to show the certificate when crossing back into the United States.

Insurance

Liability

Mexican law is considerably different from that in the United States. In the event of an accident, both parties are detained until it is determined who is responsible for what, including damage to the highway, and how the debt is to be paid. Liability coverage with a Mexican company takes care of your end of things. Liability coverage with foreign companies is not recognized, *regardless of what your insurance agent may tell you.* Without Mexican coverage, you may wind up in jail if you're involved in an accident.

Mexican vehicle liability policies include coverage for anything towed, including boats and trailers, which must be listed on the policy. For an additional fee, liability coverage can be purchased to cover boats while on the water for $83. While the risk of a boat accident is less than for vehicles, the same consequences can follow if there is no insurance coverage. Liability-only coverage for vehicles costs just $61 for a full year for any vehicle.

Physical damage

Coverage for damage to your vehicle and boat can also be purchased from a Mexican company. Sample rates from the Vagabundos del Mar Boat and Travel Club range from $101 per year for a vehicle valued up to $5,000 to $165 up to $20,000, $231 up to $40,000, and $347 up to $80,000. Some United States companies extend coverage for a short distance into México, up to about 75 miles south of the border, which doesn't take you very far.

Customs

México

Each tourist may bring into México duty-free:

- Items for personal use, such as clothes, shoes, and toiletries
- One video camera with battery packs, two cameras, 12 rolls of film or video cassettes, and one pair of binoculars
- Magazines and books
- Camping and sporting equipment
- Twenty packs of cigarettes, 50 cigars, 150 grams of loose tobacco, and three liters of alcoholic beverages (must be over 18 years of age)
- Medicines and prescription drugs with a doctor's prescription
- One portable television, one radio, one tape recorder, one video cassette player, and 20 cassettes
- One typewriter

- One musical instrument that can be carried by hand
- One boat, one Jet Ski, one ATV (all-terrain vehicle), and one sailboard
- One bicycle

The first $50 worth of dutiable items is free. Campers may have their vehicles searched, but unless a tourist is carrying commercial quantities of marketable goods, furniture, or household appliances, there should be no problem. If asked what you have, the simple answer "things to camp with" usually will suffice.

You may be searched for fruits and vegetables at Guerrero Negro going either way across the Baja Norte–Baja Sur state line, or you may simply be asked what you have. Sometimes they will take things; other times they won't. The station is located a few hundred yards south of the big steel eagle at the state line. There is another such inspection station north of La Paz at Centenario, but rarely do they require tourists to stop.

Here is what a sign at Guerrero Negro says:

"Attention Travelers:

You are entering a fruit fly free area.

Do not bring the following products without authorization:

Oranges, grapefruit, zapote, plum, guava, mango, tejocote, mamey, fruit or ornamental plants or other restricted plant products, potato gold nematode.

B.C.S. is free of hog cholera and is eradicating avian salmonella and exotic Newcastle disease of poultry.

Do not bring live pigs and pork products (fresh meat, sausage, etc.) or live birds and poultry products (fresh meat, eggs, bird dung, etc.) without corresponding zoosanitary documentation.

For further information call 2-33-11 and 2-22-19 in La Paz."

If calling from the U.S., first dial 011-52-112.

United States

Clearing customs is not a particularly pleasant experience upon returning home from an idyllic sojourn in Baja, but informed travelers can ease the strain. Customs officials state that in order to get across the border quickly you must take an active role. It is your responsibility to be prepared, to be cooperative, not to be offended by their questions, and to have whatever documents you need ready to be presented.

Your attitude has a lot to do with how quickly or slowly you get across. If you cooperate with the inspector, it speeds things up. Answer questions fully. Don't come with all your purchases wrapped. Have them in the cab with you as you arrive at the gate. Bring a list of everything you have purchased in México with the value of each item. If you will be bringing dutiable items (cameras, lenses, binoculars, radios, etc.) into México, avoid possibly having to pay duty on them when returning to the United States by taking them to a customs office beforehand. There they will record serial numbers for each item and prepare a "Certificate of Registration for Personal Effects Taken Abroad." Keep these documents with you.

It helps to understand how customs inspectors perceive the people with whom they are dealing. Protecting national sovereignty is their main concern. What we normally consider our constitutional rights were deliberately excluded by the framers of the Constitution for citizens crossing back into the United States. We can be detained legally, strip-searched without probable cause, or examined without the usual need for prior information. The only right we have is to be treated courteously. Approach customs with the attitude that you have rights and you're on the wrong foot.

It helps to accept that the burden is on us and to realize that the questions are not meant to be personal, demeaning, or degrading. Rather, they are designed to help us get across the border by sorting out what the inspectors need to know.

A lot of people react very negatively to the questions. Beyond certain questions that must be asked, each inspector must determine what to ask you personally in order to get a sense of you and speed up the process. Sometimes the best way to do this is to ask a question deliberately intended to spark a reaction, like "What are you smuggling?" A lot of people smile and laugh. Some peoples' knuckles go white or other parts of the body respond involuntarily. For instance, the carotid artery can jump under stress. We were told of one fellow who crumbled and opened the trunk to show the inspector what he was smuggling.

Consider the process from the viewpoint of the inspectors, who work under very difficult circumstances. An eight-hour shift may run 16 hours. At the San Ysidro–Tijuana port of entry, they average about 100 cars per hour with three people per car, so they talk to 300 people per hour. Of these, the usual 10 percent are on the fringes of sanity. Rain, heat, cold, and noxious fumes take their toll. Inspectors move from lane to lane at the primary gates and to the secondary gates or the pedestrian area, but are on their feet for most of the day.

Immigration and Naturalization Service (INS) and Customs Service inspectors each staff half of the primary gates. Their purpose is to sort out the arrivals who merit further scrutiny at secondary, but also to keep the primary lanes moving. We were told there's about a 20 percent increase in traffic each year and that inspectors handle upward of 100 million crossings annually at San Ysidro–Tijuana—more people than all but a few nations have.

Customs and INS inspectors receive cross training and do their jobs at the primary gates in the same way. The people at the secondary gates perform specialized work—Customs, INS, or Agriculture.

Despite years of study, the problem of long customs lines has not yet—and may never be—solved. The weather has more to do with it than anything else. If it is pleasant in San Diego, everyone heads for Tijuana. In spite of how long a line seems, though, the typical crossing is complete in 45 minutes.

Intercepting smuggled goods is the major goal of our border people. Smugglers watch the border constantly to see if inspectors are easing off near the ends of their shifts. They even have nicknames for each inspector.

Smugglers have become very sophisticated, building compartments in drive shafts and otherwise manufacturing cars with invisible joints so inspectors can't tell where things are hidden. They hire and use grandpa and grandma types or 30-year-old clean-cut couples with a child. Since smugglers go to great lengths to blend in, the customs game is to keep a few moves ahead and intercept as many of them as possible. Those of us who make up the 90 percent who are plain old tourists can contribute to the effort by submitting gracefully to the necessary inconveniences.

You can expect to be sent to the secondary gates if you have been in México any length of time. Permitted fruits available in México are bananas, cactus fruits, dates, grapes, melons, papayas, pineapples, and strawberries. All other fruits are prohibited and will be confiscated.

Most vegetables are permitted, except sweet potatoes, yams, uncooked potatoes, and avocados with seeds.

Also prohibited are pork, including sausages, cold cuts, skins, and pork tacos, and raw poultry. Be aware that when crossing into the United States at Mexicali, inspectors make periodic checks of whitefish fillets to assure that they are not the protected totuava fish. Unless the meat can be identified by patches of skin, it may be taken for laboratory identification. If it's totuava, you will be hearing from them. If not, you have lost your fish.

Each individual is allowed $400 of dutiable items. Be sure to include all fruits, vegetables, and alcoholic beverages (one-liter limit in California) on your list, whether purchased in México or brought down with you. At this point the inspector can only assume it all came from México. Before leaving home, obtain the booklet *Know Before You Go* from a United States Customs office.

Aside from the 24-hour San Ysidro–Tijuana port of entry on U.S. Interstate 5 and Baja Highway 1, there are four other Baja ports of entry:

- Otay Mesa, on the east side of Tijuana near the airport, is usually faster than the San Ysidro–Tijuana port, but it requires too much driving in heavy traffic through Tijuana to suit us. We had to change a traffic-side boat trailer tire on an overpass in Tijuana after sunset (with no place to get off the road) and have had no further desire to use Otay Mesa. It is open from 6 A.M. to 10 P.M.

- Tecate, off U.S. Highway 94 and on Baja Highways 2 and 3, is very quick to get through. It is open from 6 A.M. to midnight.

- Mexicali, on U.S. Highway 111 and Baja Highway 5, is open 24 hours.

- Mexicali east, about seven miles east of Calexico on Highway 98 and south on Hwy 7, and east of Mexicali on Madero Avenue along the border fence, is open 6 A.M to 10 P.M.

- Algodones, about 47 miles east of Calexico on U.S. Interstate 8 and three miles south on Highway 186, and about 19 miles east of Mexicali on Baja Highway 8, is open from 6 A.M. to 8 P.M.

Firearms and Drugs

Save yourself inestimable grief by leaving these seriously illegal items home. Pistols are an absolute no-no. Don't bring boxes of .22 shells for trading stock either. If they are found, it will be assumed that a gun is close at hand and your vehicle may be demolished in the search. If you are expecting to hunt, be sure you obtain all firearm permits, as well as hunting licenses and permits, beforehand.

Expect to be stopped several times at military roadblocks checking for firearms or drugs. The soldiers are uniformly polite and usually do not search tourist's vehicles. If they do, one person should accompany the soldier inside. There is a permanent roadblock a few miles south of Maneadero and one at the state line north of Guerrero Negro, manned by a garrison of career soldiers.

Bring prescriptions for all medications that require them at home to satisfy U.S. Customs and for painkillers, tranquilizers, many diet pills, and other controlled substances purchased in México to satisfy Mexican authorities. Have no street drugs or funny cigarettes. A Mexican jail is not a pleasant place to spend your vacation. Once you break the law, you cease to be a tourist and any assistance that tourists are entitled to disappears.

Vehicle Preparation

México is full of good mechanics who are very inventive in fixing things using what they have to work with. However, they are not into on-board computers, turbochargers, and other high-tech innovations. The simpler the workings of your vehicle, the better your chances of getting it repaired. The government also provides a safety net for travelers in need in the form of the Green Angels.

These green utility trucks are manned by English-speaking mechanics and cover each section of most paved highways in Baja California. They carry spare gasoline, for which you pay, and a few tools. Most importantly, they have short-wave radios linked in a network by numerous microwave towers. If they can't get you going, they can call a tow truck to take you to a shop. Tips are appreciated, but seldom offered by tourists. Feel free to help these lifesavers out in return for their assistance.

Of course, prevention is always best. Have your vehicle serviced and checked over thoroughly before leaving home and stock some basic spare parts that might come in handy if you break down in a remote area. The following items are suggested:

Pre-travel service:

- Tune-up
- Oil and filter change
- Air filter change
- Gas filter change
- Lubrication
- Check and/or pack wheel bearings
- Inspect all hoses under the hood and replace if unduly soft or brittle
- Inspect all belts and replace if frayed
- Check wiper blades and replace if necessary
- Check shock absorbers and replace if necessary
- Check and clean battery terminals (fluid level and general condition)
- Check front-end alignment
- Check tires for condition and pressure, including spares
- Check turn signals
- Check wheel lug nuts for tightness (periodically recheck in Baja, too)

Spare parts:

- Belts, one for each under the hood
- Air filter, one
- Points and plugs, one set each
- Tire, one mounted on a wheel (many sizes of tires for RVs are not available in México, so play it safe and bring your own)
- Tire tubes, one (if you have tube-type tires)
- Hitch ball, one (if you are pulling a trailer)
- Hoses, one for each under the hood
- Keys, one spare set
- Oil, enough for a change plus extra for an emergency (like the time we poured in a quart of transmission fluid by mistake and decided to drain the oil right then and there—it was time anyway)
- Oil filters, two

- Gas filters, two (if you have a gasoline-burning vehicle)
- Diesel filters, two (if you have a diesel-burning vehicle)
- Octane booster, if premium gas is required (you may have to use some low octane Nova gasoline)

Obtaining spare parts in México for vehicles and boats from the U.S. has become very difficult. Currently it is necessary to carry them by hand instead of having them shipped. Carriers are not willing to hassle with the required customs duty.

Toolbox:

We carry a simple metal toolbox measuring 19 inches long, 7 inches wide, and 7.5 inches high. It has no trays—just one big compartment into which everything is layered. Over the years, we have tossed in one item after another. Here's what it holds:

- 22-piece socket set with 1/4-inch and 3/8-inch drives in a carrying case, including 6-inch and 12-inch extensions
- 3/4-inch socket set
- 8-inch and 12-inch crescent wrenches
- Four-piece SAE flare-nut wrench set
- Nine-piece combination wrench set
- Distributor wrenches
- Monkey wrench
- Pipe wrench
- Oil filter and gas filter wrenches
- Regular pliers
- Vise-grip pliers
- Channel-lock pliers
- Lineman's pliers
- Needle-nose pliers
- Wire cutters
- 18-piece hex key set
- Claw hammer
- Hacksaw

- Keyhole saw
- Battery terminal cleaning tool
- Tape measure
- Half-round file
- Round file
- Half-round wood rasp
- Pry bar
- Two putty knife scrapers
- Wire stripping/crimping tool
- Spark plug tool
- Five blade and four Phillips head screwdrivers from small to large sizes
- Brake-adjusting tool
- Drive pins
- Assorted taps
- Cold chisel
- Scissors
- 12-volt test light
- Alligator-clip test leads
- Steel wool
- Spool of fine copper wire
- Duct tape
- Plastic ties

Essential items that won't fit in the toolbox:

- Jack, heavy enough for your vehicle
- Lug wrench
- Flashlights, two, plus extra batteries
- Jumper cables
- Small shovel
- Small ax
- Volt meter

- 110-volt tire-inflating compressor
- WD-40
- Siphoning hose

Driving Safely

Keep firmly in mind that Highway 1 from Tijuana to Cabo San Lucas and all the other paved roads in Baja were built for the trucks and buses that keep the necessities of life flowing. The highways were not designed for tourists accustomed to zipping around on freeways.

Also consider before your trip what you will do if your vehicle stops moving down the highway (for one of innumerable unpredictable reasons) and you have to go for help. Who goes and who stays with the vehicle? This amounts to a major decision fraught with conflicting imperatives.

Aside from the companionship, there is much to be said for traveling with others. On one of our trips in which we towed a boat and trailer behind our camper, the tongue broke and the boat and trailer had to be left alongside the highway while one of us drove off for a tow truck. Assuming that the boat would attract the curiosity of passersby and generate a desire to see what it contained, we were convinced that someone had to stay with it. Gloria volunteered, feeling a sense of security because a group of field-workers was just across the highway. If they had not been there, we could not have left her alone.

It would have been much simpler if we were traveling with another couple who could have parked alongside the boat while we went off to get help.

Something else to keep in mind is that turn signals are used differently in México. A driver ahead of you will use a turn signal to notify you that it's OK to come ahead and pass. You have to decide if it is safe to do so, but don't count on him turning left. However, if an intersection is coming up, it is wise to wait to see if the driver will turn. Keep this in mind when you use your left turn signal in the usual fashion—or else you may turn into someone who misread you and tried to pass.

If you want to become an old Baja hand, adhere diligently to two simple lifesaving rules:

Rule 1: Don't drive over 50 miles per hour.

Baja's roads are narrower than we're used to and don't have shoulders. Trucks and buses drive fast. You are certain to meet one just where the highway is narrowest—where concrete abutments for culverts pinch in on the pavement on each side. This is when you must have precise control of where your right wheels are, even more so if you are towing something. Slowing quickly from 50 miles per hour allows precisely controlled evasive action—safely.

Take it for granted that sooner or later you will enter a curve to meet an oncoming truck or bus taking part of your lane, but you won't be able to pull to the right because a row of boulders is in your way. Instead of flares or reflective markers, the locals use boulders to steer others away from their stalled vehicles—then often leave the rocks in place when they move on. You must be able to stop or slow down enough to let the truck or bus go by.

Rule 2: Don't drive at night.

The dangerous situations discussed in Rule 1 become impossible to deal with safely at night. Then there are the black cows, horses, and burros that roam on open range and are not visible until you are right on them. They love to feed on the side of the highway where the vegetation grows lush from rainfall sliding off the pavement and, of course, will usually stand right in the middle of the highway to contemplate their next move.

If you are thinking of driving to Cabo in two days from the border, have your affairs in order—it's suicidal.

One of Parkinson's laws of management is that work expands to fill the time available in which to do it. The corollary is that grand vacations are compressed into the limited time available in which to take them. If your Scrooge of a boss will give you only a week off and you have been dying to spend it in Cabo, forget driving—fly, that's what airplanes are for. If you must drive, forget Cabo. Settle for some other destination you can reach comfortably without violating the above rules, like San Felipe, San Quintín, or Bahía de Los Angeles. After a day of driving, take a cool, refreshing shower, then kick back. This gives you more time to get into the Baja mind-set and have a stress-free, relaxed stay in mañana land.

Fuel

Gasoline and diesel fuel are readily available from Pemex service stations on the Transpeninsular Highway and in all cities at prices roughly equal to those in the United States.

Gasoline comes in two grades: leaded Nova rated at 80 octane (blue pumps) and unleaded Magna Sin rated at 92 octane (green pumps). Some people feel that these ratings are a few points higher than the U.S. rating system. Diesel comes in red pumps.

The vehicles that we use run on unleaded regular gasoline in the United States and run just fine on Magna Sin, while Nova creates pinging. Vehicles that need premium gas in the United States should not be taken into Baja.

One of the precautions we exercise in Baja is to drive off the top one-quarter of our two tanks (full on one, half-full on the other). As soon as you pass a Pemex station with less than three-quarters of your fuel supply left, you can count on finding the next two stations temporarily out of gas. We have had to take gas out of our boat to help get stranded optimists on their way after having waited a day or two for a gas truck to arrive. This is where a realistic understanding of the word "mañana" comes in handy—rather than "tomorrow" it really means "not today."

Several games are played at gas stations to extract more money from you than you owe. It pays to have locking gas caps so that no one can start pumping until you are standing there. Otherwise, the pump may not be reset to zero. You also have to watch to see that the attendant does not suddenly reset the pump, then restart it without you knowing what you had on it. At least know the maximum number of liters your tank will hold so you can refuse to pay for more than that. Have your own calculator, since many pumps have inoperable total-price indicators. We pay in pesos to avoid varying dollar exchange rates.

Losing a little at these low-stakes games once in a while keeps us on the lookout for new variations. Look at them as contests that enliven the tedium of steady driving. On the other side of the coin, we have had some amazing experiences with attendants returning substantial overpayments when both of us later realized what happened. One fellow had written the calculations on the palm of his hand and referred right to it when we came back for a recount. Fortunately, he had not needed to wash his hands in the interim.

Some vehicles run on propane *(gas butano)*, which is sparsely available. On the Transpeninsular Highway, there are plants only in Ensenada, Colonia Vicente Guerrero, Guerrero Negro, Santa Rosalía, Ciudad Constitución, La Paz, and San José del Cabo. Propane is provided for household use rather than vehicles. While it can be obtained for vehicles, doing so is difficult.

Ferries

There is ferry service from Baja to the mainland between Santa Rosalía and Guaymas, La Paz and Topolobampo (Los Mochis), and La Paz and Mazatlán. Fares and departure times are subject to change without notice. Arrival times depend upon the weather. If you are towing something, bring it with you when obtaining your ticket so overall length can be determined.

Departures from Santa Rosalía are at 8 A.M. Sundays and Wednesdays, arriving in Guaymas about seven hours later. Departures from Guaymas are 8 A.M. Tuesdays and Fridays. The Santa Rosalía terminal is on the pier in the middle of town on Highway 1.

The ferry office in La Paz is at Cinco de Mayo and Guillermo Prieto. The departure and arrival terminal is north of town at Pichilingue. Departures for Topolobampo are at 11 A.M. daily, arriving about nine hours later. Departures from Topolobampo are at 10 P.M. daily.

Departures for Mazatlán are at 3 P.M. daily, arriving about 18 hours later. The reverse trip is on the same time schedule.

Fares increase periodically. The latest in dollars were:

Class	Guaymas	Topolobampo	Mazatlán
Salon	$13	$13	$20
Tourist	$26	$26	$39
Cabin	$39	$39	$59
Special cabin	$52	$52	$78
Autos to 16.5 ft.	$149	$129	$212
Autos to 21.5 ft.	$194	$168	$275
Auto/trailer to 29.7 ft.	$268	$232	$381
Auto/trailer to 56.1 ft.	$504	$438	$719
Bus/motor home	$359	$221	$359
Motorcycle	$19	$14	$24

A "salon" has numbered seats. "Tourist" fare is for a stateroom with two to four berths, with a washstand inside and bathrooms and toilets outside. "Cabin" fare is for a stateroom with two berths with complete bathroom facilities inside. A "special cabin" is a suite with a living room, a complete bathroom, bedrooms, and a closet.

Information and reservations can be obtained at a central source in Mazatlán by calling SEMATUR at their toll-free number, 91-800-6-9696, from inside México, or at these departure points:

- Muelle Fiscal, Apartado Postal 72, Santa Rosalía, Baja California Sur, México; phone 011-52-115-2-0013 or 0014.

- Guillermo Prieto y Cinco de Mayo, La Paz, Baja California Sur, México; phone 011-52-112-5-5700; Pichilingue Terminal phone 011-52-112-2-5005 or fax 011-52-112-5-8899.

- Muelle Fiscal, Guaymas, Sonora, México; phone or fax 011-52-622-2-3390.

- Muelle Fiscal, Topolobampo, Sinaloa, México; phone 011-52-686-2-0141 or fax 011-52-686-2-0035.

- Terminal Transbordadores, Mazatlán, Sinaloa, México; phone 011-52-69-81-7020 or 1-7021, fax 011-52-69-81-7023.

On-board services include an information and passenger assistance office; a cafeteria; a kiosk selling magazines, film, pharmacy items, and gifts; free medical service (medications must be paid for); projection of video films; a cellular telephone; toilets; and lockers.

Money

Dollars are universally accepted, but we like to have sufficient pesos to use at gas stations and other businesses with prices in pesos to avoid losing on the exchange. We stop on the United States side of the border to pick up a few hundred dollars worth, then rely on buying more at banks or exchange houses. Unfortunately, more and more banks are refusing to take traveler's checks due to extensive fraud. Debit cards and regular credit cards work at some banks for obtaining cash. ATM cards can also be used, but there have been many instances in La Paz and Cabo San Lucas of unauthorized withdrawals being made.

Telephones

There are several ways to make long distance phone calls from Baja, either to another country or within México. The newest, simplest, and cheapest method is to purchase a TELNOR or TELMEX telephone card from any of numerous shops throughout Baja for 25, 35, 50, or 100 pesos. These are inserted in any of a multitude of pay phones on sidewalks labeled *Ladatel—Red de Telephonia Publica* (look for the card slot in the upper left-hand corner). Insert the card, dial 95, the area code, then the number and start talking. When 20 seconds are left on the card, a countdown appears in the readout window. We made two calls from San Felipe to Sacramento on a 25-peso card (at that time the peso was 7.5 to the dollar, costing us all of about $1.65 per each call of about five minutes). This is without a doubt the least expensive way to call.

Unfortunately, many shops displaying *Larga Distancia* signs no longer offer the operator assistance that used to be the cheapest way to call, but now entice you to use one of the privately owned blue or black phones mentioned below. These should be avoided at all costs.

You can pick up any pay phone on the street, insert a small coin, and dial 09 for the English-speaking operator. (Most pay phones have a sign illustrating the different coins that can be used, but if in doubt, hold out a handful to someone nearby and let him/her pluck out an appropriate one.) Give the phone number and your name, then say it's collect. Charging to an international calling card will avoid a large tax, but since we have heard stories of tourists using a card in a *Larga Distancia* and later having other international calls charged to it, this may be too risky. It's simpler to use the TELNOR or TELMEX cards.

You can also dial 95-800-462-4240 from any public telephone marked *Ladatel* to get AT&T in Houston, Texas. Give the number you are calling and your calling card number, just like at home. Privately owned blue or black phones with signs offering calls to be paid for by international credit cards are found mounted on walls everywhere. You simply pick them up and dial the operator to place your call. The charge is exorbitant, as you might expect, since the establishment gets a big cut from the private company providing the service. Also, you can sign up for Mexican cellular service and use your cellular phone—but this is also a very expensive way to go.

Stick with the TELNOR or TELMEX prepaid cards, unless your constitution is strong enough to stand enormous phone bills when you get home. You may get all tensed up again and have to go back to Baja to relax.

Time Zones

Both Baja Norte and Baja Sur now observe daylight saving time. Baja Norte is in the Pacific time zone and Baja Sur is in the Mountain time zone.

Tourists have been known to miss a whale-watching reservation in Guerrero Negro by failing to set their clocks ahead an hour when crossing the state line.

Chapter 1

Northwest
Baja Norte

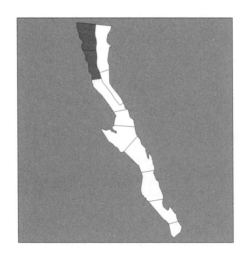

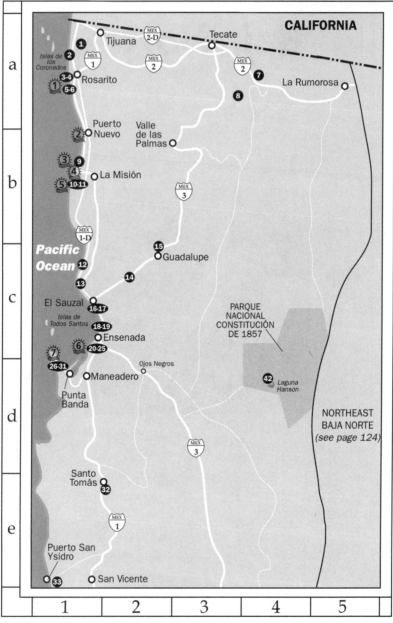

CALIFORNIA

Tijuana

MEX 2-D

Tecate

Islas de los Coronados

MEX 1

MEX 2

Rosarito

MEX 2

La Rumorosa

Puerto Nuevo

Valle de las Palmas

La Misión

MEX 3

Pacific Ocean

Guadalupe

MEX 1-D

El Sauzal

Islas de Todos Santos

Ensenada

Maneadero

Ojos Negros

PARQUE NACIONAL CONSTITUCIÓN DE 1857

Laguna Hanson

NORTHEAST BAJA NORTE
(see page 124)

Punta Banda

MEX 3

Santo Tomás

MEX 1

Puerto San Ysidro

San Vicente

Baja Map .... *page* 8

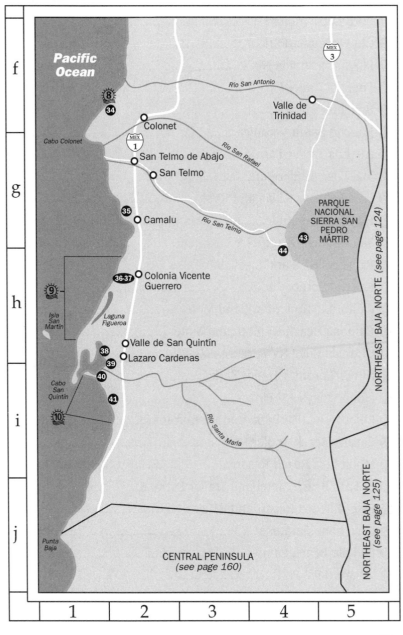

Pacific Ocean

MEX 3

Río San Antonio

8
34

Valle de Trinidad

Cabo Colonet

Colonet

MEX 1

San Telmo de Abajo

Río San Rafael

San Telmo

35

Camalu

Río San Telmo

PARQUE NACIONAL SIERRA SAN PEDRO MÁRTIR

43

44

9

Isla San Martín

36-37

Colonia Vicente Guerrero

Laguna Figueroa

Valle de San Quintín

38

Lazaro Cardenas

39

40

Cabo San Quintín

41

10

Río Santa María

Punta Baja

CENTRAL PENINSULA
(see page 160)

NORTHEAST BAJA NORTE *(see page 124)*

NORTHEAST BAJA NORTE *(see page 125)*

f

g

h

i

j

1   2   3   4   5

Northwest Baja Norte Campgrounds

Northwest Baja Norte's 10 Best Beaches

Northwest Baja Norte

The Pacific coast from the border to where Highway 1 turns inland near El Rosario is very popular with tourists because of its proximity to the United States. It is easy to throw some things in a rig on the spur of the moment and head south for a few days of relaxation and decompression from the hustle and bustle of life in Southern California.

People suffering from summer heat in inland areas can hole up on a cool southern beach and dunk themselves in the nippy Pacific waters, still carrying overtones of the frigid Arctic via the Japanese current. Accordingly, summer is the high season.

Fishing can be very good in the surf and even better offshore. Pismo clams lurk beneath the sand at low tide, and the waters draw surfers and scuba divers. Travelers with agile vehicles can make forays inland to hot springs, mountain national parks, an observatory, and other hideaways.

Those who prefer the urban scene can knock about in glitzy Tijuana and the somewhat more sedate Ensenada. Golfers will find ample opportunities for teeing off. In short, there is something for everyone in Northwest Baja California Norte.

Getting through Tijuana

The first thing you have to do is wend your way through Tijuana without getting off course. As you approach the border from the north, get in the right-hand lane. Once you're through the border gate into México and cleared out of secondary inspection, stay in the lane going up the overpass ahead beneath the sign indicating "Highway 1D" and "Rosarito, Ensenada, Scenic Road." The next signs over that lane say the same thing as the road swings left in a circle to deposit you along the south side of the border fence.

Drive carefully and don't let the local speeders rush you along. Stay to the right as you climb a big hill so you can exit to the right after the road swings left and drops down into an arroyo, following the sign to Rosarito-Ensenada. You will come onto a wider thoroughfare heading west up a steep grade. If you are towing anything, maintain your momentum. Keep following signs to Rosarito-Ensenada. A left turn over the last hill puts you onto the *cuota* (toll) road. Current tolls at each of the three tollbooths are:

Class	Pesos	Dollars
Two-axle passenger cars, pickups, and motorcycles	$12	$1.50
Two-axle buses and trucks	$23	$2.90
Three-axle buses and trucks.....................	$23	$2.90
Four-axle trucks	$42	$5.25
Five-axle trucks	$42	$5.25
Six-axle trucks..	$62	$7.75
Extra axles for passenger cars	$6	$0.75
Extra axles for buses and trucks	$10	$1.25

(dual rear wheels count as an extra axle)

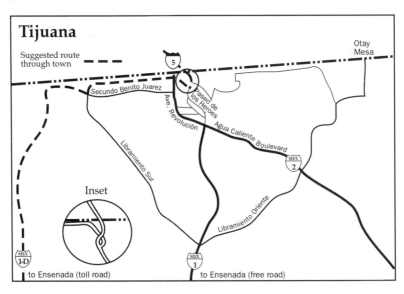

Rosarito–La Misión Area
(campgrounds 1–11, pages 92–97)

Rosarito is almost a suburb of Tijuana, but not quite, with less than 10 miles between them. For tourists it offers the first beach-town environment south of the border and thus is very popular.

Developers are building up this stretch of coast with hotels and condominiums. Still, you'll find quite a cluster of RV parks in and around Rosarito. Several in town have been around for many years and are mostly full of permanently dug-in trailers that show the debilitating effects of sitting for years in a salt-air environment. If you favor this area, look over your options before settling into one to be sure you have found the spot that suits you best. The high season is summer.

Golf

Two highly regarded golf courses are near Rosarito, and a third is about 47 miles south at Bajamar.

The Tijuana Golf and Country Club is on Agua Caliente Boulevard, past the twin towers of the Grand Hotel Tijuana. Its 18-hole course is open from 7 A.M. to 8 P.M. seven days a week. Phone 011-52-66-81-7855.

The Real del Mar Golf Club in San Antonio has 18 holes. Follow signs on the toll road, Highway 1D. Call (800) 803-6038 for reservations. Starting times begin at 10 A.M. seven days a week.

The Bajamar Oceanfront Golf Resort, about five miles south of La Misión on Highway 1, has 27 holes. Call 011-52-615-5-0151.

Sporting Events

Bullfighting is a traditional Mexican spectacle. Every summer Sunday from May to September, a *corrida de toros* is held in one or the other of Tijuana's two bullrings—the old Plaza de Toros downtown on Agua Caliente Boulevard or the newer ring by the beach against the border. Tickets can be obtained at the ring or from the ticket office downtown. Prices depend on whether you want to sit in the afternoon sun *(sol)* or shade *(sombra)* and how far you are from ringside. *Sombra* is definitely more comfortable. Reserve tickets by calling 011-52-66-86-1290.

Like bullfighting, the game of jai alai is never dull. The action can be riveting, as the hard little ball flies around almost faster than the eye can see. The skill and agility of the players is astounding. You can bet on each match, and the program tells you about every player. In the evening, when you're tired of shopping on Avenida Revolución, simply walk up the street to Calle 7, enter the palatial fronton (jai alai arena), sit down, and watch the athletes with the long basket on one hand do their work.

Horse and dog racing fans can head to the Agua Caliente Racetrack. It's been around seemingly forever, and every map shows it as a landmark. Just go east of downtown on Agua Caliente Boulevard. Greyhounds race during the week, then horses take to the track on weekends.

Shopping

Shopping in Tijuana is a major event, and can be both exciting and rewarding. Tijuana is no place to shop for day-to-day necessities, though. For that, head to Rosarito.

The center of commerce in Tijuana for traditional Mexican wares is Avenida Revolución from Calle 1 to Calle 9, plus all the side streets and alleys that branch off. There are many, many shops offering everything you can imagine. Storekeepers are fairly aggressive about herding potential customers into their establishments. That's fine— go on in and look around, and ask about prices for any items that appeal to you. Feel the storekeeper out on what price he might accept, then go on your way and start comparing prices at other shops. You'll find identical items all along the street and will gradually get an idea of what price is fair to both of you. Don't be afraid to haggle. Haggling is part of the enjoyment for seller and buyer alike. Keep a smile on your face and talk softly. Develop a rapport, taking care to admire the workmanship and quality of the goods. Politely make an offer. If you bid too low, it may be considered an insult. Developing a feel for the "real" price is important.

Tijuana is a manufacturing center for many goods, including those fashioned from leather, onyx, wood, and metal. Accordingly, you can buy these items cheaper here than in other cities because there are no freight costs to factor in. We once purchased some little onyx carvings near El Mármol, nearly 300 miles south of Tijuana. Since the onyx came from there, we thought it was the best place to purchase the manufactured product. Then the lady told us they would send the uncarved blocks to Tijuana and have the finished items shipped back. We would have fared better on Avenida Revolución.

Be wary of leather goods made from unfamiliar animal skins. If United States Customs officers suspect they are from endangered species, they might relieve you of the items for closer inspection and you may never see them again.

A more modern shopping area is Plaza Río Tijuana, the site of large department stores and upscale shops. We have made several pre-Christmas forays here armed with shopping lists for everyone in the family and always left knowing we saved a bundle. Many groups of people come across the border from the United States for a fun day of shopping here.

Be careful of the flea markets you'll encounter around Tijuana. Customs officials have found that many things sold there, particularly electronic items such as stereos and TVs, were heisted in the United States. Obtain receipts to prove that you did not purchase items at one of the flea markets that is "hot" at the moment.

Rosarito has some nice shops, particularly in the arcade at the Rosarito Beach Hotel. The free road south of Rosarito is lined with pottery shops and a few small pottery factories. Check out the prices in the factories—they're generally lower, as this is where the shops buy their products. We often stop on the way home from a Baja trip to add to our collection of Mexican pottery.

Sightseeing

The Tijuana Cultural Center in the Zona Río at Paseo de los Heroes and Avenida Independencia houses a museum, an Omnimax theater with a 180-degree wraparound screen on which special films are shown, and a performing arts theater that features changing performances. There is also a shopping arcade. The cost of admission to the theater depends on the performance. The Cultural Center is open from Monday to Friday from 11 A.M. to 7 P.M. and on weekends from 11 A.M. to 8 P.M. If you get a chance to see "Los Voladores de Papantla," don't miss their act. These men climb a tall pole, attach themselves to long ropes, then swing down to the ground in a breathtaking spiral.

Covering a city block, Mexitlan on Calle 2 and Avenida Ocampo in Tijuana, displays more than 150 scale models of México's pyramids, colonial churches, and modern buildings. There are also shows featuring music and dances from the country's various regions. After dark, hidden lights dramatically illuminate the model buildings. Mexitlan is open daily, except Tuesday, from 10 A.M. to 8 P.M. and in summer from 10 A.M. to 10 P.M. Hours are extended on holidays and weekends.

Dining

If you have ever enjoyed a Caesar's salad, you might want to stop in at Caesar's Hotel on Avenida Revolución and Calle 4 to have another. This is supposedly where it was invented.

There are lots, and we mean lots, of restaurants in Tijuana, so many we won't even try to sort them all out here. However, we do highly recommend one that we have considered special for decades—the Coronet on Calle 7 off Avenida Revolución. The quail entrée has brought us back again and again.

The village of Puerto Nuevo, south of Rosarito, specializes in lobster. If you're in town for lunch or dinner, try one of the smaller restaurants where the atmosphere is more homey and the prices a bit lower. We like Nachos on Chinchorro, the second street on the left as you enter town.

Farther south in La Misión, we particularly enjoy dining at La Fonda on the outside patio overlooking the surf.

Nightlife

Tijuana has several discos and nightclubs. Well-known establishments include: Mike's Bar, on Avenida Revolución and Calle 6; Disco Regine and Disco Cosmos, housed in the same building on Avenida Revolución and Calle 6; and 2001 Disco Club, at 3401-4 Agua Caliente Boulevard.

Ensenada Area
(campgrounds 12–33, pages 97–110)

Ensenada is not quite a border town, but since it's only 68 miles south of the United States via the fast toll road, many people from Southern California flock to the area for weekend visits. Another popular route, only four miles longer, is south from Tecate on Highway 3. Though this option takes a half hour more, it's a very pretty drive through mountains and valleys lush with vineyards, orchards, and other agri-

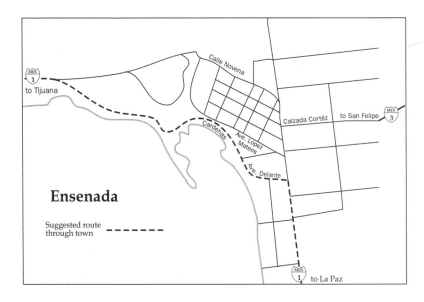

cultural communities. An exceptional benefit of reentering the United States through Tecate instead of Tijuana is much lighter traffic and ease in clearing customs. Be sure to arrive before midnight, as it closes down then until 6 A.M.

Ensenada is the most convenient place to validate your tourist card before continuing on down the peninsula. For details, see "Licenses and Permits" in the Travel Tips chapter.

Fishing

Fishing can be good out of Ensenada off Islas de Todos Santos and Punta Banda for albacore, barracuda, bonita, mackerel, kelp bass, lingcod, and other rockfish. Several fishing fleets operate out of the sportfishing dock just east of the fish market. Access and parking is very tight, as you have to thread your way around and between buildings. Once past the big speed bumps in front of the shipyards coming into Ensenada, turn right at the arterial stop sign (a big Pemex gas station is across the intersection). Go through the first light and turn at the first street to the right (the Hotel Santo Tomás is across the street). Go a very short block toward the fish market and take the first left turn, in front of the fish market. Continue and take the first right turn, then head left to the sportfishing fleet offices on the waterfront. Passenger cars and pickups do much better than motor homes on this route. Look it over before committing yourself. It may be wise to take a cab from wherever you are staying. If you are heading to the fish market, after going the very short block toward it, take the first right turn and find a parking place.

Gordo's Sportfishing has five boats ranging from 36 feet long (which can seat 12 people) to 70 feet (up to 35 people). They will go with seven to 10 passengers at the minimum. Life jackets and tackle are provided if needed. Many fishermen bring their own gear. The boats leave the dock at 7 A.M. and return at 2:30 P.M. There is always live bait. It is best to purchase tickets at the office, for you can be cheated on the street. You must receive a printed ticket. Contact them at Apartado Postal 35, Ensenada, Baja California, México; phone 011-52-617-8-2377.

Ensenada Clipper Fleet has four boats ranging from 46 feet to 85 feet long. The price includes use of a life jacket, rod and reel, hooks, and sinkers for top fishing. Boats leave daily at 7 A.M. and return at 3 P.M. Contact them at 2630 East Beyer Boulevard, Suite 678, San Ysidro, CA 92143; phone 011-52-617-8-2185 in México.

Ensenada Sportfishing Charters can be reached at 8030 La Mesa Boulevard #136, La Mesa, CA 91941; phone 011-52-617-8-2185 in México.

Smaller boats can be engaged at the docks or at Punta Banda from independent sportfishing operators or panga fishermen who sometimes rent their boats and hire themselves out as guides. Punta Banda is about 25 miles from Ensenada and takes about one hour to reach by car. Try Loco Lobo Surf and Tackle at 011-52-615-4-2144. Captain Eric Hyman has a 26-foot Searay, loaded for fishing.

Golf

The entrance road to the Baja Country Club is two miles south on Highway 1 from the Estero Beach Hotel turnoff. On the left, there is a sign and two large pillars. Drive three miles east to the entrance, then around the golf course to the left to the clubhouse.

Shopping

Ensenada is one of the best places to shop in Baja, and Avenida Lopez Mateos is the center of the action. Just strolling down Lopez Mateos and window-shopping is a delight. Bargaining is enjoyed by both shoppers and shopkeepers, provided the haggling is kept light with a tinge of humor and respect for both the merchandise and the vendor. Don't be shy about bargaining—you can be certain there is no way you will purchase an article for less than bottom price. One shop we stop at, Galeria Mexicana, on the left before the entrance to the Estero Beach Resort and RV Park (page 104) always has a variety of unique items from all over México.

The Ensenada fish market is an interesting place to shop, dine, or just look. The displays of fish are colorful and attractive, and food stalls serve up wonderful fish products. We particularly enjoy the deep-fried *vieja*. Follow directions to the sportfishing dock listed above.

Sightseeing

There is much to see and do in Ensenada. Pick up a complimentary copy of the *Baja Sun* newspaper to get tips on what to do, where to shop, where to go, how to get there, where to eat, and where to stay.

Take a tour of México's oldest winery, Bodegas Santo Tomás, at 666 Avenida Miramar between Calle 6 and Calle 7 in Ensenada. Wine tasting and a tour costs $2. Tours are given at 11 A.M., 1 P.M., and 3 P.M. every day.

Be sure to drive out to Punta Banda and see La Bufadora (the Blowhole) spout its geyser of seawater up the cliff face.

Dining

One of our favorite dining spots is El Rey Sol, at 1000 Avenida Lopez Mateos, a famous French restaurant in business since 1947. It is open from 10 A.M. to 10 P.M.

Haliotis, at 179 Avenida Delante (also known as Avenida Sangines), is a good choice for seafood; phone them at 011-52-617-6-0341.

Another good restaurant is KAIA, on Avenida Moctezuma between Calle 4 and Calle 5. It specializes in Basque cuisine, and the paella is among the finest around.

San Quintín Area

(campgrounds 34–41, pages 110–115)

This portion of Northwest Baja Norte's Pacific coast, while a bit farther south, is still within easy reach of Southern California. It is a popular destination for long weekends and extended vacations. Many people have established residences here for temporary use. For those traveling to or from southern parts of the peninsula, it also makes a convenient overnight stopping point before or after a day spent shopping in Ensenada.

Fishing

This is the preeminent activity that draws tourists to the area. Isla San Martín, Roca Ben, and other high spots in the ocean off the mouth of Bahía San Quintín offer good enough fishing to attract long-range boats from San Diego, even though it is a time-consuming and expensive boat ride. Now that fishermen can get out there easily in their own boats using the concrete launch ramps at the Old Mill Village (campground number 38)—or on a charter boat from the Old Mill establishment, Pedro's Pangas at the same location, or with San Quintín Sportfishing at Cielito Lindo Motel and RV Park (campground number 40)—they can enjoy the same great fishing at a fraction of the cost, *and* have the satisfaction of doing it on their own.

Offshore there are yellowtail, tuna, and bonita and, on the high spots, ample lingcod and rockcod. Inshore waters behind the surf harbor sand bass, corvina, halibut, perch, and other species that can also be taken in the surf from shore. In the bay, there are white sea bass, halibut, and others. Bahía San Quintín also has large blue crabs, the same critter that is considered a delicacy on the East Coast of the United States. Large Pismo clams inhabit the beaches. The Old Mill takes up to four people on each of their boats. A guide and safety equipment are provided. For reservations, call (619) 479-3476 or (800) 995-8482 or fax 011-52-617-7-7693.

To reserve a spot with Pedro's Pangas, call (888) 846-2252 or (619) 271-1167.

San Quintín Sportfishing at Cielito Lindo RV Park has 26-foot boats. Call Squidco at (619) 222-8955 or (800) 272-6236 for reservations.

Boating

The ramps are now paved with concrete, a major improvement. Keeping in the channel to the mouth of the bay requires local knowledge. Guides move or remove markers so as to protect their income. Inexperienced boaters have been known to spend the weekend stuck on mudflats. For cheap insurance, hire a guide to take you out if you cannot contrive to follow one of the Old Mill boats in the morning.

Bird-watching

Bahía San Quintín is one of Baja's prime estuaries for wintering migratory waterfowl. A growing number of dedicated bird-watchers, led by Pro Esteros, a Mexican conservation organization, are focusing their attention here to ensure the future health of the estuarine system. Fish populations use the bay for breeding, as do many birds, and other birds make this their winter grounds during their migrations.

Hunting

Waterfowl hunters find brant goose hunting to be very good in the marshes at the north end of Bahía San Quintín in winter. Quail hunting on the surrounding ranches can be very good, too.

Surfing

Surfers favor the beaches on the Pacific Ocean to the west, south to the mouth of Bahía San Quintín, and along Bahía Santa María.

Off-roading

Off-roaders find great enjoyment following wheel tracks on the peninsula between Bahía San Quintín and the Pacific Ocean. The volcanic cones that spread their lava and ash across this rugged terrain are prominent landmarks. There is much to see—and many flat tires to fix—when exploring here. Pristine campsites suitable for tent campers, vans, or small truck campers can be found on the remote Pacific shores.

Sightseeing

One side trip is to the ruins of Misión Santo Domingo de la Frontera. The Dominicans established the original mission in 1775 at a site two miles downstream from where the ruins now stand. It was moved in 1798 to obtain a more constant water supply. Aside from the usual cultivation of fruits, beans, and grains, it generated additional income through the sale of salt from San Quintín and sea otter pelts to Russian and United States traders. Epidemics struck down the native population eventually, and the mission was abandoned in 1839. Partial adobe brick walls from about five buildings are all that remain.

To get there, drive north from Colonia Vicente Guerrero on Highway 1 for about 1.5 miles. Take the signed turnoff and continue 2.5 miles east. The trip involves several crossings of Río Santo Domingo, a mere trickle, adding an adventurous note to the journey.

For a longer junket, try the Meling Ranch, about 31 miles east of Highway 1 through San Telmo. This historic, operating cattle ranch, originally known as Rancho San José, has developed facilities for tourists, including a pool. Pack trips on horses and mules can be arranged into the vast reaches of the Sierra San Pedro Mártir—a trip we have made. The ranch was founded in 1910 by Harry and Ella Johnson, only to be destroyed in 1911 during the Mexican Revolution and then rebuilt. Gold from placer deposits at Socorro was an important source of income. One of the Johnson daughters, Alberta, married Salve Meling, and the couple acquired the ranch in 1919.

The dusty dirt access road turns off Highway 1 about 6.5 miles south of Colonet, or eight miles north of Camalu. Heavy vehicles should not be taken, as there are steep grades. We drove up once with our 20-foot Born Free camper, which has its own axle behind the truck to support its rear end. One of the ladies at the Meling Ranch looked at us in wonder and asked, "You drove that up here?" We didn't know how to respond. Another 25 miles over steeper grades gets you to the National Observatory high in the pine forest of the Parque Nacional Sierra San Pedro Mártir. We wisely decided not to tackle that with our heavy rig. The ranch can put you up for the night in a room. They serve great meals.

Mountain Area
(campgrounds 42-44, pages 115–117)

The northern mountains of Baja Norte have several campgrounds that offer cool refuge from the summer heat, including two national parks in which camping is allowed at undeveloped sites. The northernmost park, Parque Nacional Constitución de 1857, covers 28,000 acres in the Sierra de Juárez and features conifer forests and a lake, Laguna Hanson. The other is Parque Nacional Sierra San Pedro Mártir, covering 160,000 acres. Its main features are conifer forests, trout streams, the highest peak in Baja—El Picacho del Diablo, at 10,154 feet in elevation—and the National Observatory. Los Manzanos Campground (campground number 44) is just outside the western border of this park.

❶ Rosarito KOA

Location: In San Antonio; Northwest Baja Norte map page 76, grid a1.

Campsites, facilities: There are 40 campsites with water and electricity, but no sewer hookups. Flush toilets, hot showers, laundry facilities, a dump station, and a small store are on the premises. Don't drink the well water, which is mineralized. The park is secured with a night watchman from 9 P.M. to 6 A.M. Tent campers are welcome. Obtain limited supplies here and go to Rosarito for the rest.

Reservations, fees: Reservations are accepted. Fees are high—$18 per night. Long-term rates are $80 per week and $185 per month.

Contact: Rosarito KOA, Apartado Postal 2082, Tijuana, Baja California, México; phone 011-52-66-13-3305 (direct) or 011-52-66-84-4814 (answering service). The U.S. address is P.O. Box 430513, San Ysidro, CA 92143.

Directions: Take the San Antonio exit off Highway 1D (the toll road) about 7.5 miles south of the Tijuana tollgate. Cross over the toll road to the east and drive up a cobblestoned driveway to the hillside site.

Trip notes: You might have guessed that the first campground you would encounter while heading south on Highway 1 is a KOA. Though it is not up to their usual standards, it is comfortable and attractive. There are lots of small trees, and the site slopes to the west so that each space has a distant ocean view. When asked what people do here, the manager said the permanents do nothing and most overnighters arrive late in the evening to stay over before crossing the border the next day. There are many things to keep you occupied, however, for those inclined to be active. Unfortunately, Tijuana is difficult to drive around, due to hectic traffic, unless you know where you are going. If you are towing anything, it isn't worth the aggravation. For RVers, the best way to do Tijuana is from one of the parks in San Ysidro or Chula Vista, California. You can get to the border by taxi or the Tijuana Trolley, which runs frequently from San Diego. Walk across the border, then catch a cab. Summer is the time to visit, as winter is chilly. For things to do in Tijuana and the surrounding area, please see page 81.

❷ Oasis Hotel and RV Resort

Location: North of Rosarito; Northwest Baja Norte map page 76, grid a1.

Campsites, facilities: There are 55 pull-through campsites with full hookups, palapas, concrete pads, tables, and barbecues. Facilities include tiled rest rooms with flush toilets and hot showers, laundry, a playground, restaurants, a live-music bar, a store, two Jacuzzis, and a sauna. For recreation there are two pools, horses for rent, billiards, Ping-Pong, miniature golf, a volleyball court, and a gym. Don't drink the water. The resort is secured with a guarded gate and employs six guards. Tent campers are not allowed. Obtain supplies in Rosarito.

Reservations, fees: Reservations are accepted. Fees are very high—$48 per night on weekends and $42 during the week. Longer-term rates can be negotiated.

Contact: Oasis Hotel and RV Resort, P.O. Box 158, Imperial Beach, CA 91933; phone 011-52-661-3-3250, 3253, or 3255 in Rosarito; fax 011-52-661-3-3252.

Directions: Drive 15 miles south of the Tijuana tollgate on Highway 1D (the toll road). The resort is on the beach at Kilometer 25.

Trip notes: Practically everything you could want to do is possible at this first-class resort. Should you want to leave, though, they also offer transportation to Tijuana, Rosarito, and Ensenada. If luxury is what you look for when camping, you will be comfortable. Summer is the time to visit, as winter is chilly. For things to do in Tijuana and the surrounding area, please see page 81.

❸ Coco Loco Trailer Park

Location: In Rosarito; Northwest Baja Norte map page 76, grid a1.

Campsites, facilities: There are nine campsites with full hookups and concrete pads. No facilities are available, not even toilets or showers. Don't drink the water. The park is secured with a gated wall, and the manager lives on the premises. Tent campers are not welcome. Obtain supplies in Rosarito.

Reservations, fees: All sites are first come, first served. The fee is very high—$25 per night.

Contact: Drive up and knock on the door.

Directions: Turn west off the main street of Rosarito at Quinta Plaza, which is one-quarter mile north of the big orange building, and head to the beach. A prominent sign at the corner says "Restaurant Bar La Hacienda de Villa." Look for the trailer park sign after driving one block.

Trip notes: The park is clean, and the location—right on Playa Rosarito—is choice. But the price tag is high, especially given the lack of facilities. Summer is the time to visit, as winter is chilly. For things to do in the Rosarito area, please see page 81.

❹ Chuy's Trailer Park

Location: In Rosarito; Northwest Baja Norte map page 76, grid a1.

Campsites, facilities: There are 26 campsites with full hookups and concrete pads. Flush toilets, hot showers, and a restaurant are on the property. Don't drink the water. A guard provides security at night. Obtain supplies in Rosarito.

Reservations, fees: Reservations are accepted. The fee is high—about $20 per night, varying according to the season.

Contact: Chuy's Trailer Park, Costa Azul 75, Rosarito, Baja California, México. There is no phone.

Directions: Turn west off the main street of Rosarito at Thrifty's, which is 100 yards north of the big orange building, and head to the beach.

Trip notes: This trailer park is crowded, and there is limited room for maneuvering a rig. Summer is the time to visit, as winter is chilly. For things to do in the Rosarito area, please see page 81.

❺ Playa Encantada No. 2

Location: South of Rosarito; Northwest Baja Norte map page 76, grid a1.

Campsites, facilities: Pit toilets are provided, but there are no other facilities. No water is available. Security is with a resident manager. Tent campers are welcome. Obtain supplies in Rosarito.

Reservations, fees: Camping is first come, first served. The fee is moderate— $8 per night.

Contact: Drive in and talk to the owner.

Directions: The beach is at Kilometer 30 on Highway 1 (the free road), about one mile south of Rosarito.

Trip notes: Park on level land on a bluff above the very nice little beach nestled between two points of land. You can lay back and enjoy the ocean just below, but you had better come fully prepared for primitive camping as the facilities are limited. Summer is the time to visit, as winter is chilly. For things to do in the Rosarito area, please see page 81.

❻ Popotla Trailer Park

Location: South of Rosarito; Northwest Baja Norte map page 76, grid a1.

Campsites, facilities: There are 33 campsites with full hookups and concrete pads. Clean, tiled rest rooms with flush toilets and hot showers, a pool, and a restaurant are on site. Don't drink the water. The park is secured with a guarded gate. Obtain supplies in Rosarito.

Reservations, fees: Reservations are accepted. Fees are high—$15 per night. Long-term rates are $84 per week and $300 per month.

Contact: Popotla Trailer Park, Kilometro 33 Carretara Ensenada, Rosarito, Baja California, México. There is no phone.

Directions: The park is at Kilometer 33 on Highway 1 (the free road), about three miles south of Rosarito.

Trip notes: Though primarily a residential facility, this trailer park does have some spaces for overnighters in a separate area. Campsites are near the ocean with a little beach, which creates a pleasant setting. Summer is the time to visit, as winter is chilly. For things to do in the Rosarito area, please see page 81.

➐ Rancho Ojai

Location: East of Tecate on Highway 2; Northwest Baja Norte map page 76, grid a4.

Campsites, facilities: The 41 full-hookup RV campsites are interspersed with some small trees and are near huge, old oaks. There also are 30 tent campsites under oaks. Facilities include tiled rest rooms with flush toilets and hot showers, central barbecues, tables, laundry, a store and a restaurant (both under construction when we visited), a clubhouse, volleyball, horseshoe pits, a playground, horse rentals, and horseback riding and hiking trails. The water is good to drink. Security is provided by a resident caretaker, with a fence and gate that's locked at 9 P.M. Obtain supplies in Tecate.

Reservations, fees: Reservations are accepted. Fees are high—$12 to $14 per night, $80 per week, $300 per month, and $2,400 per year for RVs; $10 per night, $55 per week, and $200 per month for tents.

Contact: Rancho Ojai, Apartado Postal 280, Tecate, Baja California, México; phone or fax 011-52-66-54-4772.

Directions: From Tecate, drive 13 miles east on Highway 2 to the camp on the north side of the road.

Trip notes: Until a decent turnoff is provided, you should slow down well before nearing the ranch and watch for a sign on the south side of the highway and the arched entranceway, which is plainly visible below the highway to the north. Traffic is heavy and fast, with lots of trucks and buses to contend with. In years past Rancho Ojai was a working cattle and horse ranch, but now it is being converted over for the use of campers. Some beautiful hiking and nature trails weave throughout the property. Nearby is a three-hole golf course (slated to be nine someday) at the Rancho Tecate Country Club and Resort. A greater distance away are the Valle de Guadalupe wineries, Ensenada, Tijuana, and the beaches in between. Summer is the time to come to escape the heat at lower elevations. It is cold in winter. For things to do in Tijuana and the surrounding area, please see page 81.

➑ Rancho Santa Veronica

Location: East of Tecate off Highway 2; Northwest Baja Norte map page 76, grid a4.

Campsites, facilities: This no-services campground has room for a number of RVs and tents. Huge oak trees provide shade. The property includes tiled rest rooms with flush toilets and hot showers, a hotel, a large pool, a restaurant, a playground, tennis courts, basketball and volleyball courts, picnic and barbecue areas, and off-road vehicle courses. Horses are available for rent. The water is OK to drink. Security is good due to the isolated location and staff being on the premises. Obtain supplies in Tecate.

Reservations, fees: Camping is first come, first served. The fee is low— $5 per night.

Contact: Rancho Santa Veronica, Agua Caliente Boulevard 4558-102B, Tijuana, Baja California, México; phone 011-52-66-81-7428 or fax 011-52-66-81-7429.

Directions: Drive 21 miles east of Tecate on Highway 2 to El Hongo, then head south on rotten, broken-up blacktop for four miles and on a washboard dirt road for three miles to Rancho Santa Veronica.

Trip notes: Driving off-road vehicles on the courses provided at this 5,000-acre former bull-breeding ranch is the backbone of family recreation. The full-service RV park here closed down a couple of years ago when plans for subdividing the area for homesites were drawn up. Summer is the time to visit, as winter is chilly. For things to do in Tijuana and the surrounding area, please see page 81.

❾ Alisitos Trailer Park

Location: In La Misión; Northwest Baja Norte map page 76, grid b1.

Campsites, facilities: Pit toilets are provided, but there are no other facilities. No water is available. The manager lives on the premises, so security is good. Tent campers are welcome. Obtain supplies in Rosarito.

Reservations, fees: Camping is first come, first served. The fee is very low— $3.50 per night.

Contact: Drive in and talk to the manager.

Directions: The park is at Kilometer 59 on Highway 1 (the free road), just north of the Hotel La Misión.

Trip notes: This is primitive camping on a flat area above a nice beach. The ocean is right below, creating a pleasant ambience. Summer is the time to visit, as winter is chilly. For things to do in the Rosarito area, please see page 81.

❿ Mal Paso Trailer Park

Location: South of La Misión; Northwest Baja Norte map page 76, grid b1.

Campsites, facilities: Facilities include mediocre flush toilets and cold showers. Don't drink the water. The owners live at the entrance of the compound, so security is good. It is ideal for tent camping. Obtain supplies in Rosarito.

Reservations, fees: Camping is first come, first served. The fee is low— $4 per night.

Contact: Drive in and talk to the owner.

Directions: From La Misión, drive 2.5 miles south on Highway 1D (the toll road). Cross the big creek bottom and the low ridge, then look for palms, trailers, and cabins to the right of a pedestrian overpass. Slow down and turn onto a dirt road into the RV park at Kilometer 71, just before the overpass.

Trip notes: This is one of the few places where you can camp right on the beach—and a marvelous beach it is. They have hauled in soil on top of the sand to allow for driving out to the high-tide line. The beach extends a short distance north and a long, long way south. We spent a very enjoyable night here. Summer is the time to visit, as winter is chilly. For things to do in the La Misión area, please see page 81.

⑪ Baja Seasons Villas and RVs

Location: South of La Misión; Northwest Baja Norte map page 76, grid b1.

Campsites, facilities: There are 137 campsites with concrete pads and full hookups, including satellite TV. Facilities include clean, tiled rest rooms with flush toilets and hot showers, steam rooms and saunas, laundry, a pool and spa, a restaurant and bar, a store, a clubhouse, a recreation room, a game room, a reading room, two night-lighted tennis courts, a volleyball court, a horseshoe pit, horses to rent, a putting green, and miniature golf. Also available are RV storage, safe-deposit boxes, and transportation to Ensenada. The well water is brackish, but you can get purified water in the restaurant. There is a fence around the park, a guarded gate, and 24-hour security inside. Tents are prohibited. Obtain supplies at the park store.

Reservations, fees: Reservations are accepted. Fees are very high—Oceanfront sites are $30 per night, $165 per week, and $545 per month in winter; $35 per night, $231 per week, and $775 per month in summer. Sites inside the park are $24 per night, $132 per week, and $330 per month in winter; $30 per night, $198 per week, and $545 per month in summer. Holiday rates are higher.

Contact: Baja Seasons Villas and RVs, 4492 Camino de La Plaza, Suite TIJ-1031, San Diego, CA 92173; (800) 754-4190; phone Baja at 011-52-66-28-6128 or fax 011-52-66-48-7106.

Directions: From La Misión, drive about three miles south on Highway 1D (the toll road). You can't miss the park, to your right on a long unobstructed stretch of highway at Kilometer 72.

Trip notes: Here is a first-class resort with all the amenities and a prime location on a long, long beautiful beach. We spent one night here just to experience the posh way of camping. Summer is the time to visit, as winter is chilly. For things to do in the La Misión area, please see page 81.

⑫ Playa Saldamando

Location: North of Ensenada; Northwest Baja Norte map page 76, grid c1.

Campsites, facilities: There are 40 RV campsites, all without hookups, as well as more than 500 tent sites with fire rings. Facilities include both flush toilets and out-houses, cold tiled showers, a dump station, and rental trailers. The water is not po-table, so bring your own. Two resident watchmen provide security. Tent campers are welcome. Obtain supplies in El Sauzal.

Reservations, fees: All sites are first come, first served. The fee is low—$6 per night for RVs and $4.50 for tents.

Contact: Playa Saldamando, 3965 College Avenue, San Diego, CA 92115. There is no phone.

Directions: Take the steep, half-mile-long dirt road off the southbound side of the Tijuana-Ensenada toll road (Highway 1D), about 10 miles north of Ensenada. The exit is marked with a sign. Heading south, start watching for the sign after passing the El Mirador viewpoint on the right side of the toll road.

Trip notes: Surfers, scuba divers, and anglers frequent this beach. There is a rather sharp turn off the toll road onto the dirt road, which must be taken slowly, or you can turn around at a rest stop 100 yards south of the entrance. The dirt road descends the precipitous slope of the mountainside. Small motor homes can make it, but trail-ers and larger motor homes are not recommended. Summer is the time to visit, as winter is chilly. For things to do in the Ensenada area, please see page 85.

⑬ San Miguel Village

Location: In El Sauzal; Northwest Baja Norte map page 76, grid c1.

Campsites, facilities: There are 500 campsites for tents with barbecues, electric-ity, and water, plus 50 pull-through RV sites with full hookups. Flush toilets, hot tiled showers, a dump station, a restaurant, a bar, and a gift shop are available. Don't drink the water. The manager lives on the premises and guards are on duty around the clock, so the place is secure. Obtain supplies in El Sauzal.

Reservations, fees: Reservations are accepted. Fees are moderate—$8 per night for tents or $10 per night for full-hookup sites, $60 per week, $150 per month, and $1,500 per year.

Contact: San Miguel Village, Apartado Postal 55, El Sauzal, Baja California, México; phone 011-52-617-4-6225 or fax 011-52-617-4-6124.

Directions: From the southern tollbooth on the Tijuana-Ensenada toll road (High-way 1D), drive one-half mile south on Highway 1D. From Ensenada, drive eight miles north on Highway 1.

Trip notes: The site is on a plateau above a rocky beach with great waves for surf-ing. The price is right, and the park is reasonably close to Ensenada. Summer is the best time to visit, as winter can get cold. For things to do in the Ensenada area, please see page 85.

⑭ Pancho's RV Park

Location: North of El Sauzal on Tecate Highway 3; Northwest Baja Norte map page 76, grid c2.

Campsites, facilities: There are 20 pull-through campsites with full hookups. Facilities include flush toilets, hot showers, a pool, barbecue pits, a playground, and a restaurant. Don't drink the water. There is no security. Tent campers are welcome. Obtain supplies in El Sauzal.

Reservations, fees: All sites are first come, first served. Fees are low—$5 per night and $80 per month for a site with hookups, or $3 per night for tents. Hot showers cost $1.

Contact: Drive in and talk to the owner.

Directions: From Ensenada, drive six miles north on Highway 1, then follow Tecate Highway 3 north for nine miles. The camp is at Kilometer 93.

Trip notes: The park is shady, with sites set beneath large oak trees. It is a pleasant enough place to stay, particularly for tent campers, but it is not a destination spot. Old mines in the area can be explored. Summer is the preferred time to visit. For things to do in the Ensenada area, please see page 85.

⑮ Rancho Sordo Mudo

Location: North of El Sauzal on Tecate Highway 3; Northwest Baja Norte map page 76, grid c2.

Campsites, facilities: There are 30 RV campsites, of which 20 are pull-through, 11 have full hookups, and 20 have electricity and water. The 10 tent sites have water and electricity. There are small trees at each site. Facilities include flush toilets, hot tiled showers, and laundry. The water is safe to drink. The isolated location affords security. Tent campers are welcome. Obtain supplies in Guadalupe.

Reservations, fees: Reservations are accepted. Fees are moderate—$12 per night, $50 per week, and $225 per month for RVs; $4 per night, $27 per week, and $110 per month for tents.

Contact: Rancho Sordo Mudo, P.O. Box 1376, Chula Vista, CA 91912. There is no phone.

Directions: From Ensenada, drive six miles north on Highway 1, then follow Tecate Highway 3 north about 19 miles to the campground. It's at Kilometer 75 in the Guadalupe Valley, near the Domecq Winery.

Trip notes: The owners of this campground also run a school for deaf children, and all camping fees are donated to the school. Staying here puts you within walking distance of the Domecq Winery. Tours of the winery are available by prior arrangement through the operators of the campground. A Russian colony museum is nearby in Guadalupe. Summer is the preferred time to visit. For other things to do in the Ensenada area, please see page 85.

⑯ California Trailer Park and Motel

Location: In El Sauzal; Northwest Baja Norte map page 76, grid c1.

Campsites, facilities: There are 45 campsites with full hookups, some with concrete pads. Flush toilets, hot showers, and laundry facilities are available. Don't drink the water. The park is secured with a gate. Tent campers are not welcome. Obtain supplies in El Sauzal.

Reservations, fees: Reservations are accepted. Fees are moderate—$10 per night or $150 per month.

Contact: California Trailer Park and Motel, Apartado Postal 262, Ensenada, Baja California, México; phone 011-52-617-4-6033.

Directions: The park is on the ocean side of Highway 1 just north of the Pemex plant. From Ensenada, drive six miles north on Highway 1.

Trip notes: An old, rundown RV place next door to the north is under the same name and ownership. Don't confuse it with the nice new RV facilities within the motel compound. Summer is the preferred time to visit. For things to do in the Ensenada area, please see page 85.

⑰ Ramona Beach RV Park and Motel

Location: In El Sauzal; Northwest Baja Norte map page 76, grid c1.

Campsites, facilities: There are 60 pull-through campsites for RVs with full hookups and concrete pads, and 15 tent campsites with trees, electricity, and water. A store and tiled rest rooms with flush toilets and hot showers are on site. Don't drink the water. At night, there is some lighting for security. Tent campers are welcome. Obtain supplies in El Sauzal.

Reservations, fees: Reservations are accepted. Fees are moderate—$9 per night, $60 per week, $150 per month, and $1,650 per year for RVs; $8 per night, $50 per week, $140 per month, and $1,500 per year for tents.

Contact: Ramona Beach RV Park and Motel, Apartado Postal 513, Ensenada, Baja California, México; phone 011-52-617-4-6045.

Directions: The park is on the ocean side of Highway 1 directly across from the Pemex plant. From Ensenada, drive three miles north on Highway 1.

Trip notes: Campers stay in an unattractive setting, a big, level area on the north side of the motel and store. The price is right, however, and it is fairly close to Ensenada. Summer is the preferred time to visit. For things to do in the Ensenada area, please see page 85.

18 Granada Cove RV Park

Location: On the north side of Ensenada; Northwest Baja Norte map page 76, grid c1.

Campsites, facilities: There are 45 campsites with no hookups or rest rooms. It is possible to dump RV holding tanks in the old sewer system if you ask the watchman. There is no security. Tent campers are welcome. Obtain supplies in Ensenada.

Reservations, fees: Camping is first come, first served. Fees are very low—$3 per night or 10 pesos for day use.

Contact: Drive in and park. Someone will come around to collect the fee.

Directions: The park is on the ocean side of Highway 1D at the left turn of the highway a few hundred yards south of the propane plant. Watch for the sign.

Trip notes: This old RV park has a checkered history and has been allowed to deteriorate totally. Periodically the gate is closed to prohibit entrance, but at other times it is open and access is allowed. The setting is a large graded area next to the ocean and crashing surf. There is no sand, though, merely a huge pile of boulders below that roll back and forth as the waves came and go. It is a pleasant place to spend the night, and the clicking of the boulders as they constantly shift is actually rather soothing. Tent campers can have a delightful time at an oceanside spot.

19 King's Coronita Trailer Park

Location: On the north side of Ensenada; Northwest Baja Norte map page 76, grid c1.

Campsites, facilities: There are five pull-through campsites with full hookups and concrete pads. Flush toilets and hot showers are available. Don't drink the water. The park is secured with a locked gate, and you must ask the manager, who lives next to the gate, to unlock it for you. Obtain supplies in Ensenada.

Reservations, fees: Reservations are accepted. The fee is moderate—$12 per night.

Contact: King's Coronita Trailer Park, Apartado Postal 133, Ensenada, Baja California, México; phone 011-52-617-4-4540.

Directions: The park is on the ocean side of Highway 1D, just before the road turns to the right into Ensenada around the waterfront. Watch for the sign south of the overpass to the CICESE school.

Trip notes: The park is occupied primarily by permanents and has a residential atmosphere. Summer is the preferred time to visit. For things to do in the Ensenada area, please see page 85.

⑳ Campo Playa RV Park

Location: In Ensenada; Northwest Baja Norte map page 76, grid c1.

Campsites, facilities: There are 90 pull-through campsites with full hookups and concrete pads. Clean, tiled rest rooms with flush toilets and hot showers are available. Don't drink the water. The park is fenced, but people can wander through. Tent campers are welcome. Obtain supplies in Ensenada.

Reservations, fees: Reservations are accepted. Fees are high—$16 per night, $98 per week, and $200 per month for RVs and $10 per night for tents.

Contact: Campo Playa RV Park, Apartado Postal 789, Ensenada, Baja California, México; phone 011-52-617-6-2918.

Directions: The park is on the corner of Las Dunas and Delante, which is across from the waterfront and a few blocks west of the Gigante Supermarket where Highway 1 takes a sharp right turn to the south. Street signs in this area are hard to find, and mapmakers disagree on what streets are called. As you go through Ensenada, past the statue of the so-called three heads in the Civic Plaza, keep looking to the left for Campo Playa. You can't miss it—really.

Trip notes: This is the best place to stay for fishing, dining, and sightseeing in Ensenada. If you don't want to unhook your rig and drive around town, you can call a cab. Restaurants are within walking distance, as is the Gigante Supermarket. The prominent landmark you see nearby, the 12-foot-high busts that people call the "three heads," represents the Mexican heroes Benito Juárez, Venustiano Carranza, and Miguel Hidalgo y Castillo. Summer is the preferred time to visit. For things to do in the Ensenada area, please see page 85.

㉑ Joker Hotel, RV Park, and Restaurant

Location: In Ensenada; Northwest Baja Norte map page 76, grid c1.

Campsites, facilities: There are 12 pull-through campsites with full hookups, including television. Flush toilets, hot showers, a pool, and a restaurant are available. Do not drink the water. The park is secured with a guard. Tent campers are welcome. Obtain supplies in Ensenada.

Reservations, fees: Reservations are accepted. The fee is moderate— $12 per night.

Contact: Joker Hotel, RV Park, and Restaurant, Kilometro 12.5 Highway 1, Ensenada, Baja California, México; phone 011-52-617-7-5151 or fax 011-52-617-7-4460.

Directions: Take Highway 1 to the south side of Ensenada. The park is south of the military base on the east side of Highway 1.

Trip notes: The campsites are narrow, short, and difficult to get into. They are suitable only for vehicles under 23 feet long without trailers. Summer is the best time to visit. For things to do in the Ensenada area, please see page 85.

22 Corona Beach Trailer Park

Location: South of Ensenada; Northwest Baja Norte map page 76, grid c1.

Campsites, facilities: There are 60 pull-through campsites with electricity and water. Flush toilets, cold showers, and a recreation hall are provided. Don't drink the water. The park is secured with a fence, and the owner lives on the premises. Tent campers are welcome. Obtain supplies at shops along Highway 1.

Reservations, fees: Reservations are accepted. Fees are moderate—$10 per night and $260 per month.

Contact: Corona Beach Trailer Park, Apartado Postal 1149, Ensenada, Baja California, México. There is no phone.

Directions: Take the Estero Beach Hotel turnoff from Highway 1 about six miles south of Ensenada. Go west on the paved street toward the beach, then turn right on the first paved road. When the pavement becomes dirt, look north for a yellow water tower with "Corona Beach" painted on it.

Trip notes: This is a large, flat site behind residences on the beach of Bahía Todos Santos, which normally has very mild surf. It is a nice place to camp. Horses can be rented for rides on the beach; the going rate is $10 an hour. Try a gallop in the surf— it's fun! Summer is the preferred time to visit. For other things to do in the Ensenada area, please see page 85.

23 Mona Lisa Beach Resort

Location: South of Ensenada; Northwest Baja Norte map page 76, grid c1.

Campsites, facilities: There are 15 RV campsites with full hookups and concrete pads with some palapas, tables, fire rings, and trees. There are 30 tent campsites with some palapas and tables, trees, and central water for washing. On the property are clean, tiled rest rooms with flush toilets and hot showers, a restaurant, a curio store, motel rooms, and horse rentals. Don't drink the water; purified bottled water is available. The park is secured with a fence and patrolmen, and the owner lives on the premises. Obtain supplies at shops along Highway 1.

Reservations, fees: Reservations are accepted. Fees are moderate—$12 per night, $60 per week, and $225 per month for RVs, with a 10 percent discount for yearly stays. Tent sites are $12 per night and $40 per week.

Contact: Mona Lisa Beach Resort, Apartado Postal 607, Ensenada, Baja California, México; phone 011-52-617-7-5100; phone or fax 011-52-617-7-4920.

Directions: Take the Estero Beach Hotel turnoff from Highway 1 about six miles south of Ensenada. Go west on the paved street toward the beach, then turn right on the first paved road. When the pavement becomes dirt, you'll see Mona Lisa to your left on the beach. There are signs to follow.

Trip notes: A homey atmosphere pervades this very nice, neat, small compound. Rules require you to arrive with an empty holding tank, so as not to overload their septic system. The owner will turn you away if he suspects you are packing a full load. Many people prefer to visit in summer, since winter can be cold. It is, however, less crowded in winter, the rates are lower, and the fishing is good. For things to do in the Ensenada area, please see page 85.

㉔ El Faro Beach Motel and Trailer Park

Location: South of Ensenada; Northwest Baja Norte map page 76, grid c1.

Campsites, facilities: There are 20 campsites with electricity and water on the beach below the restaurant, and many more sites with no hookups behind the seawall to the right. Facilities include flush toilets, cold showers, a restaurant that's open in the summer, and a dump station. Don't drink the water, which comes out of a cistern. The park is secured with a fence. Tent campers are welcome at the beach campsites. Obtain supplies at shops along Highway 1.

Reservations, fees: Reservations are accepted. The fee is moderate—$12 per night with electricity and $10 without.

Contact: El Faro Beach Motel and Trailer Park, Apartado Postal 1008, Ensenada, Baja California, México; phone 011-52-617-7-4630 or fax 011-52-617-7-4620.

Directions: Take the Estero Beach Hotel turnoff from Highway 1 about six miles south of Ensenada. Go west on the paved street toward the beach and continue west when the road turns to dirt. You will see El Faro.

Trip notes: This is a crowded place, and as such can get fairly noisy. It is right on the beach, however, and we spent a very pleasant night at one of the attractive sites. You can rent horses to ride on the beach; the going rate is $10 an hour. Try it. Summer is the preferred time to visit. For things to do in the Ensenada area, please see page 85.

㉕ Estero Beach Resort and RV Park

Location: South of Ensenada; Northwest Baja Norte map page 76, grid c1.

Campsites, facilities: There are 70 RV campsites with full hookups, concrete pads, and trees, and 100 tent campsites with trees but no electricity or water. The tiled rest rooms are clean, with flush toilets and hot showers. Also available are a restaurant, a store, a launch ramp into the estero, tennis courts, horses, bicycles, volleyball courts, a recreation center with billiards, Ping-Pong, and games, a children's playground, shops, and an exhibit center and museum displaying treasures from various Mexican cultures. A beach club offers sailing, windsurfing, Jet Skiing, waterskiing, and snorkeling equipment. Don't drink the water. The park is secured with a guarded gate and 24-hour guard service. Obtain supplies at shops along Highway 1.

Reservations, fees: Reservations are accepted. The fee is high—$16 per night with a 10 percent monthly discount for RVs, and $12 per night for tents.

Contact: Estero Beach Resort and RV Park, Apartado Postal 86, Ensenada, Baja California, México; phone 011-52-617-6-6230, 6235, or 6225; fax 011-52-617-6-6925.

Directions: Take the Estero Beach Hotel turnoff from Highway 1 about six miles south of Ensenada. Go west on the paved street and follow signs to the office where you will register. The RV park is on the bay a little farther ahead.

Trip notes: All the amenities are available at this full-fledged resort. The RV park has many shade trees and is on the edge of the huge Estero de Punta Banda Reserve, home to a wide variety of aquatic birds, including loons, grebes, pelicans, cormorants, herons, egrets, hawks, and coots. Estero de Punta Banda is about 4.5 miles long and shaped somewhat like a dumbbell, with the north end about one mile wide and the south end about two miles wide. Punta Estero separates the estero from Bahía Todos Santos. There is a one-half-mile gap between the north end of Punta Estero and the point of land housing the Estero Beach Hotel. Beneath this gap is a shallow bar that creates breakers at low tide and during storms.

The resort rents equipment for all manner of water sports—you can get lessons if you want. Windsurfing is one of the more popular pursuits in the estero. In awe, we watched an elderly couple adroitly mount their individual boards at the ramp and sail off together with great aplomb. Fishermen launch their trailer boats here for $5 and brave the entrance sandbar for offshore fishing around Islas de Todos Santos, but they are careful to cross it at high tide each way. It can be dangerous, as friends of ours learned when they bounced on the bottom between large swells. Summer is the best time to visit. For things to do in the Ensenada area, please see page 85.

26 Loco Lobo Paradise

Location: In Punta Banda; Northwest Baja Norte map page 76, grid d1.

Campsites, facilities: There are four campsites with water and electric hookups for rigs up to 28 feet long, plus 16 campsites for tents. Beach palapas, young trees, tables, barbecues, and a dump station are provided, and there are plans to add satellite TV access. Facilities include tiled rest rooms with flush toilets and hot showers, a store, and a restaurant. Don't drink the water, which is brackish. Security is provided with a fence, lighting, a 24-hour guard in the office, and the owner living nearby. Obtain supplies in Punta Banda.

Reservations, fees: Reservations are accepted. Fees are moderate—$10 per night for two people, plus $2 for each additional person over age eight. The weekly rate is $60.

Contact: Loco Lobo Paradise, P.O. Box 8458, Chula Vista, CA 91912; phone or fax 011-52-615-4-2144 in México.

Directions: Heading west from Maneadero on the paved road to La Bufadora, drive 6.2 miles. The park is on the beach at Bahía Todos Santos.

Trip notes: Water sports enthusiasts take note: Kayaks, paddleboats, rowboats, surfboards, boogie boards, and fishing poles are for rent. Fishing charters can be arranged. And supplies for surfing, fishing, boating, and camping are available.

㉗ La Jolla Beach Camp

Location: In Punta Banda; Northwest Baja Norte map page 76, grid d1.

Campsites, facilities: There is plenty of room to camp on the beach without hookups in front of permanent residences. Flush toilets, hot showers, a restaurant, a dump station, a launch ramp, and horse rentals are available. Don't drink the water. The park is secured with a guarded gate. Tent campers are welcome. Obtain supplies in Punta Banda.

Reservations, fees: All sites are first come, first served. Fees are low—$6 per night for two people or $140 per month.

Contact: Drive in and talk to the owner.

Directions: Heading west from Maneadero on the paved road to La Bufadora, drive eight miles. The camp is on the beach at Bahía Todos Santos at Kilometer 12.5.

Trip notes: On holidays this park is jammed with tourists. It's a large place with lots of activity at any time of year. Small boats can be launched into the surf of Bahía Todos Santos for fishing and scuba diving around the Punta Banda Peninsula. If you don't have your own boat, you can arrange to fish or dive with Jessie and Sons. They're located one mile west of La Jolla Beach Camp on the paved road. La Bufadora Dive is located at La Bufadora. Contact Dale Erwin, Apartado Postal 102, Maneadero, Baja California, México. On the south side of the peninsula, you should visit La Bufadora (the Blowhole). Park in the cluster of curio shops at the end of the road and walk 100 yards to the viewing area. Every wave forces water into a narrow slot and upward onto the face of the cliff with a resounding boom. Summer is the best time to visit. For other things to do in the Ensenada area, please see page 85.

㉘ Villarino RV Park

Location: In Punta Banda; Northwest Baja Norte map page 76, grid d1.

Campsites, facilities: There are 35 campsites with full hookups. Facilities include flush toilets, hot showers, a restaurant, a full-service store, boat rentals, tables, fire rings, grills, a playground, a volleyball court, a horseshoe pit, motorbike and hiking trails, horse rentals, a launch ramp, and large tents with cots to rent for $5 per night. Don't drink the water. The park is secured with a guard gate. Tent campers are welcome. Obtain supplies in Punta Banda.

Reservations, fees: Reservations are accepted. Fees are moderate—$10 per night per person. Discounts of 25 to 40 percent per week are available, depending on the number of people in your party. The monthly rate is $240.

Contact: Villarino RV Park, Apartado Postal 842, Ensenada, Baja California, México; phone 011-52-617-6-4246 or fax 011-52-617-6-1309.

Directions: Heading west from Maneadero on the paved road to La Bufadora, drive eight miles. The park is on the beach at Bahía Todos Santos at Kilometer 12.5, next door to La Jolla Beach Camp.

Trip notes: Each space has its own tree in this well-tended camping area that is generally not as crowded as neighboring La Jolla Beach Camp (campground number 27). See the trip notes for that listing to learn about all the action on the Punta Banda Peninsula. Summer is the best time to visit. For things to do in the Ensenada area, please see page 85.

㉙ Ejido Campo No. 5

Location: West of Punta Banda; Northwest Baja Norte map page 76, grid d1.

Campsites, facilities: This is a primitive camping area with no facilities or security. Water is not available. Obtain supplies in Punta Banda.

Reservations, fees: Camping is first come, first served. Fees are very low.

Contact: Drive in to the entrance station.

Directions: From Punta Banda, drive about 1.5 miles west on the paved road to La Bufadora.

Trip notes: The paved road to Punta Banda has climbed high on the intervening ridge, and the dirt road leading down the mountainside to this primitive campground close to the ocean is very steep. Tent campers in small vehicles will find the camping to be quite pleasant, but most drivers with larger rigs would not risk the hazard of getting here. Summer is the best time to visit. For things to do in the Ensenada area, please see page 85. For things to do on the Punta Banda Peninsula, see La Jolla Beach Camp (campground number 27).

㉚ Ejido Campo No. 7

Location: West of Punta Banda; Northwest Baja Norte map page 76, grid d1.

Campsites, facilities: This is a primitive camping area with no facilities or security. Water is not available. Obtain supplies in Punta Banda.

Reservations, fees: Camping is first come, first served. Fees are very low.

Contact: Drive in to the entrance station.

Directions: From Punta Banda, drive about three miles west on the paved road to La Bufadora.

Trip notes: The paved road to Punta Banda has climbed high on the intervening ridge, and the dirt road leading down the mountainside to this primitive campground close to the ocean is very steep. Tent campers in small vehicles will find the camping to be quite pleasant, but most drivers with larger rigs would not risk the hazard of getting here. Summer is the best time to visit. For things to do in the Ensenada area, please see page 85. For things to do on the Punta Banda Peninsula, see La Jolla Beach Camp (campground number 27).

㉛ Ejido Campo No. 8

Location: West of Punta Banda; Northwest Baja Norte map page 76, grid d1.

Campsites, facilities: This is a primitive camping area with no facilities or security. Water is not available. Obtain supplies in Punta Banda.

Reservations, fees: Camping is first come, first served. Fees are very low.

Contact: Drive in to the entrance station.

Directions: From Punta Banda, drive about 4.5 miles west on the paved road to La Bufadora.

Trip notes: The paved road to Punta Banda has climbed high on the intervening ridge, and the dirt road leading down the mountainside to this primitive campground close to the ocean is very steep. Tent campers in small vehicles will find the camping to be quite pleasant, but most drivers with larger rigs would not risk the hazard of getting here. Summer is the best time to visit. For things to do in the Ensenada area, please see page 85. For things to do on the Punta Banda Peninsula, see La Jolla Beach Camp (campground number 27).

㉜ El Palomar RV Park

Location: In Santo Tomás; Northwest Baja Norte map page 76, grid e2.

Campsites, facilities: There are 23 campsites, of which six are pull-through. Fifteen sites have full hookups, and eight have just electricity and water. Facilities include rustic rest rooms with flush toilets and hot showers, three pools, a restaurant/bar, a curio store, barbecue pits, an area for off-road motorbikes, satellite TV access, a motel, a gas station, and hunting and fishing guide services. Don't drink the water. The park is secured with a chain across the entrance road. Tent campers are welcome. Obtain supplies in Maneadero.

Reservations, fees: All campsites are first come, first served. Fees are moderate—$12 per night or $150 per month.

Contact: El Palomar RV Park, 4492 Camino de La Plaza #232, San Ysidro, CA 92173. There is no phone.

Directions: From Maneadero, drive 18.5 miles south on Highway 1. The campground is on the north side of the road. Register at the office in the store across the road.

Trip notes: This park is set in a recreation area for people from Ensenada who flock here on weekends for picnics, swimming, and other activities. Quail hunters come to hunt on ranches up the valley of the Río Santo Tomás, and anglers come to fish in the ocean down the valley. At the north end of the olive grove below the highway, there is a small pile of melted adobe marking the last remains of the Misión de Santo Tomás de Aquino, which was built by the Dominicans in 1794. Summer is the preferred time to visit. For things to do in the Ensenada area, please see page 85.

Warning: The entrance road down into the RV park is steep, and the drive coming up can be difficult since you must look out for trucks and buses whizzing by on Highway 1. We had to go into four-wheel drive once to crawl slowly out into traffic while dragging our 10,000-pound boat behind us.

🚐 Malibu Beach Sur RV Park

Location: South of Puerto San Ysidro; Northwest Baja Norte map page 76, grid e1.

Campsites, facilities: There are 14 pull-through campsites with full hookups and concrete pads. Electricity is provided by a generator from 5 P.M. to 10 P.M. Facilities include laundry and tiled rest rooms with flush toilets and hot showers. Don't drink the water. The owner lives on the premises, so security is good. Tent campers are welcome. Obtain supplies in San Vicente.

Reservations, fees: Camping is first come, first served. The fee is moderate—$10 per night for RVs or tents.

Contact: Drive in and talk to the owner.

Directions: Drive south of Santo Tomás on Highway 1 for 17 miles, then follow a very rough paved road 12 miles west to Erendira on the ocean. Continue three miles south across the river on a rough dirt road winding through tomato fields.

Trip notes: The park has a delightful location on a bluff above a very nice beach. We pulled in one afternoon planning to check it out then continue on to Ensenada, but we couldn't tear ourselves away. We spent a most pleasant night serenaded by the surf. Castro's Camp, at Puerto San Ysidro four miles north of the village of Erendira, is known for good fishing in the kelp and on the bottom. You can charter a *panga* there if you'd like to try your luck. Summer is the preferred time to visit. For things to do in the Ensenada area, please see page 85.

34 San Antonio del Mar Beach

Location: Northwest of Colonet; Northwest Baja Norte map page 77, grid f2.

Campsites, facilities: It is possible to camp on the beach with four-wheel-drive vehicles. There are no facilities. With the right vehicle it is a great spot for tent camping. Obtain supplies in Colonet.

Reservations, fees: Camping is first come, first served. The fee is very low— $3 per night, assuming someone comes to collect it.

Contact: Drive in and camp.

Directions: On the north side of Colonet close to the bridge over the river, turn west at the San Antonio del Mar sign onto a good dirt road and drive seven miles. Beach access is among several beach houses.

Trip notes: The beach and dunes are extensive and well suited for vehicles that can traverse soft sand. There is nothing here for travelers with motor homes or trailers. Summer is the preferred time to visit. For things to do in the San Quintín area, please see page 88.

35 Punta San Jacinto Trailer Park

Location: North of Camalu; Northwest Baja Norte map page 77, grid g2.

Campsites, facilities: There are several semideveloped RV campsites, plus room for RV and tent camping along the beach. Pit toilets and one hot shower are provided. Don't drink the water. A resident manager provides security. Obtain supplies in Camalu.

Reservations, fees: Camping is first come, first served. The fee is low— $5 per night.

Contact: Drive in and camp. The manager will come around and collect the fee.

Directions: At Kilometer 150 on Highway 1 between Colonet and Camalu (about five miles north of Camalu), turn west on a graded dirt road and drive 4.5 miles to the beach.

Trip notes: This is a popular spot for surfers. The wreck of a large ship is just offshore. Summer is the preferred time to visit. For things to do in the San Quintín area, please see page 88.

36 Mesón Don Pepe RV Park and Restaurant

Location: South of Colonia Vicente Guerrero; Northwest Baja Norte map page 77, grid h2.

Campsites, facilities: There are 23 campsites (19 pull-through) with full hookups and trees. Facilities include simple, clean, tiled rest rooms with flush toilets and hot showers, laundry, and a restaurant. The water is safe to drink. There is no formal security, but there are no real problems. Tent campers are welcome in a special grassy area. Obtain supplies of all sorts in San Quintín.

Reservations, fees: Reservations are accepted. Fees are low—tents are $5 per night, vans and campers are $7, and motor homes and trailers are $8.50. Discounts are available for longer stays: 10 percent off per week, 25 percent per month, and 40 percent per year.

Contact: Mesón Don Pepe RV Park and Restaurant, Apartado Postal 7, Colonia Vicente Guerrero, Baja California, México; phone 011-52-616-6-2216 or fax 011-52-616-6-2268.

Directions: Head one mile south of Colonia Vicente Guerrero on Highway 1. Watch for the park sign before the crest of the hill, south of the Pemex station.

Trip notes: Mesón Don Pepe is one of our regular stops when we're traveling to or from Guerrero Negro. The restaurant is dependably good. We are particularly fond of the fried rabbit. Anglers and surfers use nearby Playa San Ramon, which is 2.5 miles west of the campground on a sandy road. Fishing can be good for perch and corbina. In and around San Quintín there's a large agricultural community dedicated to growing tomatoes and strawberries, most of which are shipped north to the United States. Summer is the best time to visit. For things to do in the San Quintín area, please see page 88.

37 Posada Don Diego RV Park, Restaurant, and Bar

Location: South of Colonia Vicente Guerrero; Northwest Baja Norte map page 77, grid h2.

Campsites, facilities: There are 100 campsites (15 pull-through) with concrete pads, of which 40 have full hookups and 60 have only electricity and water. Facilities include flush toilets, hot showers, fire rings, tables, laundry, a restaurant, a bar, a dump station, a volleyball court, and a horseshoe pit. Don't drink or cook with the water, which is brackish and comes from a well. The owners live on the premises, so there are no problems with security. Tent campers are welcome in a special area. Obtain supplies in San Quintín.

Reservations, fees: Reservations are accepted. Fees are moderate—$10 per night with a 10 percent discount for weeklong stays. Long-term rates are $160 per month.

Contact: Posada Don Diego RV Park, Apartado Postal 126, Colonia Vicente Guerrero, Baja California, México; phone 011-52-616-6-2181.

Directions: Head one mile south of Colonia Vicente Guerrero on Highway 1 to the dirt access road adjacent to the propane plant 100 yards south of the Mesón Don Pepe RV Park sign. There is no sign for Don Diego's from the north, though there is a sign on the roof of a shed visible from the south. The park is one-half mile west, past Mesón Don Pepe RV Park.

Trip notes: The park covers a good deal of ground with big spaces and lots of room for large groups. We have stayed here many times when traveling south with groups of Vagabundos. Summer is the preferred time to visit. For information about nearby Playa San Ramon, see Mesón Don Pepe RV Park (campground number 36). For things to do in the San Quintín area, please see page 88.

㊳ The Old Mill Village

Location: South of San Quintín; Northwest Baja Norte map page 77, grid h1.

Campsites, facilities: There are 20 camping spots (five pull-through), all with full hookups and concrete pads. An overflow area with no hookups is also available. The rest rooms are clean and tiled with flush toilets and hot showers. Facilities include fire rings, grills, a restaurant, a bar, bait and tackle shop, a small store, a free launch ramp, a horseshoe pit, a volleyball court, and rental boats with guides. Don't drink the water in the RV park. The water served in the restaurant is pure. The manager lives on the premises, so there are no problems with security. Tent campers are welcome. Obtain supplies in San Quintín.

Reservations, fees: Reservations are accepted. Fees are high—$10 per night for tents and $15 for RVs.

Contact: Phone (800) 995-8482 or (619) 479-3476, fax 011-52-617-7-7693. There is no available mailing address.

Directions: At the sign about 2.5 miles south of the military camp south of San Quintín, turn off Highway 1 and follow the signs 3.5 miles west on a graded dirt road to the shore of Bahía San Quintín.

Trip notes: Yes, there really is an old gristmill, the remains of a failed attempt at farming by English settlers in the late 1800s. In front of the park, the embankment of an abandoned railroad trestle narrows the tide through a raceway going into the upper bay. For decades, there were camping facilities here under different management and the name Molino Viejo. The park has been upgraded and expanded with first-class renovations, making this a popular destination, particularly in summer. One major improvement: The owners have realigned and graded the access road. Hauling in big offshore boats like ours used to be a chore. Now it's a snap. The restaurant is excellent, one of the best in Baja. Their lobster omelet and seafood dinners are renowned. The refurbished mill that houses the restaurant and bar is very attractive. Summer is the best time to visit. For things to do in the San Quintín area, please see page 88.

⑳ Old Pier Motel and RV Park

Location: South of San Quintín; Northwest Baja Norte map page 77, grid i2.

Campsites, facilities: There are seven campsites with no hookups. Tiled flush toilets, cold showers (hot showers are available in the motel rooms), concrete fire pits, and a restaurant are available. Don't drink the water. Security is not a problem due to the remote location and access to the campground being routed through the motel and restaurant entrance. Tent campers are welcome. Obtain supplies in San Quintín.

Reservations, fees: All sites are first come, first served. The fee is very low—$3 per night. Weekly discounts can be negotiated.

Contact: Old Pier Motel and RV Park, Apartado Postal 111, San Quintín, Baja California, México. There is no phone.

Directions: Driving down Highway 1, ignore the Old Pier sign. Turn off at the Old Mill sign about 2.5 miles south of the military camp south of San Quintín, then head 2.5 miles west to the Old Pier sign pointing south. Turn left and continue 1.5 miles.

Trip notes: An old cemetery used by English settlers in the last century is nearby to the south, and just to the north is a reconstruction of an original house and outbuildings from that era. This is an ideal place for tent camping, as it sits on the edge of a bluff under trees with a grand, long view of Bahía San Quintín and the rugged peninsula on the far side. Bird-watching in the marshes around the bay can be magnificent. A staircase down the 20-foot-high bluff gives access to the shoreline. Summer is the most popular time for camping. For things to do in the San Quintín area, please see page 88.

⑳ Cielito Lindo Motel and RV Park

Location: South of San Quintín; Northwest Baja Norte map page 77, grid i1.

Campsites, facilities: At the motel, there are eight RV campsites (five pull-through) with full hookups and seven sites with palapas for tent and van campers. There's plenty of space at the beach for tent camping with no facilities. Trees, a good restaurant, a barbecue area, and a charter boat business with a small tackle shop are on the property. Every month a free fiesta is held. Don't drink the brackish water. Security is provided by resident owners. Obtain supplies in San Quintín.

Reservations, fees: Reservations are accepted. Fees are low—$5 per night and $65 per month.

Contact: Cielito Lindo Motel and RV Park, Apartado Postal 7, San Quintín, Baja California, México; phone (619) 222-8955 or (800) 272-6236 for reservations.

Directions: Drive about eight miles south of San Quintín on Highway 1 to the La Pinta Hotel sign. Turn west on the paved road and continue about 3.5 miles past the hotel to Cielito Lindo. Watch for the signs. For the beach campground, continue past the motel toward the ocean and a couple of prominent concrete block buildings.

Trip notes: The delightful oceanside campground is a lovely spot behind the dunes and close to the surf on one of Baja's truly great beaches. Playa Santa María extends several miles to the south and offers good fishing for perch and corbina, as well as lots of Pismo clams. In years past, we were able to pluck big ones off the beach every morning after the waves of the previous night's high tide had scooped them out of the sand for us. Fishing can be just as satisfying. While fishing one evening on the point between the beach and the inner bay, a dolphin came close to shore, caught a large leopard shark, and proceeded to toss the shark high in the air, catch it, and toss it again. In one hour there that night, we caught a leopard shark, an angel shark, a bat ray, a stingray, and a guitarfish. All in all, it was a very memorable evening. Summer is the preferred time to visit. For more on the San Quintín area, please see page 88.

Note: Before camping in the beach area, inquire about security there.

❹ El Pabellón RV Park

Location: South of San Quintín; Northwest Baja Norte map page 77, grid i2.

Campsites, facilities: In addition to the many places to park at the edge of the dunes and farther back, there are 14 campsites with water faucets and sewer hookups. The two rest room buildings are clean and have flush toilets and hot showers. Concrete outdoor sinks and fish cleaning tables are available. Don't drink the water. There is no security. It's ideal for tent camping. Obtain supplies in San Quintín.

Reservations, fees: All sites are first come, first served. The fee is low— $5 per night.

Contact: Drive in and talk to the attendant.

Directions: Proceed about nine miles south of San Quintín on Highway 1 and look for the El Pabellón sign one mile south of the junction of Highway 1 with the old highway—it comes in at a sharp angle on the right. Follow the dirt road one mile to the park on the beach.

Trip notes: Tent campers revel in this place, a choice spot on magnificent Playa El Pabellón, which runs for miles in both directions. When we first asked the attendant where to park, he gave a wide sweep of his arm and with a huge smile bellowed, "Anywhere!" If you can, camp between the widely spaced rows of shrubs on the leveled-off area at the edge of the dunes. The shrubs break the wind and afford a little privacy. It is the best-run park operated by an *ejido* in Baja. Interestingly enough, it is not one of the old parks built for them by the government. *Pangas* can be chartered for fishing trips behind the breakers or out to Isla San Martín. The fishermen sell Pismo clams, stone crab claws, lobster, and fish from their *pangas,* which operate through the surf in front of the campground. Surf fishing can be good for perch and corbina. Summer is the preferred time to visit. For other things to do in the San Quintín area, please see page 88.

42 Parque Nacional Constitución de 1857

Location: East of Ensenada; Northwest Baja Norte map page 76, grid d4.

Campsites, facilities: This is primitive camping with no developed facilities or services. There is no water. Security is not a problem due to the remote location. Obtain supplies in Ensenada.

Reservations, fees: All sites are first come, first served. There is no fee.

Contact: Drive in and camp.

Directions: You can access the park from the north or south, but the most preferred route is from the south. Take Highway 3 southeast from Ensenada toward San Felipe about 25 miles to Ojos Negros. Turn left (north) on a short paved road into the village. At its end, turn right onto a graded dirt road. Continue eight miles, then turn right at the junction. Go another 12 miles and turn left. The park is about 27 miles farther, a drive of approximately two hours. Proceed through the pines to Laguna Hanson, which may be dry, and pick a campsite. This road may be impassable after a rain. Pickup trucks are advised. Don't try this in a motor home or trailer without scouting it out.

The northern route has some rough stretches and is less traveled. From Tecate, drive east on Highway 2 about 32 miles to El Condor, where a graded dirt road heads south about 37 miles to the park. After 16 miles, it joins another graded dirt road coming in from La Rumorosa on Highway 2, about 10 miles east of El Condor. The main road bears east passing El Topo Rancho, climbs a steep grade, and enters the park. Pickup trucks are advised.

Trip notes: Parque Nacional Constitución de 1857 offers an uncrowded, relaxing camping experience. Sleeping in the cool mountains in a forested setting is a different way to enjoy Baja, which is usually identified by its coastal attractions. Folks with a yen for exploring will enjoy tramping around among the park's pine trees. Spring, summer, and fall are the times to visit.

43 Parque Nacional Sierra San Pedro Mártir

Location: Southeast of Ensenada; Northwest Baja Norte map page 77, grid g4.

Campsites, facilities: This is primitive camping with no developed facilities or services except for pit toilets at the base of the access road up to the observatory. There is no water. Security is not a problem due to the remote location. Obtain supplies in Ensenada.

Reservations, fees: All sites are first come, first served. There is no fee.

Contact: Drive in and camp.

Directions: The best way to access the park is to turn east off Highway 1 about eight miles south of Colonet at the village of San Telmo de Abajo. A sign for San Telmo (about six miles) and the Meling Ranch (about 21 miles) marks the start of a graded dirt road that leads approximately 60 miles to the park, a drive of three hours.

Trip notes: Hiking, fishing, mountain climbing, even the National Observatory—the Sierra San Pedro Mártir national park has it all. Tent camping in this mountain setting far from the crowded coastal areas of Baja is a delight. Just set up camp wherever you desire. A particularly attractive campsite is in a pine forest at the base of the observatory access road. The upper elevations of the mountains are covered with conifer trees interspersed with meadows (and aspen) generating year-round streams harboring a unique trout species—the Nelson rainbow. From the high points, sweeping views may be had of the desert plain around San Felipe, the Sea of Cortéz, and the Sonoran coast on the Mexican mainland. It is pleasant to settle back against a towering Jeffrey pine and contemplate that arid region baking in the summer heat so far below you. Spring, summer, and fall are the best times to visit.

Note: Some steep grades must be tackled en route to the Meling Ranch and even steeper ones beyond that. Motor homes and trailers are not suited for the drive. The road in from Highway 1 can be incredibly dusty, up to several inches deep, and vehicles become enveloped in clouds of the stuff, which penetrates every crack.

44 Los Manzanos Campground

Location: Southeast of Ensenada near Parque Nacional Sierra San Pedro Mártir; Northwest Baja Norte map page 77, grid h4.

Campsites, facilities: There is room for 10 to 25 vehicles with no hookups. Flush toilets and hot showers are available, and a generator provides electricity to the common facilities. The water is good to drink. Security is not a problem due to the remote location. Obtain supplies in Ensenada.

Reservations, fees: Reservations are accepted. Fees were initially to be the same as for the owner's other establishment, Mesón Don Pepe RV Park and Restaurant (campground number 36), where fees are low—tents are $5 per night, vans and campers are $7, and motor homes and trailers are $8.50, with discounts available for longer stays.

Contact: Drive in and see the manager or contact Mesón Don Pepe RV Park, Apartado Postal 7, Colonia Vicente Guerrero, Baja California, México; phone 011-52-616-6-2216 or fax 011-52-616-6-2268.

Directions: The best access is from Highway 1 about eight miles south of Colonet in the village of San Telmo de Abajo. A sign for San Telmo (about six miles) and the Meling Ranch (about 21 miles) marks the start of a graded dirt road that leads about 60 miles to the Parque Nacional Sierra San Pedro Mártir, a drive of three hours. Los Manzanos is two miles before the park. Motor homes and trailers are not recommended due to steep grades.

Trip notes: An ideal location for tent camping, this forested mountain setting offers seclusion far from the crowds that you are more likely to encounter while staying on the coast. However, at last report there was no one in attendance at Los Manzanos, which opened in spring of 1997. You might want to head up the road two miles to Parque Nacional Sierra San Pedro Mártir (campground number 43), which is open to camping everywhere and has more attractive campsites with pit toilets.

Northwest Baja Norte's 10 Best Beaches

① Playa Rosarito

Location: In Rosarito; Northwest Baja Norte map page 76, grid a1.

Directions: The beach runs along the front of the city of Rosarito.

Trip notes: Both Coco Loco Trailer Park (campground number 3) and Chuy's Trailer Park (campground number 4) are on this long beach, the best known feature of Rosarito. The wide, clean stretch of sand is good for surfing and fishing. While it is an urban spot and as such is heavily used, it is highly regarded by the people who flock to Rosarito because it's the first good beach south of the border. Southern California beaches are so horribly crowded that Rosarito is greatly appreciated by those eager to spend a weekend in a more attractive setting. Rosarito has everything you might need in the way of services or supplies. Summer is the preferred time to visit, as winter is chilly. For things to do in the Rosarito area, please see page 81.

② Cantamar Dunes

Location: South of Rosarito; Northwest Baja Norte map page 76, grid b1.

Directions: The dunes are next to Highway 1 (the free road) and extend for three miles between Kilometers 47 and 52, about 13 miles south of Rosarito. Exit the toll road at Cantamar.

Trip notes: There is a nice beach on the ocean below the dunes. The big activity here is driving all-terrain vehicles on the dunes. Obtain supplies in Rosarito. Summer is the preferred time to visit, as winter is chilly. For things to do in the Rosarito area, please see page 81.

③ Playa La Fonda

Location: South of Rosarito; Northwest Baja Norte map page 76, grid b1.

Directions: The beach is at Kilometer 59 on Highway 1, about 20 miles south of Rosarito. Take the Alisitos exit off the toll road.

Trip notes: From the bluffs above, you'll catch your first view of this beach as it curves enticingly around the irregular projections of the coastline. The sand is fine and clean. Spending a night at Alisitos Trailer Park (campground number 9), which sits on the bluff, allows you to take full advantage of the setting: Watching the moon's reflection on the sea and sand below is a romantic experience for any couple. This is a great place to stroll barefoot, letting the sand ooze between your toes, and to dash out in the receding wetness of the last wave. Get the things you need in Rosarito.

Summer is the preferred time to visit, as winter is chilly. For things to do in the Rosarito area, please see page 81.

④ Playa La Misión

Location: At La Misión; Northwest Baja Norte map page 76, grid b1.

Directions: The beach extends for about one mile north of the Río Guadalupe at Kilometer 69 on the toll road (the free road goes inland at La Misión, just to the north). At La Misión, 24 miles south of Rosarito on Highway 1D, the free road (old Highway 1) crosses under the toll road (Highway 1D). Drive two miles south on the toll road to the parking area on the west side of the highway in the arroyo of the Río Guadalupe.

Trip notes: We have enjoyed this wide, soft sand beach while visiting friends who have a house in La Misión. The rocky prominence blocking the north end affords elevated spots for sitting and scanning the ocean for the plumes of gray whales as they migrate south in the fall and north in the spring. During weekends, the beach can be very crowded near the south end. It is especially popular with locals. Surf fishing can produce perch and corbina. Obtain supplies in Rosarito. Summer is the preferred time to visit, as winter is chilly. For things to do in the La Misión area, please see page 81.

⑤ Playa Mal Paso

Location: South of La Misión; Northwest Baja Norte map page 76, grid b1.

Directions: The beach extends about 2.5 miles. Access it from Mal Paso Trailer Park (campground number 10) at Kilometer 71, Baja Seasons (campground number 11) at Kilometer 72, or La Salina (the salt pan) at Kilometer 73.

Trip notes: This is one of the most spectacular beaches in all of Baja, a wide strip of sand that sweeps in an unbroken line from one end to the other. Since there are only three access points, a little walking will yield as much solitude as a person could need. The sand is clean and soft, and the beat of the surf is soothing and relaxing. At Mal Paso Trailer Park, it is possible to drive out on imported clay soil and camp close to the surf line. In fact, few beaches in Baja allow vehicular access so close to the surf. The song of the sea lulls campers into a peaceful, restorative sleep.

Beachgoers might see grunion here during the fishes' frenzied nocturnal mating ritual—a startling sight for those who have never witnessed the hilarious spectacle. These seven-inch smelt spawn through the spring and summer only on three or four nights following each full or new moon and then for a one- to three-hour period immediately after high tide. Females swim onto the beach accompanied by several males, dig themselves into the sand, and lay their eggs. The males discharge their milt on the sand near the female and go back to the water. The female then frees herself and returns to the sea. The eggs remain buried in the sand for about 10 days, until the next series of high tides washes them out. As the baby grunion hatch and immediately swim off, fishermen dash about, scooping them up after each wave and filling their buckets. Grunion are good broiled or battered and deep-fried.

The nearest supplies are in Rosarito. Summer is the preferred time to visit, as winter is chilly. For things to do in the La Misión area, please see page 81.

{6} Bahía Todos Santos Beaches

Location: South of Ensenada; Northwest Baja Norte map page 76, grid c1.

Directions: Starting from Corona Beach Trailer Park (campground number 22) on the north, the beaches extend about 1.5 miles past Mona Lisa Beach Resort (campground number 23) and El Faro Beach Motel and Trailer Park (campground number 24) to Estero Beach Resort and RV Park (campground number 25).

Trip notes: Even though we use the plural, this is really one long beach. Various segments have different names, depending upon what is behind them: Playas Hermosa, Corona, Mona Lisa, and Estero. The bay is polluted near Ensenada but farther south, toward the estero, it is cleaner. We have had a great deal of enjoyment on these very wide beaches, whether riding horses, walking, wading in the surf, or just sitting and watching the gulls and shorebirds as the waves roll in. Supplies can be picked up out on Highway 1 or on the side streets. Visit in summer, as winter gets chilly. For things to do in the Ensenada area, please see page 85.

{7} Playa Punta Banda

Location: In Punta Banda; Northwest Baja Norte map page 76, grid d1.

Directions: The beach runs along the north side of the Punta Banda Peninsula. From Maneadero on Highway 1, take the Punta Banda road for about eight miles to the beach.

Trip notes: The beach in front of Loco Lobo Paradise (campground number 26), La Jolla Beach Camp (campground number 27), and Villarino RV Park (campground number 28) is very popular with campers. Small boats can be launched into the surf of the bay for fishing and diving along the point. Obtain supplies in Punta Banda or back in Maneadero. Visit in summer, as winter gets chilly. For things to do in the Ensenada area, please see page 85.

{8} Playa San Antonio del Mar

Location: Northwest of Colonet; Northwest Baja Norte map page 77, grid f2.

Directions: Access is by a seven-mile dirt road leaving Highway 1 near the north end of the Colonet bridge at the San Antonio del Mar sign. It is about 65 miles south of Maneadero.

Trip notes: There are dunes behind the large beach and plenty of room for camping. (See campground number 34, San Antonio del Mar Beach). People like to cruise in their all-terrain vehicles in the dunes, surf, and cast into the surf for perch and corbina. The road in is best handled by pickups or four-wheel-drive vehicles. Colonet has the basic supplies. Summer is the time to visit, as winter is chilly.

⑨ Playa San Ramon

Location: Northwest and west of San Quintín; Northwest Baja Norte map page 77, grids h1–h2.

Directions: Access the beach west of Posada Don Diego RV Park (campground number 37) on a soft sand road that leads to the dunes or by rough four-wheel-drive roads west of San Quintín.

Trip notes: Surfers like this wide sand beach that extends for about 12 miles south of the Río Santo Domingo, ending at some cliffs. There are lots of Pismo clams to dig for, and the surf fishing for perch and corbina is good. Obtain supplies in San Quintín. Summer is the time to visit, as winter is chilly. For things to do in the San Quintín area, please see page 88.

⑩ Bahía Santa María Beaches

Location: South of San Quintín; Northwest Baja Norte map page 77, grids i1–i2.

Directions: The northern beach, Playa Santa María, is reached at Cielito Lindo Motel and RV Park (campground number 40). The southern beach, Playa Pabellón, is reached at El Pabellón RV Park (campground number 41). Access is also by sandy roads off the road into Cielito Lindo and off Highway 1.

Trip notes: This one magnificent, wide beach extends unbroken from the mouth of Bahía San Quintín for about 10 miles south to Arroyo Socorro. Many sand dollars dot the beach and if you dig around in the sand you'll find Pismo clams. Surf fishing can be good for perch and corbina, and the waves attract surfers. San Quintín has a full array of supplies. Summer is the time to visit, as winter is chilly. For things to do in the San Quintín area, please see page 88.

Protective small caves eroded into the walls of Guadalupe Canyon provide retreats for silent comtemplation. Indians used these, too, as evidenced by numerous ancient pictographs.

Chapter 2

Northeast
Baja Norte

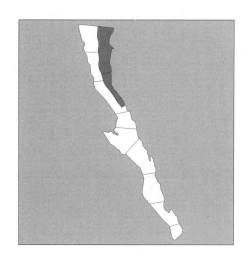

Northeast Baja Norte

Baja Map .... *page* 8

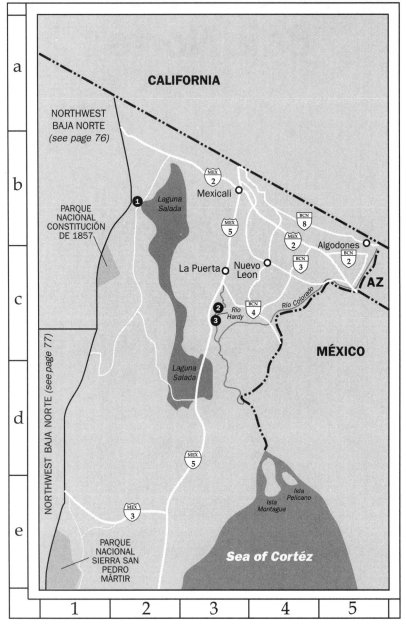

CALIFORNIA

NORTHWEST
BAJA NORTE
(see page 76)

PARQUE
NACIONAL
CONSTITUCIÓN
DE 1857

Laguna
Salada

MEX 2

Mexicali

MEX 5

BCN 8

MEX 2

BCN 3

Algodones

BCN 2

La Puerta

Nuevo
Leon

AZ

2

3

Río
Hardy

BCN 4

Río Colorado

MÉXICO

Laguna
Salada

NORTHWEST BAJA NORTE *(see page 77)*

MEX 5

MEX 3

Isla
Pelicano

Isla
Montague

PARQUE
NACIONAL
SIERRA SAN
PEDRO
MÁRTIR

Sea of Cortéz

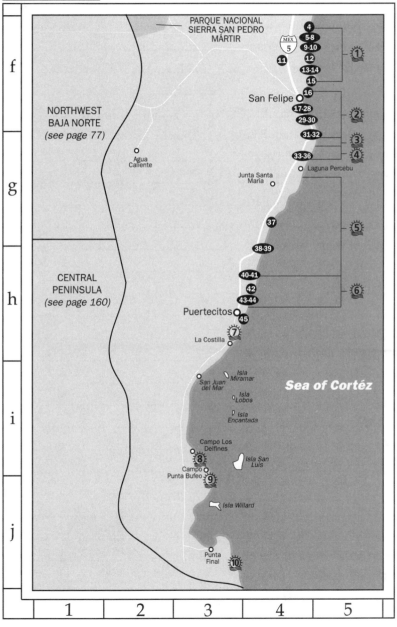

PARQUE NACIONAL
SIERRA SAN PEDRO
MÁRTIR

MEX 5

4
5-8
9-10
11   12
13-14
15
16

San Felipe

17-28
29-30
31-32
33-36

1
2
3
4

NORTHWEST
BAJA NORTE
(see page 77)

Agua
Caliente

Laguna Percebu

Junta Santa
María

37

38-39

5

CENTRAL
PENINSULA
(see page 160)

40-41
42
43-44

6

Puertecitos
45

La Costilla

7

Isla
Miramar

San Juan
del Mar

Isla
Lobos

Isla
Encantada

Sea of Cortéz

Campo Los
Delfines

8

Campo
Punta Bufeo

9

Isla San
Luis

Isla Willard

Punta
Final

10

Northeast Baja Norte Campgrounds

Northeast Baja Norte's 10 Best Beaches

Northeast Baja Norte

Readily accessible from Southern California through Mexicali, this stretch of the Baja California Peninsula is very popular. Winter is the prime season, while summer is the most uncomfortable with high desert temperatures. The area is easy to get to for long weekends, and even for short ones if you are willing to push it. San Felipe, the center of activity, is a mere 124 miles south of the U.S.-Mexico border on Highway 5—the nearest Baja resort on the Sea of Cortéz.

From San Felipe, the paved road leading 54 miles south to Puertecitos has its limitations. It is badly marred with potholes and has numerous small *vados* (dips into stream channels). Unlike elsewhere in Baja, these *vados* are not always announced to drivers by warning signs. The waterways they drop into are mostly narrow, creating a sudden plunge and an equally sudden ascent on the other side. Popping into one at high speed could be disastrous. This road must be taken at moderate speed, preferably in daylight.

The large tourist population disperses itself into a huge collection of campos, playas, and RV parks on the water between Río Hardy on the north and Puertecitos on the south. Pavement ends at Puertecitos, and the rugged dirt road on south to Bahía Gonzaga and ultimately Highway 1 at Laguna Chapala is suitable only for high-clearance vehicles.

Sierra de Juárez Area
(campground 1, page 132)

The Sierra de Juárez tilts gradually upward to the east, then drops precipitously down a 5,000-foot escarpment to the desert floor at sea level. The Rumorosa Grade on old Highway 2 is steep, curvy, and scenic, with startling vistas of the desert far below. There is also a parallel toll road with an easier gradient. The eastern slope has several palm-lined streams cut through solid rock, with water running from pool to pool. Exploring is best done in winter, as the rock-lined canyons become ovenlike in the summer heat.

Río Hardy Area
(campgrounds 2–3, pages 132–133)

The Río Hardy is about 40 miles south of the border and 80 miles north of San Felipe. It is not on the Sea of Cortéz and, accordingly, people go there for different activities—freshwater fishing, game-bird hunting, and waterskiing. The river is fed mainly by agricultural drain water.

San Felipe and Puertecitos Areas
(campgrounds 4–45, pages 134–154)

Originally a fishing village, San Felipe has had 45 years since the arrival of paved roads to stimulate development of a strong tourist clientele. With the totuava fish population depleted and currently protected, the shrimp fishery all but moribund, and commercial fishing in the northernmost reaches of the Sea of Cortéz closed by presidential decree, tourism, including sportfishing, now supports the local economy. The growth of hotels, campgrounds, and resort developments is continuous. Great beaches are the main attraction.

Starting about 10 miles north of San Felipe and continuing another 54 miles south to Puertecitos, there is a series of campos and playas on the Sea of Cortéz, each with its own sign and access road off Highway 5. Even when they adjoin each other, there are separate access roads. Along some stretches of highway, such roads appear every quarter mile.

While most of these campos lease sites by the year and do not serve overnight travelers, some indicate on their signs that they have camping facilities. These vary from nothing except a place to pitch a tent or park a rig to full-service establishments. Frequent campers check them all out, then settle into a favorite and return year after year. Newcomers with nothing to guide them are completely befuddled and can exhaust all their available time driving down one access road after another.

The Puertecitos camping experience is out of the ordinary, requiring an attitude adjustment. The large number of visitors who seek out this area desire the simplicity and tranquillity of desert living on a beach far from the trappings of urbanized society. Sunrises and sunsets take on special significance; the comings and goings of the extreme daily tides become endlessly fascinating. The satisfying pleasures of life are oriented to natural phenomena rather than contrived amusements. There is much opportunity for intriguing activities, yet there is no need to do anything. Camping here can touch on the essence of mañana-land and foster a great refreshing of the spirit, or it can be the epitome of privation in a primitive existence.

Fishing

In the vicinity of Puertecitos, anglers will find corvina, bay bass, triggerfish, barracuda, sierra, pargo, and grouper. Around San Felipe, you can expect corvina, croaker, and various types of bass. If you don't have your own boat, you can usually rent a *panga* wherever there are local commercial fishermen. Ask other campers who have been there awhile how the fishing is, as it comes and goes.

Alex's (Alejandro's) Sportfishing in San Felipe has a good reputation with foreign residents. His office is on the Malecón (the city waterfront), and he is usually nearby. He speaks good English and charges fair prices for half-day trips.

Boating

Many visitors bring cartop boats or small trailered boats to San Felipe and Puertecitos for fishing. Others tow large trailered boats to begin an extended cruise of the Sea of Cortéz—at times with the planned destination being Cabo San Lucas or mainland México ports such as Bahía Kino, San Carlos, Guaymas, or points even farther south. Starting from San Felipe or Puertecitos can save many miles of highway trailering farther into Baja or onto the mainland.

Boaters must learn to deal with the special conditions created by the area's extreme tidal ranges. They must coordinate launching and retrieving with high tides and avoid anchoring in shallow water at high tide. Boaters can launch using a special vehicle at Ruben's RV Park (campground number 19). Four launch ramps are available at high tide—at Ruben's, El Cortéz Motel, and Club de Pesca RV Park (campground number 28) in San Felipe, and the ramp in Puertecitos—for about $5 each. No longer are there any free launch ramps in the area.

Off-roading

Running around the desert and on the beaches in various off-road vehicles (ORVs) is a major activity in these parts. People use all manner of vehicles, many of them homemade. A common denominator is that they are lightweight and have soft, fat tires. There are motor scooters, trail bikes, dune buggies, sand rails, all-terrain vehicles (ATVs), two-wheelers, three-wheelers, four-wheelers, and so on.

Tidepooling

The high tidal range of 20 feet or more exposes hundreds of yards of seafloor at low tide, inviting exploration. The incoming tide moves swiftly enough to warrant attentiveness and brisk walking to avoid being dunked, however.

Mountaineering

West of San Felipe and Puertecitos are the two northernmost ranges of the many mountains that form the high spine of the peninsula—the northern Sierra de Juárez and the southern Sierra San Pedro Mártir. The great eastern escarpment of Baja's highest peak, the 10,154-foot El Picacho del Diablo, looms up behind San Felipe, offering a mountain climbing adventure, but one that only experts should attempt. It is an extremely grueling and dangerous ascent.

The eastern canyons of both ranges are steep and feature hidden pools and palm groves. Huge boulders and smooth water-worn rock faces are difficult and risky to surmount. Summer heat can turn these canyons into ovens. Exploring them for their hidden nooks is best done in the cool of winter. You might observe other intrepid mountaineers, desert bighorn sheep, in these canyons.

Excursions

If you don't have the equipment to get off the pavement or on the water, you can have someone take you for a fee. Enchanted Island Excursions in San Felipe offers cruises to Isla de Las Encantadas (the Enchanted Islands) and remote beaches, leads off-road dune buggy trips, and takes clients fishing in a *panga.* Call them at 011-52-657-7-1431 or -1885 in Baja.

Dining

Two good dining choices in San Felipe are El Nido (348 Mar de Cortéz; phone 011-52-657-7-1028) and George's Restaurant and Bar (336 Mar de Cortéz Sur; no phone).

❶ Guadalupe Canyon Hot Springs and Campground

Location: West of Mexicali; Northeast Baja Norte map page 124, grid b2.

Campsites, facilities: There are 30 campsites accommodating from one to seven vehicles, all without hookups. Each site has picnic tables, barbecue pits, palapas, trees, and private concrete and rock hot tubs with valves to control the temperature of geothermal mineral water. Facilities include hot showers, flush toilets, a pool with 80-degree Fahrenheit natural water, a restaurant (open on weekends), a small store, gas and oil sales, and cellular phone service. Tent camping is very popular, as access is most suitable for small vehicles. Potable water (all water here is mineral), food, ice, and firewood must be brought in by campers. Due to the remote location, security is not a problem.

Reservations, fees: Reservations are recommended on weekends. Fees are high—$15 per night for the small campsite and $30 to $45 for the large group sites. Discounts for weekly, monthly, or year-long stays are available.

Contact: Guadalupe Canyon Hot Springs and Campground, P.O. Box 4003, Balboa, CA 92661; phone or fax (714) 673-2670.

Directions: Take Highway 2 (the free road) east from Tecate approximately 66 miles or west from Mexicali about 28 miles, then head south on a graded dirt road at the "Cañon de Guadalupe" sign near Kilometer 28. After about 27 miles, turn right (west) at a large sign and continue about six miles on a winding dirt road and the final two miles over a rough road with steep, narrow rocky spots and soft sand off the tracks. Passing can be tough and is not recommended for motor homes or trailers.

Trip notes: Three camps are available near the Guadalupe Canyon Hot Springs. Number 1 is the first you'll encounter and the one you are dealing with when you call or write as directed above. Camps 2 and 3 adjoin camp number 1 on the uphill side and are under different management, which does not advertise or provide services other than the hot tubs. Fees in those are much lower. We stayed in one and liked it. The camps are open year-round and are busiest on weekends. You can arrange for a guide to take you exploring in Indian caves and to view rock art for $20. Other features include waterfalls, hiking and rock climbing terrain, and, of course, the hot springs. Heavy rains can wash out the road, another reason to call before going. Winter is the time to come, as summer is hot.

❷ Campo Sonora

Location: South of Mexicali; Northeast Baja Norte map page 124, grid c3.

Campsites, facilities: There are seven campsites with palapas, very dirty toilets, and a small restaurant that is open in summer for drinks and snacks. Don't drink the water. The park is secured with a chain at the entrance to the parking lot. Tent campers are welcome. Obtain supplies in Mexicali.

Reservations, fees: All sites are first come, first served. The fee is low—$7 per night.

Contact: Drive in and talk to the owner.

Directions: From the border just north of Mexicali, head about 40 miles south on Highway 5. The park is at Kilometer 58.

Trip notes: The good news? The camp is set on the Río Hardy, where you can fish for carp and perch. There are also nearby hunting opportunities for waterfowl and white-winged doves. The bad news? This is a very minimal facility and a poorly maintained one at that. Noise from the adjacent highway can be disturbing. A note of warning: It is difficult to find a place to purchase supplies without going back to Mexicali, so it's best to enter México fully prepared for your entire trip if you'll be staying here. Visit in winter, as summer can be hot.

③ Campo Mosqueda

Location: South of Mexicali; Northeast Baja Norte map page 124, grid c3.

Campsites, facilities: There are 50 campsites, of which 20 have electricity. On the premises are clean rest rooms with flush toilets and cold showers, a restaurant, and a lake. Don't drink the water. The owner lives on the premises, so security is good. Tent campers are welcome. Obtain supplies in Mexicali.

Reservations, fees: All sites are first come, first served. The fee is low—$7 per night.

Contact: Drive in and talk to the owner.

Directions: From the border just north of Mexicali, head about 40 miles south on Highway 5. Turn off at Kilometer 60, which is well marked with a large sign, and drive one mile.

Trip notes: Being so close to the border makes this a very convenient destination. It is a large, attractive campground with lots of trees and palms. Some of the campsites border a small, pretty man-made lake. If you like freshwater fishing, you'll be happy; the lake is stocked with catfish and largemouth and smallmouth bass. Fees are $1 per rod and $3 per kilogram of fish caught. Waterskiing and bird hunting for waterfowl and white-winged doves are also excellent. A note of warning: It is difficult to find a place to purchase goods without going back to Mexicali, so it's best to enter México fully supplied for your entire trip if you will be staying here. Visit in winter, as summer can be hot.

④ Campo Los Amigos

Location: North of San Felipe; Northeast Baja Norte map page 125, grid f4.

Campsites, facilities: There's room for an indeterminate number of campers. Facilities include hot showers (available for $1), toilets, a few palapas, and tables. Don't drink the water. The manager lives on the premises, so security is good. Tent campers are welcome. Obtain supplies in San Felipe.

Reservations, fees: All sites are first come, first served. Fees are low—$2 for day use and $5 for overnight camping.

Contact: Drive in and talk to the manager.

Directions: From San Felipe, drive about 10 miles north on Highway 5, then turn east at Kilometer 173 and continue one mile on a wide, hard-packed dirt road.

Trip notes: This campground is at the northern end of the string of campos and playas along the Sea of Cortéz north of San Felipe. The shoreline to the north turns into extensive mudflats extending south from the mouth of the Colorado River. To the south there is a fine beach. Winter is the time to come, as summer is hot. For things to do in the San Felipe area, please see page 129.

⑤ Playa Grand

Location: North of San Felipe; Northeast Baja Norte map page 125, grid f4.

Campsites, facilities: Pit toilets and 14 palapas are provided. Don't drink the water. The manager lives on the premises, so security is good. Tent campers are welcome. Obtain supplies in San Felipe.

Reservations, fees: All sites are first come, first served. The fee is low.

Contact: Drive in and talk to the manager.

Directions: From San Felipe, drive about 10 miles north on Highway 5, then turn east at Kilometer 173 and continue one mile on a good dirt road.

Trip notes: Playa Grande is worth a visit. The beach lives up to its name, extending north and south in front of the camp. Camping here is an enjoyable experience, even though the facility is a bit run-down. Winter is the time to come, as summer is hot. For things to do in the San Felipe area, please see page 129.

⑥ Campo Jalisco

Location: North of San Felipe; Northeast Baja Norte map page 125, grid f4.

Campsites, facilities: Of the 19 campsites, all with palapas, 14 are on the beach. Neither water nor electricity are provided, though there are flush toilets and cold showers. Don't drink the water. The owner lives on the premises, so security is good. Tent campers are welcome. Obtain supplies in San Felipe.

Reservations, fees: Camping is first come, first served. The fee is moderate—$10 per night.

Contact: Drive in and the owner will collect your fee.

Directions: From San Felipe, drive about 10 miles north on Highway 5, then turn east at Kilometer 175 and continue one mile on a wide, hard-packed dirt road.

Trip notes: Though this small RV park offers the bare minimum in services, it is smack-dab on a magnificent beach—wide and long with toe-tickling sand. When someone asks us for a beautiful, quiet, no-frills beach camp in the San Felipe area where they can get away from it all, we mention Campo Jalisco. Winter is the time to come, as summer is hot. For things to do in the San Felipe area, please see page 129.

❼ Campo Hacienda Beach

Location: North of San Felipe; Northeast Baja Norte map page 125, grid f4.

Campsites, facilities: Set up your RV or tent wherever you please, as there are no marked campsites. Flush toilets and cold showers are sometimes available. For $1 you can shower at Campo Jalisco next door. The owner lives on the premises and keeps a cable across the road, so security is good. Obtain supplies in San Felipe.

Reservations, fees: Camping is first come, first served. Fees are low—$6 per night and $35 per week.

Contact: Drive in and the owner will collect your fee.

Directions: From San Felipe, drive about 10 miles north on Highway 5, then turn east at Kilometer 175 and continue one mile on a wide, hard-packed dirt road.

Trip notes: Here you camp on the same great beach as at Campo Jalisco (see campground number 6), but in a slightly different setting. Winter is the time to come, as summer is hot. For things to do in the San Felipe area, please see page 129.

❽ El Dorado Ranch RV Park

Location: North of San Felipe; Northeast Baja Norte map page 125, grid f4.

Campsites, facilities: There are 100 campsites (42 pull-through), all with full hookups, palapas, and very small trees. The front row just above the beach has 15 campsites with tables. Flush toilets, cold showers, a pool, a store, a restaurant, rental horses, tennis courts, and dune buggy tours are available. Don't drink the water. Security is tight, as you must enter through a manned gate. Tent camping is not provided for, though the brochures show a tent set up. Obtain supplies in San Felipe.

Reservations, fees: Reservations are accepted. The fee is high—$25 per night.

Contact: El Dorado Ranch RV Park, P.O. Box 3809, Calexico, CA 92232; phone 011-52-657-7-1278 in México, (800) 404-2599 in the United States.

Directions: From San Felipe, drive about 10 miles north on Highway 5, then turn east at Kilometer 176 and continue one mile on a wide, hard-packed dirt road.

Trip notes: Though campers may stay here, the primary goal of El Dorado Ranch RV Park is to sell memberships with permanent RV spaces or homesites. The park is on a beautiful beach and has more amenities than other RV facilities north of San Felipe. Winter is the time to come, as summer is hot. For things to do in the San Felipe area, please see page 129.

⑨ Pete's Camp El Paraiso

Location: North of San Felipe; Northeast Baja Norte map page 125, grid f4.

Campsites, facilities: There is a lot of space for RV and tent camping on the beach. Facilities include hot showers (for $1), flush toilets, a restaurant, a bar, a nine-hole golf course, and an RV dump station. Ask for drinking water. The manager lives on the premises and the camp is well populated with permanent residents, so security is good. Obtain supplies in San Felipe.

Reservations, fees: Reservations are accepted. The fee is moderate—$8 per night.

Contact: For reservations, phone (909) 676-4224.

Directions: From San Felipe, drive about eight miles north on Highway 5, then turn east at Kilometer 178 and continue one mile on the good dirt road.

Trip notes: An old campground, Pete's Camp El Paraiso has built up a substantial following over the years. It was crammed full on the weekend we visited, while the other campgrounds north of San Felipe were deserted. Don't come if you're in the mood for serenity; the place can be downright boisterous, as the clientele consists primarily of the beach-vehicle and partying crowd. Winter is the time to come, as summer is hot. For things to do in the San Felipe area, please see page 129.

⑩ La Playa Encantada

Location: North of San Felipe; Northeast Baja Norte map page 125, grid f4.

Campsites, facilities: There are 30 palapas, along with showers and flush toilets that don't work. Water and security are not provided. Tent camping is appropriate. Obtain supplies in San Felipe.

Reservations, fees: All sites are first come, first served. When we visited, there was no one to ask about the fee, nor was it posted.

Contact: Drive in and park.

Directions: From San Felipe, drive about eight miles north on Highway 5, then turn east at Kilometer 178 and continue one mile on the good dirt road.

Trip notes: This beach camp adjoins Pete's Camp El Paraiso across a fence (see campground number 9). The first time we were here, the place was new but not yet functioning. Two years later it appeared abandoned yet was still accessible. Before driving down to the beach, walk the last pitch of road to see if you can handle it. The camping area is so narrow it would be difficult for a truck and trailer to turn around. Winter is the time to come, as summer is hot. For things to do in the San Felipe area, please see page 129.

⑪ El Cachanilla RV Park

Location: North of San Felipe; Northeast Baja Norte map page 125, grid f4.

Campsites, facilities: There are 95 campsites (20 pull-through), all without hookups. Facilities include central palapas, barbecues, a dump station ($2 fee), tiled rest rooms with flush toilets and hot showers ($1 fee), laundry, a small store, RV storage, a mechanical shop, air supply for tires, and a clubhouse with a pool table, a TV, darts, and a library. Don't drink the water. Security is provided by a watchman. Tent campers are welcome. Obtain supplies in San Felipe.

Reservations, fees: Reservations are accepted. Fees are low—$5 per night, $30 per week, or $100 per month.

Contact: El Cachanilla RV Park, P.O. Box 3809, Calexico, CA 92232; phone 011-52-657-7-1278 for reservations.

Directions: From San Felipe, drive about seven miles north on Highway 5, then turn west at Kilometer 179 and continue one mile on the good dirt road.

Trip notes: This park is part of the El Dorado Ranch operation. Some members stay here for the low rates and drive over to El Dorado Ranch RV Park (campground number 8) to take advantage of the amenities and play on the beach. For nonmembers there is little to recommend the place except for the low rates, as it is out in the desert with only a very distant view of the Sea of Cortéz. Winter is the time to come, as summer is hot. For things to do in the San Felipe area, please see page 129.

⑫ Campo Los Compadres

Location: North of San Felipe; Northeast Baja Norte map page 125, grid f4.

Campsites, facilities: Pit toilets and several palapas are provided for RVers and tenters. Don't drink the water. The manager lives on the premises, so security is good. Obtain supplies in San Felipe.

Reservations, fees: All sites are first come, first served. The fee is moderate—$10 per night.

Contact: Drive in and talk to the manager.

Directions: From San Felipe, drive about seven miles north on Highway 5, then turn east at Kilometer 180 and continue one mile on the good dirt road.

Trip notes: You camp on a gentle slope that leads down to a nice beach and has plenty of room for rigs or tents. The beach is wide and stretches far in both directions. We spent a pleasant night watching the tide come in and go out and enjoyed poking around in little tidepools among the boulders. We also admired the display of fireworks launched skyward from Pete's Camp El Paraiso to the north and marveled at the variety and number of beach vehicles coming and going. A little boy was sent down to collect the fee, which he stoutly insisted was $2 more than we had been told upon arrival. We didn't have the heart to complicate his life by arguing. Winter is the time to come, as summer is hot. For things to do in the San Felipe area, please see page 129.

⓭ San Diego Beach

Location: North of San Felipe; Northeast Baja Norte map page 125, grid f4.

Campsites, facilities: There are hot showers and palapas. Don't drink the water. The manager lives on the premises, so security is good. Tent campers are welcome. Obtain supplies in San Felipe.

Reservations, fees: All sites are first come, first served. The fee is low—$7 per night.

Contact: Drive in and talk to the manager.

Directions: From San Felipe, drive about six miles north on Highway 5, then turn east at Kilometer 182 and continue one mile on the fair dirt road.

Trip notes: You'll find little room to maneuver a vehicle on this tiny, pretty beach. It is suitable only for small rigs and tents—don't try it with a trailer. Winter is the time to come, as summer is hot. For things to do in the San Felipe area, please see page 129.

⓮ Playa del Sol

Location: North of San Felipe; Northeast Baja Norte map page 125, grid f4.

Campsites, facilities: There are 45 campsites with palapas for RVs and tents. Neither water nor electricity are provided, though there are flush toilets and hot showers ($1 fee). Don't drink the water. Security is provided by a resident owner. Obtain supplies in San Felipe.

Reservations, fees: Reservations are accepted. The fee is low—$5.50 per night.

Contact: Playa del Sol, Apartado Postal 128, San Felipe, Baja California, México, or P.O. Box 3635, Calexico, CA 92232. There is no phone.

Directions: From San Felipe, drive about six miles north on Highway 5, then turn east at Kilometer 183 and continue one mile on the fair dirt road.

Trip notes: The campsites are set on several terraces rising above a beautiful beach—a long, wide strip of powdery sand. Winter is the time to come, as summer is hot. For things to do in the San Felipe area, please see page 129.

⓯ Playa Blanca

Location: North of San Felipe; Northeast Baja Norte map page 125, grid f4.

Campsites, facilities: Run-down toilets and some palapas are provided. Don't drink the water. There is no security. Obtain supplies in San Felipe.

Reservations, fees: All sites are first come, first served. The fee is moderate—$10 per night.

Contact: Drive in and talk to the manager.

Directions: From San Felipe, drive about five miles north on Highway 5, then turn east at Kilometer 184 and continue 1.5 miles to the Sea of Cortéz.

Trip notes: Playa Blanca, a wide beach, extends far in both directions. It offers some trees and plenty of room for RV and tent camping. An abandoned one-story hotel sits on the dunes above a nice stretch of beach, attracting the occasional sightseer. The open camping area is astride a beach-vehicle route, so it can get loud. Winter is the time to come, as summer is hot. For things to do in the San Felipe area, please see page 129.

⓰ Campo Numero Uno

Location: In San Felipe; Northeast Baja Norte map page 125, grid f4.

Campsites, facilities: Each of the 65 full-hookup campsites comes with palapas, tables, and barbecues. On the premises you'll find tiled rest rooms with flush toilets, cold showers, a dump station, and a restaurant, which is open only at busy times. Don't drink the water. The camp is secured by a resident manager, a guard, and a gated fence. Tent campers may use any of the sites. Obtain supplies in San Felipe.

Reservations, fees: All sites are first come, first served. Fees are moderate—$10 per night, $50 per week, or $150 per month.

Contact: Drive in and talk to the manager, or phone 011-52-657-7-1139.

Directions: Take Highway 5 into San Felipe, 124 miles south of Mexicali. The park is behind the hill on Avenida Mar de Cortéz Norte, on a narrow sand beach with rocks that are exposed at low tide. All the other northside beach parks are on the waterfront street east of Avenida Mar de Cortéz. Follow the signs.

Trip notes: The northernmost campground on the beach in San Felipe, Campo Numero Uno is a pleasant spot for folks who want to rough it in a tent or RV. Being off the beaten track, it is not well known. Winter is the time to come, as summer is hot. For things to do in the San Felipe area, please see page 129.

⓱ Marco's RV Park

Location: In San Felipe; Northeast Baja Norte map page 125, grid f4.

Campsites, facilities: There are 15 campsites with full hookups, concrete pads, palapas, and tables. Flush toilets and hot showers are provided. Don't drink the water. The park is secured with a gate. Tent campers are prohibited. Obtain supplies in San Felipe.

Reservations, fees: All sites are first come, first served. Fees are moderate—$8 per night, $50 per week, or $200 per month.

Contact: Drive in and talk to the manager, or phone 011-52-655-7-2579.

Directions: Take Highway 5 into San Felipe, 124 miles south of Mexicali. The park is on the land side of the waterfront street, just north of Ruben's RV Park (a landmark by virtue of being the largest RV park in that neighborhood).

Trip notes: The properties on the other side of the street are set beside the Sea of Cortéz, so Marco's lacks the main attraction in this area—a beachfront location. It has built up a loyal clientele, however, with many people returning just for the privacy. Winter is the time to come, as summer is hot. For things to do in the San Felipe area, please see page 129.

🅲 Playa Bonita RV Park

Location: In San Felipe; Northeast Baja Norte map page 125, grid f4.

Campsites, facilities: For RVs, there are 11 pull-through sites with full hookups, concrete pads, palapas, barbecues, and tables under trees. For tents, there are 16 sites with palapas, tables, some barbecues, electricity, and water. Flush toilets, tiled hot showers, and laundry facilities are provided. Don't drink the water. The park is secured with gates. Obtain supplies in San Felipe.

Reservations, fees: Reservations are accepted. Fees are high—for RVs, $16.50 per night in winter, $22 in summer, and $27.50 on holidays; for tents, $11 per night in winter, $16.50 in summer, and $22 on holidays. Motor homes are slightly higher. There is a 20 percent discount for monthly stays.

Contact: Playa Bonita RV Park, 475 East Badillo Street, Covina, CA 91723; phone 011-52-657-7-1215 in San Felipe. For reservations, phone (909) 595-4250 or fax (818) 966-1487 in the United States.

Directions: Take Highway 5 into San Felipe, 124 miles south of Mexicali. The park is on the waterfront street on the north side of town, north of Ruben's RV Park.

Trip notes: Playa Bonita RV Park is a very nice little facility on a wide, extensive beach. Since it fills up in winter, early birds get to settle into the few choice campsites overlooking the water. Winter is the time to come, as summer is hot. For things to do in the San Felipe area, please see page 129.

🅳 Ruben's RV Park

Location: In San Felipe; Northeast Baja Norte map page 125, grid f4.

Campsites, facilities: There are 50 pull-through campsites with full hookups, tables, and shade structures topped with balconies that afford ocean views. On the premises are flush toilets, hot showers, a restaurant, and a special vehicle used for launching boats. Don't drink the water. The park is well populated and is secured with a gate. Tent campers are welcome. Obtain supplies in San Felipe.

Reservations, fees: Reservations are accepted. Fees are moderate—$12 per night, $70 per week, $225 per month, or $1,400 per year.

Contact: Ruben's RV Park, Apartado Postal 196, San Felipe, Baja California, México; phone 011-52-657-7-1442.

Directions: Take Highway 5 into San Felipe, 124 miles south of Mexicali. The park is on the beach, on the waterfront street on the north side of town.

Trip notes: In front of Ruben's there's a great beach, a huge parcel of bright white sand, making this a very popular spot. Tenters often pitch their tents on the balconies atop the shade structures to get a better ocean view. It is a large campground and at times is a beehive of activity. Boaters can launch their watercraft using an ancient four-wheel-drive army truck at just about any tide for $20 to $40, depending on the size of the boat; there also is a launch ramp available. Winter is the time to come, as summer is hot. For things to do in the San Felipe area, please see page 129.

⑳ Josefina's RV Park

Location: In San Felipe; Northeast Baja Norte map page 125, grid f4.

Campsites, facilities: There are 21 campsites with full hookups, concrete pads, balconies, and tables. Flush toilets and hot showers are provided. Don't drink the water. A manager lives on the premises, and the park is secured with a gate. Tent campers are welcome. Obtain supplies in San Felipe.

Reservations, fees: All sites are first come, first served. Fees are moderate— $12 per night to camp on the beach or $10 for a site back from the beach.

Contact: Drive in and talk to the manager.

Directions: Take Highway 5 into San Felipe, 124 miles south of Mexicali. The park is on the beach on the north waterfront street, adjoining Ruben's RV Park on the south.

Trip notes: This very pleasant little RV park is on the same big beach as Ruben's (campground number 19). The people staying here when we came urged us not to tell anyone about it, and no one knew what the name was. There is no sign, and the camp appears to be part of Ruben's, which is not the case. We've been here a couple of times and haven't been able to find anyone in charge. The manager at Ruben's told us the name was Josefina's RV Park, but another source came up with Campo La

Palapa. We just love these little mysteries. Winter is the time to come, as summer can sizzle. For things to do in the San Felipe area, please see page 129.

㉑ Vista del Mar RV Park

Location: In San Felipe; Northeast Baja Norte map page 125, grid f4.

Campsites, facilities: There are 20 campsites with full hookups, concrete pads, tables, barbecues, and palm trees. Flush toilets and hot showers are provided. Don't drink the water. A manager lives on the premises, and the park is secured with a gate. Tent campers are welcome. Obtain supplies in San Felipe.

Reservations, fees: Reservations are accepted. Fees are moderate—$12 per night or $10 without electricity.

Contact: Drive in and talk to the manager.

Directions: Take Highway 5 into San Felipe, 124 miles south of Mexicali. The park is at the corner of Avenidas Mar de Cortéz and Puerto Vallarta.

Trip notes: This is a very clean park on a slope with a brick driveway and well-manicured grounds. Though it has an ocean view, it is not on the beach—which is the main attraction in San Felipe. Winter is the time to come, as summer is hot. For things to do in the San Felipe area, please see page 129.

㉒ Campo Posada del Mar

Location: In San Felipe; Northeast Baja Norte map page 125, grid f4.

Campsites, facilities: There are 60 two-story palapas with full hookups, concrete pads, trees, tables, and barbecues. Both RVs and tents can be accommodated. Flush toilets, hot showers, and rooms are available. Don't drink the water. Security is provided by a gate and a residential manager. Obtain supplies in San Felipe.

Reservations, fees: Reservations are accepted. Fees are moderate to high—$10 to $20 per night.

Contact: Campo Posada del Mar, 555 Golfo de California, San Felipe, Baja California, México; phone 011-52-657-7-1543.

Directions: Take Highway 5 into San Felipe, 124 miles south of Mexicali. The park is in town at the junction of Golfo de California and San Felipe.

Trip notes: Tucked among city streets away from the Sea of Cortéz, this campground holds little attraction for tourists. Winter is the time to come, as summer is hot. For things to do in the San Felipe area, please see page 129.

㉓ La Jolla RV Park

Location: In San Felipe; Northeast Baja Norte map page 125, grid f4.

Campsites, facilities: There are 55 pull-through campsites with full hookups and palapas. Both RVs and tents can be accommodated. Facilities include flush toilets, hot showers, laundry, a pool, and a Jacuzzi. Don't drink the water. A manager lives on the premises. Obtain supplies in San Felipe.

Reservations, fees: Reservations are accepted. The fee is high—$15 per night.

Contact: La Jolla RV Park, P.O. Box 978, El Centro, CA 92244; phone 011-52-657-7-1222.

Directions: Take Highway 5 into San Felipe, 124 miles south of Mexicali. The park is in the middle of town at Avenidas Manzanillo and Mar Bermejo.

Trip notes: The park is situated in a quiet residential neighborhood. However, it is not on the beach, which is what most people who come to San Felipe want. Winter is the time to come, as summer is hot. For things to do in the San Felipe area, please see page 129.

㉔ Campo San Felipe

Location: In San Felipe; Northeast Baja Norte map page 125, grid f4.

Campsites, facilities: There are 34 pull-through RV sites with full hookups, concrete pads, palapas, and tables. Six tent sites have palapas, electricity, and water. Tiled rest rooms with flush toilets and hot showers and laundry facilities are available. Don't drink the water. A resident owner and a watchman provide security. Obtain supplies in San Felipe.

Reservations, fees: Reservations are accepted. Fees are moderate to high—$11 to $17 per night or $300 per month for RVs and $11 for tents. Both get one day free for weeklong stays.

Contact: Campo San Felipe, 301 Avenida Mar de Cortéz, San Felipe, Baja California, México; phone 011-52-657-7-1012.

Directions: Take Highway 5 into San Felipe, 124 miles south of Mexicali. The park is on the beach in the southern part of town on Avenida Mar de Cortéz.

Trip notes: This popular park, which adjoins Playa de Laura RV Park to the south, has been a haven for RVers and tent campers for many, many years. It's in the heart of town, within walking distance of shops, restaurants, and other attractions. Winter is the time to come, as summer is hot. For things to do in the San Felipe area, please see page 129.

㉕ Playa de Laura RV Park

Location: In San Felipe; Northeast Baja Norte map page 125, grid f4.

Campsites, facilities: There are 45 campsites (35 full-hookup pull-through), all of which may be used by tent campers, with concrete pads, palapas, tables, barbecues, and some shade structures topped with balconies. Tiled rest rooms with flush toilets and hot showers are provided, and campers can launch boats over the sand. Don't drink the water. The park is well populated and secure with a watchman. Obtain supplies in San Felipe.

Reservations, fees: Camping is first come, first served. Fees are high— $13 to $18 per night, $91 to $115 per week, or $360 to $432 per month.

Contact: Playa de Laura RV Park, Avenida Mar de Cortéz #333, San Felipe, Baja California. México; phone 011-52-657-7-1128.

Directions: Take Highway 5 into San Felipe, 124 miles south of Mexicali. The park is on the beach in the southern part of town on Avenida Mar de Cortéz.

Trip notes: We have stayed in this popular park and appreciated the large beach and its proximity to restaurants. The place was a bit too congested for us, however, and things can get pretty raucous. Winter is the time to come, as summer is hot. For things to do in the San Felipe area, please see page 129.

26 Baja Mar RV Sport Beach Club

Location: In San Felipe; Northeast Baja Norte map page 125, grid f4.

Campsites, facilities: There are 70 campsites with full hookups, concrete pads, palapas, tables, and barbecues. All sites accommodate both RV and tent campers. Facilities include tiled rest rooms with flush toilets and hot showers and laundry. Don't drink the water. Security is provided by a resident manager. Obtain supplies in San Felipe.

Reservations, fees: Camping is first come, first served. Fees are high—$14 to $19 per night, with tents and automobiles at the low end and RVs and beachfront sites at the high end. One day is free for weekly stays. The monthly rate is $300 to $375.

Contact: Baja Mar RV Sport Beach Club, Mar de Cortéz Sur, San Felipe, Baja California, México. There is no phone.

Directions: Take Highway 5 into San Felipe, 124 miles south of Mexicali. The park is on the beach in the southern part of town on Avenida Mar de Cortéz, on the south side of Playa de Laura RV Park.

Trip notes: Recently opened, this modern, attractive, full-service park is right in the middle of town and fronts on the beach. Winter is the time to come, as summer is hot. For things to do in the San Felipe area, please see page 129.

27 Victor's RV Park

Location: In San Felipe; Northeast Baja Norte map page 125, grid f4.

Campsites, facilities: There are 50 pull-through campsites with full hookups and concrete pads. Flush toilets and hot showers are provided. Don't drink the water. The park is secure. Tent campers are welcome. Obtain supplies in San Felipe.

Reservations, fees: Camping is first come, first served. Fees are high—$15 per night, $75 per week, $200 per month, or $2,000 per year.

Contact: Victor's RV Park, P.O. Box 1227, Calexico, CA 92232. There is no phone.

Directions: Take Highway 5 into San Felipe, 124 miles south of Mexicali. The park is on the beach in the southern part of town on Avenida Mar de Cortéz.

Trip notes: This is a very popular park with a number of permanents, which gives it a residential atmosphere. It fills up quickly and is a little tight for maneuvering. Winter is the time to come, as summer is hot. For things to do in the San Felipe area, please see page 129.

28 Club de Pesca RV Park

Location: In San Felipe; Northeast Baja Norte map page 125, grid f4.

Campsites, facilities: There are 40 campsites with electricity, water, palapas, and concrete pads. Sites located away from the beach have sewer hookups. Flush toilets, hot showers, a dump station, a recreation room, a launch ramp, and a store are on the property. Don't drink the water. There is 24-hour security. Tent campers are welcome. Obtain supplies in San Felipe.

Reservations, fees: Reservations are accepted. Fees are high—$18 per night for a site on the beach and $13 in back. If you stay a week, you get one day free; stay a month and receive a 30 percent discount. Long-term rates are $1,560 per year.

Contact: Club de Pesca RV Park, Apartado Postal 90, San Felipe, Baja California, México; phone 011-52-657-7-1180.

Directions: Take Highway 5 into San Felipe, 124 miles south of Mexicali. The park is on the beach in the southern part of town at the south end of Avenida Mar de Cortéz.

Trip notes: This is primarily a residential park containing privately owned houses and mobile homes. Though there is room for travelers, the residential atmosphere seems a bit incompatible with the tourist experience. The wide beach is a playground for people with ATVs, trail bikes, sand rails, dune buggies, and other fat-tired, sand-floating vehicles. Strollers may even find it enjoyable—provided they're agile enough to get out of the way. Boat launching costs about $5. Winter is the time to come, as summer is hot. For things to do in the San Felipe area, please see page 129.

29 Mar del Sol RV Park

Location: In San Felipe; Northeast Baja Norte map page 125, grid f4.

Campsites, facilities: There are 106 campsites with concrete pads, of which 85 have full hookups and 21 have no hookups. Flush toilets and hot showers in clean, tiled rest rooms, laundry facilities, a pool, a restaurant, and brick walkways are on the property. Don't drink the water. The park is secured with a gate. Tent campers are welcome. Obtain supplies in San Felipe.

Reservations, fees: Reservations are accepted. Fees are high—$20 per night for sites with full hookups and $12 for tents.

Contact: Mexico Resorts International, 4126 Bonita Road, Bonita, CA 91902; (619) 472-6767 or (800) 336-5454. Phone Mar del Sol RV Park in Mexico at 011-52-657-7-1088.

Directions: Take Highway 5 into San Felipe, 124 miles south of Mexicali. The park is on the beach in the southern part of town off the paved road to the airport, just north of the harbor and south of Las Misiones Hotel. Watch for the sign.

Trip notes: Overnight guests at this well-maintained facility can camp in the front row in full view of the Sea of Cortéz and the beach, a focal point of fun. The beach is wide, with lots of room for running dune buggies and other off-road vehicles—a plus if you like cruising along the waterfront, a minus if you're trying to take a siesta. Eventually, the small trees and palms on the grounds will grow to shade-giving proportions. We have found this to be a first-class operation—very clean and comfortable, though short on tranquillity, given all the vehicular activity. Winter is the time to come, as summer is hot. For things to do in the San Felipe area, please see page 129.

30 San Felipe Marina Resort and RV Park

Location: South of San Felipe; Northeast Baja Norte map page 125, grid f4.

Campsites, facilities: There are 143 campsites with full hookups (30- and 50-amp electrical outlets), cable TV, concrete pads, palapas, barbecues, and trees. Facilities include flush toilets and hot showers in clean, tiled rest rooms, laundry, pools, a store, a restaurant, a health spa, and tennis courts. A marina is under construction. Don't drink the water unless they have begun treating it (there are plans to do so). Security is provided 24 hours daily. Tents are not allowed. Obtain supplies in San Felipe.

Reservations, fees: Reservations are accepted. Fees are high—$22 to $24 per night, $132 to $144 per week, and $375 per month.

Contact: San Felipe Marina Resort and RV Park, Apartado Postal 315, San Felipe, Baja California, México; phone 011-52-657-7-1435 and fax 011-52-657-7-1827 in San Felipe, or phone (619) 558-0295 in the United States.

Directions: From San Felipe, take Highway 5 south about three miles. The park is adjacent to the paved airport road well above the beach.

Trip notes: The wide beach below the elevated camping area is Playa San Felipe, which extends southward for another 7.5 miles. Beach vehicles can run the entire 10-mile stretch between San Felipe and Punta Estrella. The owners of San Felipe

Marina Resort and RV Park want to make this an exclusive members-only resort and will undoubtedly attain their goal. When they do, the park will no longer have spaces available for nonmembers. Winter is the time to come, as summer is hot. For things to do in the San Felipe area, please see page 129.

③① Campo San Fernando

Location: South of San Felipe; Northeast Baja Norte map page 125, grid g5.

Campsites, facilities: There are 48 campsites with water and sewer hookups for both RVs and tents. Tiled rest rooms with flush toilets and hot showers are provided. Don't drink the water. The camp is fenced, and the owner lives on site. Obtain supplies in San Felipe.

Reservations, fees: Reservations are accepted. Fees are moderate—$12 per night for RVs and $10 for tents.

Contact: Campo San Fernando, P.O. Box 23, Calexico, CA 92232; phone 011-52-657-7-1259.

Directions: Drive south on Highway 5 from the San Felipe airport road (5.5 miles south of the center of San Felipe) about three miles and turn east on the dirt road into the park. Watch for the sign.

Trip notes: The park is perched on a bluff above the Sea of Cortéz with a stupendous view in all directions. One special feature is the sulfur springs, which send hot water bubbling up among rocks at low tide creating small pools. Some people like dunking their bodies into the smelly water. Winter is the time to come, as summer is hot. For things to do in the San Felipe area, please see page 129.

③② El Faro RV Park

Location: South of San Felipe; Northeast Baja Norte map page 125, grid g5.

Campsites, facilities: There are 135 pull-through campsites with full hookups and concrete pads. On the premises are flush toilets, hot showers, and a pool. Don't drink the water. The park is secured with a gate. Tent campers are not welcome. Obtain supplies in San Felipe.

Reservations, fees: Reservations are accepted. The fee is very high—$25 per night.

Contact: El Faro RV Park, Apartado Postal 107, San Felipe, Baja California, México; phone 011-52-657-7-1886.

Directions: Drive south on Highway 5 from the San Felipe airport road (5.5 miles south of the center of San Felipe) about four miles. Take the turnoff at Kilometer 15 and continue a few hundred yards to the park. Watch for the sign.

Trip notes: One of the more upscale campgrounds in the San Felipe area, El Faro is, however, a bit removed from restaurants, fishing charters, and so forth. Below it lies the northern stretch of beautiful, wide Playa Punta Estrella. Winter is the time to come, as summer is hot. For things to do in the San Felipe area, please see page 129.

33 Villa Marina RV Park

Location: South of San Felipe; Northeast Baja Norte map page 125, grid g4.

Campsites, facilities: There are 36 campsites with concrete pads, young trees, tables, and barbecues, but no hookups. Facilities include a shaded pavilion on the beach, water for washing (do not drink it; bottled water is available), a dump station, and tiled rest rooms with flush toilets and hot showers. Security is provided by a resident watchman and a gate. Tent campers are welcome. Obtain supplies in San Felipe.

Reservations, fees: Reservations are accepted. Fees are moderate—$10 per night, $60 per week, or $175 per month. Yearly rates are $1,500 for a site on the beach and $700 in back.

Contact: Villa Marina RV Park, Apartado Postal 172, San Felipe, Baja California, México; phone or fax 011-52-657-7-1342.

Directions: Drive south on Highway 5 from the San Felipe airport road (5.5 miles south of the center of San Felipe) about five miles.

Trip notes: This is a new RV park and is still under development. When electricity is brought in, the addition of facilities such as a pool, laundry, a store, and a restaurant will be possible. Winter is the time to come, as summer is hot. For things to do in the San Felipe area, please see page 129.

34 Rancho Vista Hermosa

Location: South of San Felipe; Northeast Baja Norte map page 125, grid g4.

Campsites, facilities: Toilets are provided, but there is no drinking water and no security. Tent campers are welcome. Obtain supplies in San Felipe.

Reservations, fees: All sites are first come, first served. The fee is low—$5 per night.

Contact: Drive in and talk to the manager.

Directions: Drive south on Highway 5 from the San Felipe airport road (5.5 miles south of the center of San Felipe) about five miles. The park is on the beach, a few hundred yards off the road. Watch for the sign.

Trip notes: This is the northernmost in a string of beach campos and playas on the Sea of Cortéz between San Felipe and Puertecitos. Campers who regularly come to this area find the campground that best suits their tastes and stick with it faithfully. Many eventually bring in a trailer and leave it parked in a campsite leased on an annual basis to return to, trip after trip, year after year, gradually adding improvements as it becomes a permanent fixture on the landscape. Winter is the time to come, as summer is hot. For things to do in the San Felipe area, please see page 129.

🕳 Las Conchas RV Park

Location: South of San Felipe; Northeast Baja Norte map page 125, grid g4.

Campsites, facilities: There are 20 pull-through or tent campsites, all without hookups. Facilities include concrete pads, palapas, tables, barbecues, lights, water for washing (do not drink it), a dump station, and tiled rest rooms with flush toilets and hot showers. Security is with a resident watchman. Obtain supplies in San Felipe.

Reservations, fees: Reservations are accepted. Fees are moderate—$10 per night for RVs or tents, $50 per week, or $200 per month.

Contact: Las Conchas RV Park, P.O. Box 526, Calexico, CA 92232; phone 011-52-655-2-4376.

Directions: Drive south on Highway 5 from the San Felipe airport road (5.5 miles south of the center of San Felipe) about seven miles. The park is on the beach.

Trip notes: Some 300 feet of beautiful beachfront is the star attraction at this new park. As time goes on, improvements will undoubtedly be made, including the addition of electricity. Winter is the time to come, as summer is hot. For things to do in the San Felipe area, please see page 129.

🕳 Rancho Punta Estrella Beach

Location: South of San Felipe; Northeast Baja Norte map page 125, grid g4.

Campsites, facilities: There are 48 campsites with water and electric hookups for both RVs and tents, palapas, barbecues, flush toilets, and cold showers. Don't drink the water. Security is provided by a resident manager. Obtain supplies in San Felipe.

Reservations, fees: Camping is first come, first served. Fees are high—$15 per night and $70 per week.

Contact: Drive in and talk to the manager.

Directions: Drive south on Highway 5 from the San Felipe airport road (5.5 miles south of the center of San Felipe) about eight miles, then turn east and continue one mile to the beach. Watch for the sign.

Trip notes: A huge area between the highway and the RV park has been cleared of vegetation, indicating that ambitious plans for development are afoot. The beach is huge, sprawling north, south, and away from the Sea of Cortéz. Winter is the time to come, as summer is hot. For things to do in the San Felipe area, please see page 129.

③⑦ Campo García

Location: North of Puertecitos; Northeast Baja Norte map page 125, grid g4.

Campsites, facilities: There's room for an indeterminate number of campers in vehicles or tents. Toilets are provided, but there are no other facilities. Don't drink the water. The manager lives on the premises. Obtain major supplies in San Felipe. Limited groceries and fuel can be purchased in Puertecitos, which has a Pemex station and a small store.

Reservations, fees: All sites are first come, first served. The fee is moderate—$10 per night.

Contact: Drive in and talk to the manager.

Directions: The camping area is on the beach, about 27 miles south of the San Felipe airport road (5.5 miles south of the center of San Felipe) and one-half mile off Highway 5, the paved road to Puertecitos. Watch for the sign.

Trip notes: Campo García seems to attract a lot of families who return regularly to stay in annually leased sites. The entrance road is in good shape. Winter is the time to come, as summer is hot. For things to do in the Puertecitos area, please see page 129.

③⑧ Punta Baja

Location: North of Puertecitos; Northeast Baja Norte map page 125, grid h4.

Campsites, facilities: There's room for an indeterminate number of campers in vehicles or tents. No facilities are provided. There is no security. Obtain major supplies in San Felipe. Limited groceries and fuel can be purchased in Puertecitos, which has a Pemex station and a small store.

Reservations, fees: All sites are first come, first served. The fee is low.

Contact: Drive in and talk to the manager.

Directions: Drive south on Highway 5 from the San Felipe airport road (5.5 miles south of the center of San Felipe) about 33 miles, then turn east and continue one mile to the beach. Watch for the sign.

Trip notes: Expect a primitive camping experience. There are no facilities, but you do get a beach that stretches far in both directions. Puertecitos is closer than San Felipe. Winter is the time to come, as summer is hot. For things to do in the Puertecitos area, please see page 129.

③⑨ Campo Turistico Vallarta

Location: North of Puertecitos; Northeast Baja Norte map page 125, grid h4.

Campsites, facilities: There are five palapas with concrete pads, plus some pit toilets. Tent campers are welcome. Obtain major supplies in San Felipe. Limited groceries and fuel can be purchased in Puertecitos, which has a Pemex station and a small store.

Reservations, fees: All sites are first come, first served. The fee is moderate—$8 per night.

Contact: Drive in and talk to the manager.

Directions: Drive south on Highway 5 from the San Felipe airport road (5.5 miles south of the center of San Felipe) about 34 miles, then turn east and continue 1.5 miles to the beach. Watch for the sign.

Trip notes: This camp fronts on sand dunes behind a rocky beach. The entrance road is a little longer than those leading to the campgrounds to the north, since the highway swings inland. Winter is the time to come, as summer is hot. For things to do in the Puertecitos area, please see page 129.

40 Rancho El Zimarrón

Location: North of Puertecitos; Northeast Baja Norte map page 125, grid h4.

Campsites, facilities: Tent campers are welcome. Don't drink the water. There is no security. Obtain major supplies in San Felipe. Limited groceries and fuel can be purchased in Puertecitos, which has a Pemex station and a small store.

Reservations, fees: All sites are first come, first served. While there was no one here to collect the fee when we visited, we expect the rate is low.

Contact: Drive in and talk to the manager.

Directions: Drive south on Highway 5 from the San Felipe airport road (5.5 miles south of the center of San Felipe) about 44 miles, then turn east and continue one mile to the beach. Watch for the sign.

Trip notes: Come here for truly primitive camping. Winter is the time to come, as summer is hot. For things to do in the Puertecitos area, please see page 129.

41 Campo La Violeta

Location: North of Puertecitos; Northeast Baja Norte map page 125, grid h4.

Campsites, facilities: Tent campers are welcome. Toilets, rental boats, and trailer storage are available. Don't drink the water. The manager lives on the premises. Limited groceries and fuel can be obtained in Puertecitos, which has a Pemex station and a small store.

Reservations, fees: All sites are first come, first served. The fee is low.

Contact: Drive in and talk to the manager.

Directions: Drive south on Highway 5 from the San Felipe airport road (5.5 miles south of the center of San Felipe) about 44 miles, then turn east and continue one mile to the beach. Watch for the sign.

Trip notes: This place is set amidst a cluster of campos and playas near Puertecitos. Winter is the time to come, as summer is hot. For things to do in the Puertecitos area, please see page 129.

㊷ Jacaranda

Location: North of Puertecitos; Northeast Baja Norte map page 125, grid h4.

Campsites, facilities: Tent campers are welcome. Don't drink the water. There is no security. Limited groceries and fuel can be obtained in Puertecitos, which has a Pemex station and a small store.

Reservations, fees: All sites are first come, first served. There is no fee.

Contact: Drive in and talk to the manager.

Directions: Drive south on Highway 5 from the San Felipe airport road (5.5 miles south of the center of San Felipe) about 47 miles, then turn east and proceed to the beach. Watch for the sign.

Trip notes: People in search of a primitive camping spot might want to try this place. Talk to the locals about fishing techniques. Winter is the time to come, as summer is hot. For things to do in the Puertecitos area, please see page 129.

㊸ Speedy's Campo

Location: North of Puertecitos; Northeast Baja Norte map page 125, grid h4.

Campsites, facilities: Tent campers are welcome. There are pit toilets and a little store. Don't drink the water. No security is provided. Limited groceries and fuel can be obtained in Puertecitos, which has a Pemex station and a small store.

Reservations, fees: Camping is first come, first served. There is no fee.

Contact: Drive in and talk to the manager.

Directions: Drive south on Highway 5 from the San Felipe airport road (5.5 miles south of the center of San Felipe) about 48 miles, then turn east and proceed a short distance to the beach. Watch for the sign.

Trip notes: This campground is set in a little cove, but it's just off the highway. There's not much in the way of privacy, as people seem to be constantly pulling in off the road. Speedy runs the store by the campground; we're not sure why there is no fee to camp here, unless it's because he's more interested in selling goods to campers than in charging them for a space. Winter is the time to come, as summer is hot. For things to do in the Puertecitos area, please see page 129.

44 Octavio's Campo Playa Escondida

Location: North of Puertecitos; Northeast Baja Norte map page 125, grid h4.

Campsites, facilities: Tent campers are welcome. Pit toilets and cold showers are provided. Don't drink the water. There is no security. Limited groceries and fuel can be obtained in Puertecitos, which has a Pemex station and a small store.

Reservations, fees: Camping is first come, first served. The fee is low—$5 per night.

Contact: Drive in and talk to the manager.

Directions: Drive south on Highway 5 from the San Felipe airport road (5.5 miles south of the center of San Felipe) about 49 miles, then turn east and proceed one-half mile to the beach. Watch for the sign.

Trip notes: A small cove with a nice beach is the setting for this campground. Anglers can rent *pangas* for fishing trips in the offshore waters. There is no set price for doing so; you pay whatever you can negotiate. Local commercial fishermen are often happier to take a tourist out for money than struggle with their nets. If a *pangero* is not catching much, he'll take you out for a reasonable fee. If he is catching a lot, though, he won't take you at all. Fishing charter businesses are different—they set prices but are always willing to negotiate. Winter is the time to come, as summer is hot. Puertecitos is a mere mile away. For things to do in the area, please see page 129.

45 Puertecitos Campground

Location: In Puertecitos; Northeast Baja Norte map page 125, grid h4.

Campsites, facilities: There are 17 campsites with electricity (available from sundown to 10 P.M.), concrete pads, beach palapas, young palm trees, and tables. Toilets and a restaurant are on the property. Don't drink the water. The camp is secured with a watchman at the entrance to the town. Tent campers are welcome. Limited groceries and fuel can be obtained in Puertecitos, which has a Pemex station and a small store.

Reservations, fees: All sites are first come, first served. Fees are moderate—$6 per night for tents and $8 for RVs, with discounts for weekly stays.

Contact: Drive in and talk to the manager.

Directions: Drive south on Highway 5 from the San Felipe airport road (5.5 miles south of the center of San Felipe) about 50 miles. The campground is in town.

Trip notes: Not only does this campground claim a great location on a sandy beach at the edge of a pretty inlet extending south to the Sea of Cortéz, it also has the only restaurant in town. Other facilities are being improved. Local commercial fishermen will charter their *pangas* for reasonable rates and guide you to fishing grounds around Islas de Las Encantadas, a group of five islands and exposed rocks about 15 miles south off the shores of Puertecitos. You'll find great fishing for white sea bass, bay bass, triggerfish, sierra, yellowtail, dorado, skipjack, and grouper.

If you're hauling your own boat, the steep, rough concrete and rock launch ramp at the point is suitable for large craft—it's also free. There is a hot sulfur spring near the ramp on the north side of the point, about one-quarter mile from the RV park. At low tide, it creates several hot pools in natural depressions in the rocky beach in which you can dunk yourself. These pools are best enjoyed during the maximum tidal action at full and new moons. Tides can have a range of 20 feet or more. Visit in winter, as summer is hot. For more information on things to do in the Puertecitos area, please see page 129.

Northeast Baja Norte's 10 Best Beaches

① Playa Las Almejas

Location: North of San Felipe; Northeast Baja Norte map page 125, grids f4–f5.

Directions: Heading 10 miles north of San Felipe on Highway 5, you can access the beach in many places via dirt roads.

Trip notes: This is the extremely popular eight-mile-long beach north of San Felipe, roughly between Campo Los Amigos (campground number 4) on the north and Playa Blanca (campground number 15) on the south. Fishing is fair for corvina, croaker, and bass. You may find it difficult to secure privacy, due to all the off-road-vehicle traffic, however. The beach can be driven from one end to the other in beach vehicles. Pick up supplies in San Felipe. Winter is the time to come, as summer is hot.

② Playa San Felipe

Location: In San Felipe; Northeast Baja Norte map page 125, grids f4–g5.

Directions: Take Highway 5 into the town of San Felipe. You can access the beach in a highway vehicle at several RV parks and numerous other places.

Trip notes: The mainstay of San Felipe's tourist business, this beach runs through town and beyond for about 10 miles to Punta Estrella. Beach vehicles can drive along most of the beach. Fishing is fair for corvina, croaker, and bass. Pick up supplies in San Felipe. Winter is the time to come, as summer is hot.

③ Playa Punta Estrella

Location: South of San Felipe; Northeast Baja Norte map page 125, grid g5.

Directions: Highway vehicles can access the beach via campgrounds between El Faro RV Park (campground number 32) and Rancho Punta Estrella Beach (campground number 36). Sand tracks allow access by four-wheel-drive vehicles, and beach vehicles can drive on the beach.

Trip notes: Extending some five miles south from Punta Estrella to Punta Diggs, this wide, sandy beach about 11 miles south of San Felipe is popular for camping and fishing. The Huatamote Wash enters the Sea of Cortéz about one-half mile north of Punta Diggs, creating a lagoon that can block the beach. The slope of land is very shallow along this stretch of coast. At low tide, the water can recede more than one-quarter mile, exposing a vast expanse of flats to explore. Fishing is fair for corvina, croaker, and bass. Pick up supplies in San Felipe. Winter is the time to come, as summer is hot.

④ Playa El Provenir

Location: South of San Felipe; Northeast Baja Norte map page 125, grid g5.

Directions: About 15 miles south of San Felipe, the beach is accessible by four-wheel-drive vehicles over sand tracks.

Trip notes: Extending south of Punta Diggs for about four miles, this is a wide sand beach with extensive low tidal flats. The Parra Wash may create a lagoon about two miles south of Punta Diggs that can interrupt vehicle traffic along the beach. Punta Diggs and other points in this area are low and not very prominent. Fishing is fair for corvina, croaker, and bass. Pick up supplies in San Felipe. Winter is the time to come, as summer is hot.

⑤ Beaches between Bahía Santa María and Punta San Fermin

Location: North of Puertecitos; Northeast Baja Norte map page 125, grids g4–h4.

Directions: Highway vehicles can reach these beaches via campgrounds between Campo García (campground number 37) and Rancho El Zimarrón (campground number 40). Four-wheel-drive vehicles can use numerous sand tracks, and beach vehicles can navigate the beaches.

Trip notes: An almost continuous stretch of wide sand beach with hundreds of yards of tidal flats extends from Bahía Santa María (about 25 miles south of San Felipe) for about 24 miles to Punta San Fermin. The land here is level, with few distinguishing features. The northern half has numerous camps along the beach that are easily accessible from the paved road one-half mile or less away, leading to congestion on popular weekends. The southern half is more remote and less populated as the highway is farther inland and there are only a couple of camps. Fishing is fair for corvina, croaker, and bass. Pick up supplies in San Felipe. Winter is the time to come, as summer is hot.

⑥ Beaches between Punta San Fermin and Octavio's Campo

Location: North of Puertecitos; Northeast Baja Norte map page 125, grid h4.

Directions: Highway vehicles can use access roads between Rancho El Zimarrón (campground number 40) and Octavio's Campo Playa Escondida (campground number 44), which is one mile north of Puertecitos. Many sand tracks are suitable for four-wheel-drive vehicles.

Trip notes: Beaches are nearly continuous for about four miles between these two points. The wide, sandy swaths are backed by low-lying land and fronted by extensive tidal flats, as is common north to Punta Estrella. You can fish for corvina, bay bass, triggerfish, barracuda, sierra, pargo, and grouper in the vicinity. Limited groceries and fuel can be obtained in Puertecitos, which has a Pemex station and a small store. Winter is the time to come, as summer is hot.

⑦ Playa La Costilla

Location: South of Puertecitos; Northeast Baja Norte map page 125, grid h3.

Directions: This beach is six miles south of Puertecitos, on the graded road heading south to Bahía San Luis Gonzaga.

Trip notes: An offshore reef protects this beach, making it ideal for swimming. Shorefishing is good for bass, corvina, barracuda, and triggerfish. Security is provided by a resident manager. The only facilities are pit toilets. Pick up major supplies in San Felipe; limited groceries and fuel can be obtained in Puertecitos. Winter is the time to come, as summer is hot. A word of warning: The road south of Puertecitos becomes very rough and requires high-clearance vehicles traveling dead slow. It's rough enough to damage motor homes and trailers.

⑧ Playa Bufeo

Location: South of Puertecitos; Northeast Baja Norte map page 125, grid i3.

Directions: Drive south from Puertecitos for 38 miles on a very rough road, or exit Highway 1 at Laguna Chapala and head 43 miles north on a somewhat better road. Turn east on a dirt road and continue three-quarters of a mile to the beach.

Trip notes: This very pretty, wide white sand beach is tucked into a gently curving cove that extends about two miles north of the rocky outcrop of Punta Bufeo. The point provides protection from southerly and easterly winds. Fishing is good for bass, corvina, grouper, pargo, yellowtail, sierra, and triggerfish. The Punta Bufeo Resort, a restaurant, and an airstrip are near the beach. Come in fully supplied. Emergency necessities can be scrounged up at Bahía Gonzaga about eight miles south. Winter is the time to come, as summer is hot.

⑨ Playa El Faro

Location: South of Puertecitos; Northeast Baja Norte map page 125, grid j3.

Directions: Drive south from Puertecitos for 42 miles on a very rough road, or exit Highway 1 at Laguna Chapala and head 39 miles north on a somewhat better road. The beach is three miles north of Punta Willard (the Bahía Gonzaga area) on the Puertecitos-to-Bahía San Luis Gonzaga road.

Trip notes: More than just beautiful to look at, this beach is very good for swimming. Fishing is good for bass, yellowtail, pompano, grouper, barracuda, and triggerfish. Come fully stocked, though emergency supplies can be scraped up around Bahía Gonzaga. Winter is the time to come, as summer is hot.

🔟 Bahía Calamajue

Location: South of Puertecitos; Northeast Baja Norte map page 125, grid j3.

Directions: Leave Highway 1 at Laguna Chapala and drive 12 miles north to the Calamajue road, then continue 27 miles northeast to Calamajue.

Trip notes: A great sandy beach lies at the south end of the bay but is accessible only to adventurous souls with four-wheel-drive vehicles. Fishing is good for bass, yellowtail, grouper, and triggerfish. Come fully stocked, since you'll be a long way from anywhere. Winter is the time to come, as summer is hot.

Chapter 3

Central Peninsula

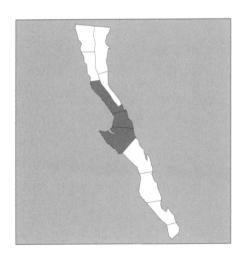

Central Peninsula

Baja Map .... *page* 8

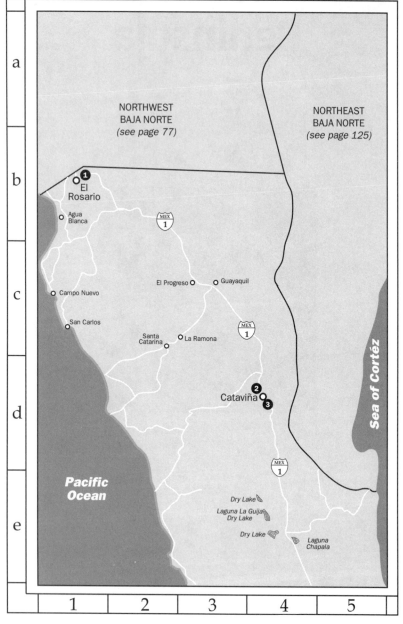

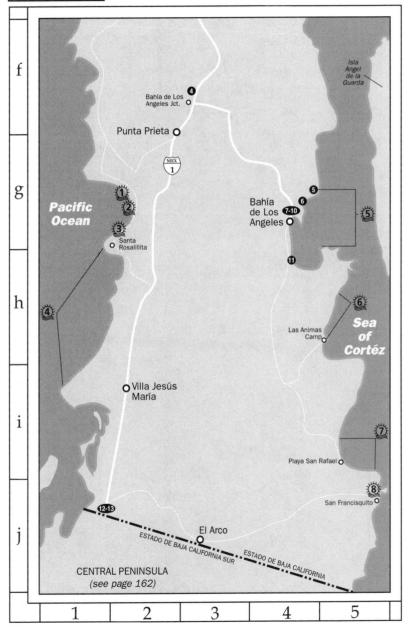

Pacific Ocean

Bahía de Los Angeles Jct.

Punta Prieta

MEX 1

Santa Rosalillita

Villa Jesús María

Isla Ángel de la Guarda

Bahía de Los Angeles

Sea of Cortéz

Las Animas Camp

Playa San Rafael

San Francisquito

El Arco

ESTADO DE BAJA CALIFORNIA SUR

ESTADO DE BAJA CALIFORNIA

CENTRAL PENINSULA
(see page 162)

161

Central Peninsula

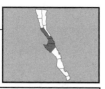

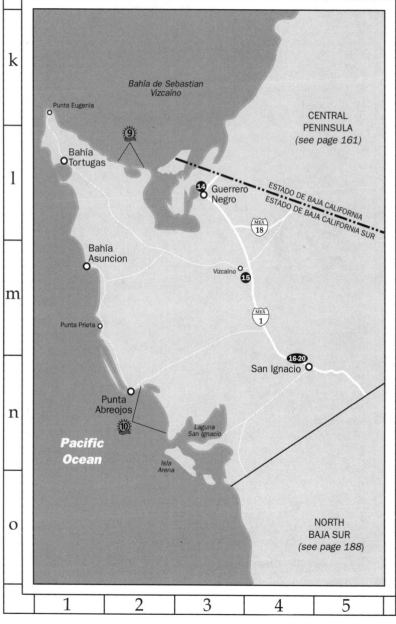

k

Bahía de Sebastian Vizcaíno

Punta Eugenia

CENTRAL PENINSULA
(see page 161)

l

Bahía Tortugas

Guerrero Negro **14**

ESTADO DE BAJA CALIFORNIA
ESTADO DE BAJA CALIFORNIA SUR

MEX 18

Bahía Asuncion

Vizcaíno **15**

m

MEX 1

Punta Prieta

16-20
San Ignacio

n

Punta Abreojos

Laguna San Ignacio

Pacific Ocean

Isla Arena

o

NORTH BAJA SUR
(see page 188)

1   2   3   4   5

Central Peninsula Campgrounds

Central Peninsula's 10 Best Beaches

Central Peninsula

The middle portion of the Baja California Peninsula has been least affected by tourist development. It is essentially wild, remote country traversed lengthwise by Highway 1. Bahía de Los Angeles boasts the greatest concentration of campgrounds and activities. Guerrero Negro and San Ignacio are rapidly becoming tourist centers in their own right, focusing on gray whale watching and exploring caves decorated with ancient paintings of larger-than-life human and animal figures.

Some of the most unusual plants to be found anywhere can be seen while driving Highway 1 through this part of Baja. A few miles east of El Rosario, the first *cirios* come into view. These otherwordly plants are at the extreme northern edge of their range and seem stunted, though it is difficult to know just what constitutes normality with these oddballs. Tapering from a plump base to wispy, whiplike branches, their tan bark studded with tiny stubs of branchlets, they resemble nothing familiar. Following rains, small green leaves and delicate white flowers pop out, the plant sucks up all the water it can, then drops leaves and flowers and harbors its internal water supply until the next irrigation. The only other place in the world that *cirios* are found is in a small patch in Sonora—further proof that the Baja Peninsula was once firmly attached to mainland México.

The first giant *cardón* cacti appear at about the same place. These in the "fringe" habitat are hardly giants, but farther inland they become so. Their appearance is much like that of the more familiar saguaro of Arizona, though they have multiple trunks. *Cardón* have strong internal hardwood rods that support their mass and serve as stout building material for ranch structures. In dry times, the flesh shrinks inward with pronounced ribbing. Following rain they swell with water and appear almost round.

Farther south on Highway 1, the third of Central Baja's most prominent plants appears—the elephant tree. It actually looks like branched, spreading trees found the world over, except that the trunk and limbs are grossly round and fat. The plant may seem a bit shriveled in dry times. There are two large versions of these in Baja—one gray, the other pinkish.

Around Cataviña, midway between the Pacific Ocean and the Sea of Cortéz, is the Desert Natural Park. For miles, Highway 1 threads its way between massive piles of enormous rounded boulders, among which are scattered magnificent specimens of *cirios, cardón,* and elephant trees, along with a full array of other Baja desert vegetation.

The scenery is on a grand scale, bluish mountains across vast desert plains and Highway 1 stretched far out in front of you. Many dirt side roads beckon off-road explorers, but crews of large RVs must continue on their pilgrimage to distant coastlines offering other things to do. The delights of Bahía de Los Angeles are in mind for many, and the lure of seeing gray whales and cave paintings out of Guerrero Negro and San Ignacio attracts more tourists each year.

Obtaining fuel can be a problem between El Rosario and Villa Jesús María, located 21 miles north of Guerrero Negro, or Bahía de Los Angeles, so top off all tanks at El Rosario and Cataviña; the latter may be temporarily out of fuel or service. The former Pemex station at Bahía de Los Angeles junction has had its pumps removed.

Highway 1 Area
(campgrounds 1–4, 12–20, pages 170–172, 175–180)

For most people, the stretch of Highway 1 extending from El Rosario south past San Ignacio is little more than a corridor of travel en route to the enticing camping areas on the Sea of Cortéz. There are a few scattered campgrounds along the 300-plus miles of essentially inland road to accommodate weary travelers for a night. Those with eyes that see more than the black ribbon rolling beneath their vehicle will be entranced by the odd plants and rock formations that grace this landscape and may find the long drive fascinating.

The dammed lake on the way into San Ignacio is fed by a powerful spring, a natural wonder that gives life to an enormous expanse of date palms. The many blessings visited on San Ignacio seem to have influenced its citizens, who are exceptionally gracious and hospitable. Stay a few days and absorb as much of it as you can. You will be better for the experience.

Sightseeing

San Ignacio is a lovely place for strolling. The town square is unique, dominated by huge, ancient Indian laurel trees that cast dense shade. Be sure to visit the magnificent Misión de San Ignacio Kadakaamán, across the street from the square, and the adjoining Cave Paintings Museum. If you will be taking the very rough road that heads south past Laguna San Ignacio to Ciudad Insurgentes—an alternate to Highway 1, which requires crossing the peninsula twice—San Ignacio is the takeoff point. This road allows people with high-clearance vehicles to access some pretty remote places before eventually hooking back up with Highway 1.

Whale Watching and Cave Paintings

More and more local businesses conduct excursions to see whales and cave paintings. There are two good outfitters in Guerrero Negro: Malarrimo Motel and RV Park (campground number 14) leads whale-watching and cave trips. Laguna Tours focuses on whales; you can reach them at 011-52-115-7-0050.

You'll find several guide services for both whale watching and cave paintings in San Ignacio. The oldest is Oscar Fischer at Motel La Posada, Avenida Carranza 22, Pueblo Nuevo, San Ignacio, Baja California Sur, México; phone 011-52-115-4-0313. Ask for directions if you are in town.

El Padrino RV Park (campground number 20) leads whale-watching excursions. Ecoturismo Kuyima, another local business, takes larger groups than the others; call 011-52-115-4-0070. If you choose to drive yourself to Laguna San Ignacio and arrange there to have a guide take you out, don't be discouraged by the rough road that you must follow.

As for cave paintings, you can either arrange for a guide in town or drive up into the mountains and engage one there. Before heading out, everyone must obtain a free permit from the office of the National Institute for Archaeology and History (INAH), located next to the Cave Paintings Museum.

Numbering over a hundred so far, Baja's cave paintings have been found only in the mountains of the central peninsula from west of Bahía de Los Angeles in the north to west of the southern end of Bahía Concepción in the south. The best are here in the Sierra de San Francisco north of San Ignacio. The larger-than-life art works depict individual figures of humans, animals, birds, and fish in black, red, yellow, and white. They cover the cave walls—actually shallow overhangs—with newer paintings overlaying older ones. Some caves provide greater protection that others and contain paintings that have retained their vibrant hues. In more exposed locations little is left except spots of paint. Recent research conducted by the Barcelona Group placed these magnificent works at somewhere between 3,500 and 5,000 years old, with the last ones being created around 350 A.D.

Bahía de Los Angeles Area
(campgrounds 5–11, pages 172–175)

You can reach this area in one long day's drive from San Diego. At times, the 42-mile paved road in from Highway 1 deteriorates and can be slow going until you reach another repaired stretch. One of the most stunning views in Baja is the first sight of Bahía de Los Angeles from high in the hills. The reds and browns of the many islands in the bay contrast vividly with the bright blues of sky and water.

The small town has the basic necessities, including both Nova and Magna Sin gasoline. However, there are perennial problems with electricity and water, with service sometimes limited to an hour a day or only on certain days. In other words, camping is somewhat more rustic than in other Baja locales. But for those of us who are captivated by the place it is worth the extra effort. The most spectacular stand of *cirios, cardón,* and elephant trees we have seen is along the road in from Highway 1. And wildflower fans won't be disappointed: In spring there are profuse, colorful displays of flowers in every color imaginable. Some years the carpets of blooms extend as far as the eye can see. Even the *cirios* and ocotillo come out with showy red flowers.

Fishing

This narrowed midriff area on the Sea of Cortéz with its numerous islands creates upwellings of nutrient-rich water that supports a resident fin whale population, sport fish, and migratory game fish plus myriad seabirds. Fishing is the main activity for tourists. Most people bring their own boats and launch at one of three ramps, an unusually high concentration in launch-ramp-poor Baja.

Bahía de Los Angeles is famous for its feeding frenzies, with sharp-toothed game fish driving massive balls of bait to the surface, attracting hundreds of birds that dive madly into the maelstrom. Fishing is good for grouper, yellowtail, bass, barracuda, sierra, and triggerfish. At times, huge schools of yellowfin tuna enter the midriff area and provide great fishing.

Guillermo's rents boats and guides. Boats leave at 7 A.M. and return at 3 P.M. (For more information, see campground number 9.) Diaz RV Park also rents *pangas* from 6 A.M. to 1 P.M. (For more information, see campground number 10.)

Off-roading

Some interesting side roads will take you into the mountains behind the village and south toward San Francisquito—if you are prepared to handle the rugged and hazardous desert conditions.

Sightseeing

English-speaking naturalist Raul Espinoza takes groups of six to eight people in a 26-foot *panga* to explore islands and view whales, dolphins, and seabirds. He also guides land tours that examine Indian pictographs, desert flora and fauna, and the Misión de San Francisco de Borja. In the United States, phone him at (818) 899-7876. In Baja, he can be located in Bahía de Los Angeles at Campo La Ventana on the road to La Gringa (see campground number 6). There is a sign.

Guillermo's takes groups of up to six people sightseeing by boat.

In the village of Bahía de Los Angeles, there is a very interesting archaeological museum, a real must-see.

❶ Sinai RV Park, Motel, and Restaurant

Location: In El Rosario; Central Peninsula map page 160, grid b1.

Campsites, facilities: There are 24 campsites, of which 12 have full hookups. Flush toilets, hot showers, laundry facilities, and a restaurant are on the premises. Don't drink the water. The owner lives on site. Tent campers are welcome. Obtain supplies in El Rosario.

Reservations, fees: All sites are first come, first served. Fees are moderate—$13 per night or $50 per week.

Contact: Sinai RV Park, Motel, and Restaurant; phone 011-52-616-5-8818.

Directions: As you head south on Highway 1, follow the road as it turns sharply left in El Rosario. Look for the park in about one mile on the left.

Trip notes: El Rosario is not a prime tourist destination. Still, you should take a look at the ruins of one of two separate missions bearing the name Misión Nuestra Señora del Santísimo Rosario Viñadaco. The spot where the mission was founded in 1774 flooded out and, in 1802, the mission was relocated, only to be abandoned in 1832. The relocated mission has only a few remnants of adobe walls but is easily seen about a mile west of town on the south side of the stream. You'll find it beside the dirt road leading west, along with a sign that tells its history. (The ruins of the first mission have melted down and can't be seen at all.) In the fall, look for masses of red chiles drying on the south-facing hillsides south of town on the highway. It is a very colorful display. Top off your fuel tanks here because the next gas stations down the line may be out. Winter is the best time to visit, as summers are hot.

❷ Central Desert RV Park (ejido)

Location: In Cataviña; Central Peninsula map page 160, grid d4.

Campsites, facilities: There are 67 pull-through campsites, a few of which may have electricity. Flush toilets and hot showers sometimes are available. Don't drink the water. Tent campers are welcome. Obtain supplies in El Rosario.

Reservations, fees: All sites are first come, first served. The fee is low—$7 per night.

Contact: Drive in and talk to the manager.

Directions: From El Rosario, drive about 76 miles south on Highway 1. The park is in Cataviña, just north of La Pinta Hotel.

Trip notes: There is no security at Central Desert RV Park, so camping alone here is not recommended. Instead, go a short distance south to Rancho Santa Ynéz, campground number 3.

❸ Rancho Santa Ynéz

Location: South of Cataviña; Central Peninsula map page 160, grid d4.

Campsites, facilities: You camp in a large, level parking area next to a small restaurant. The water is good to drink. Being at the ranch headquarters affords security. Tent campers are welcome. Obtain supplies in El Rosario.

Reservations, fees: Camping is first come, first served. The fee is very low— $4 per night.

Contact: Drive in and park.

Directions: From El Rosario, drive about 76 miles south on Highway 1 to Cataviña. Continue one-half mile south on Highway 1, then turn left at the sign and go three-quarters of a mile east.

Trip notes: Long before the highway was paved, Rancho Santa Ynéz was one of the original stopping places for travelers. Nostalgic old-timers still enjoy dropping in to feast on the excellent tacos served in the restaurant flanking this campground. Winter is the time to visit, as summers are very hot. The campground is within the Desert Natural Park (Parque Natural del Desierto Central), a jumbled mass of enormous old, old granite boulders as big as houses. *Cirios* plants, giant *cardón* cacti, and elephant trees grow throughout the area. Other features include Indian rock art sites and running streams with tall palms. It is a fascinating place in which to poke around and explore, with exciting photo opportunities at every turn. Top off your fuel tanks at Cataviña, as it is about 124 miles to the next gas station at Villa Jesús María.

❹ Parador Punta Prieta Trailer Park (ejido)

Location: At the junction of Highway 1 and the road to Bahía de Los Angeles; Central Peninsula map page 161, grid f3.

Campsites, facilities: There are 40 pull-through campsites with concrete pads and no hookups. Tent campers are welcome. Obtain supplies in El Rosario or Guerrero Negro.

Reservations, fees: All sites are first come, first served. The fee is low— $5 per night.

Contact: Drive in and talk to the manager.

Directions: From El Rosario, drive about 141 miles south on Highway 1. The park is at the junction of Highway 1 and the road to Bahía de Los Angeles, one-quarter mile north of the Pemex station.

Trip notes: If darkness sneaks up on you as you're driving on Highway 1, this park provides a place to pull off the road and sleep for the night. Other than that, few tourists have reason to stop here. There is, however, an interesting cactus garden to examine among the RV spaces. Top off your fuel tanks if the Pemex station is operating. Winter is the time to visit, as summers are hot. There is no security, and camping alone is not recommended.

❺ Playa La Gringa

Location: North of Bahía de Los Angeles; Central Peninsula map page 161, grid g4.

Campsites, facilities: There are no facilities. Obtain supplies in Bahía de Los Angeles.

Reservations, fees: All sites are first come, first served. There is no fee.

Contact: Drive in and park.

Directions: The beach is at the end of the dirt road north of the Bahía de Los Angeles village, which is about 183 miles south of El Rosario. Coming into town, make a sharp left turn at the Conasupa sign onto the dirt road to the airport. Drive eight-tenths of a mile, then turn right at the Brisa Marina RV Park sign. After a half mile, turn left at the Reuben's sign. You are now on a wide, washboard dirt road that will take you past numerous turnoffs to private beach camps within view. Some of the signs announce camping for a small fee—$2 or so. La Gringa is six miles north, at the end of the road.

Trip notes: There are camping spots all along the beach and a fish camp just short of a narrow spit of land going out to Punta La Gringa. (The beach was named for an American woman who tried to establish a camping operation here years ago. You can still see the ruins of a concrete rest room she built.) A narrow road leads on through a low saddle between hills and ends on a rocky beach facing Isla Smith. This is such a scenic location that it is pleasant just to be here. While kicking back, one of our friends saw a whale shark cruise by offshore. Fishermen in small boats that can be launched across the beach do well, since they are close to the prime fishing grounds around Isla Smith. Winter is the best time to visit, as it is very hot in summer. For things to do in the Bahía de Los Angeles area, please see page 168.

❻ Campo La Ventana

Location: North of Bahía de Los Angeles; Central Peninsula map page 161, grid g4.

Campsites, facilities: Beachfront parking is provided for several RVs or tent campers. You'll find some palapas and trees, an outhouse, a cold-water shower, and a dump station. Limited water for washing, but not drinking, is available. Security is provided by a resident guard. Obtain supplies in Bahía de Los Angeles.

Reservations, fees: Camping is first come, first served, though prior contact can be made. The fee is low—$5 per night.

Contact: Cydney Henderson, 12323 Carl Street, Pacoima, CA 91331; (818) 899-7876.

Directions: The campground is approximately two miles north of Bahía de Los Angeles. Signs on the highway indicate where to turn off.

Trip notes: Stay at this beachfront campground and you'll enjoy a nice view across the water to Isla Smith. Owner Raul Espinoza is a naturalist who leads tours on land and water (refer to "Sightseeing" on page 169). Summers are hot in these parts, so come in winter, spring, or fall.

❼ Brisa Marina RV Park (ejido)

Location: North of Bahía de Los Angeles; Central Peninsula map page 161, grid g4.

Campsites, facilities: There are 50 pull-through campsites with no hookups. You may pitch tents wherever you want. No security is provided. Obtain supplies in Bahía de Los Angeles.

Reservations, fees: All sites are first come, first served. There is no fee.

Contact: Drive in and park.

Directions: The park is north of Bahía de Los Angeles. Coming into town, make a sharp left turn at the Conasupa sign onto the dirt road to the airport. Drive eight-tenths of a mile, then turn right at the Brisa Marina RV Park sign. After a half mile, you'll see the Reuben's sign; continue straight for another two-tenths of a mile to the beach.

Trip notes: You can park here, but you'll be closer to the water if you go in front of the facility, to the side of the turtle ponds. They're maintained by Tony Resendez, who lives 100 yards north. If you ask, he might let you camp in his compound for a small fee. Winter is the best time to visit, as it is very hot in summer. For things to do in the Bahía de Los Angeles area, please see page 168.

❽ Villa Vitta Hotel, Restaurant, and RV Park

Location: In Bahía de Los Angeles; Central Peninsula map page 161, grid g4.

Campsites, facilities: There are 100 pull-through campsites with electricity hookups and sewage disposal. Facilities include flush toilets and hot showers at the hotel (available to campers for a fee), a pool, a restaurant, a bar, a store, and a launch ramp. Don't drink the water. The park is secured with a gate. Tent campers are welcome. Obtain supplies in Bahía de Los Angeles.

Reservations, fees: All sites are first come, first served. The fee is moderate—$10 per night.

Contact: Villa Vitta Hotel, Restaurant, and RV Park, 509 Ross Drive, Escondido, CA 92029; (619) 741-9583.

Directions: The RV park is on the beach, across the road from the Villa Vitta Hotel and Restaurant. Register in the hotel office.

Trip notes: The camping area is shadeless and unattractive. The rest room building there was nonfunctional the last time we saw it, necessitating a hike across the road to use the facilities in the hotel—which was considerably inconvenient. Still, Villa Vitta has the best launch ramp in Bahía de Los Angeles. They charge $10 for launching, which includes both putting in and taking out. The owner has plans for improvements, including putting a gas pump on the pier. Hopefully these will materialize. Winter is the best time to visit, as it is very hot in summer. For things to do in the Bahía de Los Angeles area, please see page 168.

⑨ Guillermo's Hotel, RV Park, Restaurant, Bar, and Store

Location: In Bahía de Los Angeles; Central Peninsula map page 161, grid g4.

Campsites, facilities: There are 40 pull-through campsites with full hookups. Flush toilets, hot showers, a restaurant, a bar, a store, and a launch ramp are on the premises. Don't drink the water, which is on only part of the day. There is no security. Tent campers are welcome. Obtain supplies in Bahía de Los Angeles.

Reservations, fees: Reservations are accepted. The fee is moderate—$8 per person per night.

Contact: Guillermo's RV Park, Monte de Oca #190A, Frac. Buena Venture, Ensenada, Baja California, México; phone 011-52-665-0-3206 or 3207.

Directions: The RV park is south of Villa Vitta on the beach.

Trip notes: We have stayed at Guillermo's several times over the years and find that it suits our needs. The owners are gracious and helpful, and the restaurant is very good. One bonus: Use of the launch ramp is free for guests of the hotel and RV park. Winter is the best time to visit, as summer is very hot. For things to do in the Bahía de Los Angeles area, please see page 168.

⑩ Diaz RV Park

Location: In Bahía de Los Angeles; Central Peninsula map page 161, grid g4.

Campsites, facilities: The five campsites have full hookups. Facilities include poorly maintained flush toilets and cold showers, a restaurant, a store, and a launch ramp (the fee is $5, free for guests). Don't drink the water. The spigot near the gas station is supposed to have drinking water from the spring. Other water is piped in from elsewhere. There is no security. Obtain supplies in Bahía de Los Angeles.

Reservations, fees: All sites are first come, first served. The fee is low—$5 per night.

Contact: Drive in and register at the restaurant.

Directions: The RV park is in Bahía de Los Angeles, on the south side of the gas station.

Trip notes: At this time, Diaz RV Park is not being maintained very well and has fallen into a state of disrepair. Tenters are welcome. For things to do in the Bahía de Los Angeles area, please see page 168.

⓫ Gecko Camp

Location: South of Bahía de Los Angeles; Central Peninsula map page 161, grid h4.

Campsites, facilities: There are 10 campsites with palapas but no hookups. Toilets and a ramp for small boats are provided. Water is not available. There is no security. Tent campers are welcome. Obtain supplies in Bahía de Los Angeles.

Reservations, fees: All sites are first come, first served. The fee is low— $3 to $5 per night.

Contact: Drive in and talk to the attendant.

Directions: Coming into the village of Bahía de Los Angeles, turn right when you see the rock wall dead ahead, then take the first left turn and proceed about 3.5 miles south on a rough dirt road to the camp on the beach.

Trip notes: This secluded camp offers more privacy than you'll get right in town. Some people prefer the place for that very reason. It is a good choice for tent campers, being right on the water with a view of the mountains. The beaches here are a little more rocky than others in the area. Winter is the best time to visit, as summer is very hot. For things to do in the Bahía de Los Angeles area, please see page 168.

⓬ La Espinita Motel, RV Park, and Restaurant

Location: North of Guerrero Negro; Central Peninsula map page 161, grid j2.

Campsites, facilities: The restaurant has rest rooms and a parking lot for RVers. (The owner may even let you use the shower, if you ask.) Obtain supplies in Guerrero Negro.

Reservations, fees: Camping is first come, first served. There is no fee.

Contact: Drive in and park.

Directions: La Espinita is on Highway 1, about one-half mile north of the big steel eagle marking the Baja Norte–Baja Sur state line. Guerrero Negro is about 222 miles south of El Rosario on Highway 1.

Trip notes: Campers are welcome to spend the night in the parking lot of the restaurant. Beyond that, we have yet to see the place live up to the definition of an RV park. It's basically a busy truck stop on the highway. The owner has been very helpful to tourists with mechanical breakdowns. For things to do in Guerrero Negro, please see the trip notes for Malarrimo Motel, RV Park, Restaurant, and Bar (campground number 14).

⑬ Guerrero Negro RV Park (ejido)

Location: North of Guerrero Negro; Central Peninsula map page 161, grid j2.

Campsites, facilities: There are 40 pull-through campsites with concrete pads. Some in the western and southern portions of the park have full hookups. Electricity varies from 80 to 150 volts, extremes that can cause damage. Modest rest rooms with flush toilets and hot showers are on the premises. Don't drink the water. The park has a gate and a surrounding fence; a resident manager also provides security. Tent campers are welcome. Obtain supplies in Guerrero Negro.

Reservations, fees: All sites are first come, first served. The fee is moderate—$10 per night.

Contact: Drive in and talk to the manager.

Directions: The RV park is on Highway 1 at the Baja Norte–Baja Sur state line, next to La Pinta Hotel. Guerrero Negro is about 222 miles south of El Rosario on Highway 1.

Trip notes: The local *ejido* makes an effort to keep facilities up and running, but the cost of electricity can exceed income. Over the years, it has been hit or miss: Sometimes there are hookups and the rest rooms are functioning properly, and at other times nothing works—or the park is closed altogether. Guerrero Negro is a convenient place to stop on pilgrimages south, and this park does the job when open. For things to do in Guerrero Negro, please see the trip notes for Malarrimo Motel, RV Park, Restaurant, and Bar (campground number 14).

⑭ Malarrimo Motel, RV Park, Restaurant, and Bar

Location: In Guerrero Negro; Central Peninsula map page 162, grid l3.

Campsites, facilities: There are 36 campsites with full hookups and concrete pads. Facilities include clean rest rooms with flush toilets and hot showers, a pool table, and a restaurant. Don't drink the water. The park is behind the restaurant and motel. A guard provides security. Tent campers are welcome. Obtain supplies in Guerrero Negro, which has a wide selection of stores.

Reservations, fees: Reservations are accepted. The fee is moderate—$10 to $12 per night.

Contact: Malarrimo Motel, RV Park, Restaurant, and Bar, Boulevard Emiliano Zapata s/n, Infonavit, Guerrero Negro, Baja California Sur, México; phone and fax 011-52-115-7-0100 or phone 011-52-115-7-0250.

Directions: Guerrero Negro is about 222 miles south of El Rosario on Highway 1. As you enter town, you'll see the motel and RV park on the right side of the road.

Trip notes: We have gravitated to this place over the years, as it's the most dependable campground in the area. The restaurant is widely renowned for its food—don't miss the Friday night fiesta. Another plus is that owner Enrique Achoy is very good about helping you find whatever you need in Guerrero Negro. Though this is a company town devoted to producing salt—and said to be the largest such operation in the world—tourism is becoming big business. In particular, winter whale watching at nearby Scammon's Lagoon is attracting more and more tourists. Whale-watching trips in *pangas* can be booked at Malarrimo. (You can reach the lagoon by driving about eight miles south of Guerrero Negro on Highway 1 to a sign, then about 17 miles south on a graded dirt road.)

Many people also come for the winter bird-watching in the extensive marshes west of town, where you might see gulls, shorebirds, ducks, and ospreys. A word about the weather: The climate is better in summer, but getting to Guerrero Negro involves driving through hot desert. Winters, though, can be chilly. Many times during winter we have come north from the southern peninsula in shorts and T-shirts and been forced to bundle up in long pants and jackets once in Guerrero Negro. The change can be a shock.

A water purification plant in town on the south side of the main street has a hose that you can use to fill your RV tank.

Another asset in Guerrero Negro is Pescados y Mariscos, the seafood warehouse owned by Señora María del Socorro Espinoza. To get there: From the main street in town, turn north on the next street west of the grocery store and just east of the water tower. Drive to the end of the road. It is on the left, across from the power-generating plant. You'll savor the largest and most tender scallops we have ever encountered, as well as fresh lobster and fish—at prices that are very reasonable.

Note: There is a permanent army base at the state line, and the soldiers stop everyone to check for drugs and firearms. They are uniformly polite and very professional. For information on what they will accept at the agricultural check station between the state line and town, see "Customs" in the Travel Tips chapter.

⑮ Kadakaamán RV Park

Location: In Vizcaíno; Central Peninsula map page 162, grid m4.

Campsites, facilities: There are five campsites with electricity and water. Flush toilets and hot showers are on the premises. Don't drink the water. Meals can be taken in the owner's home, which adjoins the park. The park is secure, as the owner's home is so close. Tent campers are welcome. Obtain supplies in Guerrero Negro.

Reservations, fees: All sites are first come, first served. The fee is low—$5 per night.

Contact: Drive in and talk to the manager.

Directions: From Guerrero Negro, drive south on Highway 1 for about 45 miles to the park, which is on the east side of Vizcaíno.

Trip notes: This would be a convenient place to pull off if you're caught on the road at nightfall. Other than that, there is nothing much to do unless you plan on leaving Highway 1 here and heading west for Malarrimo Beach—not a suitable trip for motor homes or trailers. For more on the beach, see page 166.

⓰ San Ignacio RV Park (ejido)

Location: In San Ignacio; Central Peninsula map page 162, grid n4.

Campsites, facilities: There are 20 pull-through campsites with full hookups that sometimes work. Modest rest rooms with flush toilets and cold showers are on the premises. Don't drink the water. The park is secure, with a gate and a surrounding fence. A resident family also provides security. Tent campers are welcome. Obtain supplies in San Ignacio.

Reservations, fees: All sites are first come, first served. The fee is low—$6 per night.

Contact: Drive in and talk to the manager.

Directions: From Guerrero Negro, drive south on Highway 1 for about 89 miles to San Ignacio. The park is in town, behind the Pemex station.

Trip notes: This is a noisy spot, being right behind and on a hill above the town's gas station. There is no reason to stay here save desperation. For things to do in San Ignacio, please see page 166.

⓱ Campo La Muralla

Location: In San Ignacio; Central Peninsula map page 162, grid n4.

Campsites, facilities: There will be 20 full-hookup campsites and a large open area for dry camping when construction is completed and electricity is installed. Facilities will include palapas, tiled rest rooms with flush toilets, and hot showers. A small store and restaurant also are planned. Don't drink the water. The park will be secure, with a gate and a surrounding fence. A resident manager will also provide security. Tent campers will be welcome. Obtain supplies in San Ignacio.

Reservations, fees: All sites are first come, first served. The fee currently is very low—$3 per night, but will increase to about $7 when services are in place.

Contact: Drive in and talk to the manager.

Directions: From Guerrero Negro, drive south on Highway 1 for about 89 miles to

San Ignacio. Heading into town, watch for the sign on the right about one-tenth of a mile from the highway.

Trip notes: The owner seems intent on completing the park as planned, and construction was well under way when we visited. This may turn out to be the best RV park in San Ignacio, with good facilities, a store, a restaurant, and shade trees. For things to do in San Ignacio, please see page 166.

⑱ Don Chon's RV Park

Location: In San Ignacio; Central Peninsula map page 162, grid n4.

Campsites, facilities: You'll find numerous places to camp in a large date palm grove. No facilities are available. A fence and a resident family provide security. It is a great spot for tent camping. Obtain supplies in San Ignacio.

Reservations, fees: All sites are first come, first served. The fee is very low— $3 per night.

Contact: Drive in and talk to the manager.

Directions: From Guerrero Negro, drive south on Highway 1 for about 89 miles to San Ignacio. Heading into town, watch for the handmade sign on a car door to your left, about one-quarter mile from the highway.

Trip notes: With so many palm trees, this is not the place for big motor homes or trailers. Tenters, however, will be very happy. If you want to try it in your big rig anyway, park and walk it out first. The setting is pleasant, adjoining a permanent freshwater lake that is unique to San Ignacio. For things to do in town, please see page 166.

⑲ Martin Quezada RV Park

Location: On the outskirts of San Ignacio; Central Peninsula map page 162, grid n4.

Campsites, facilities: There's plenty of room to park. Facilities include a water spigot and a pit toilet. Don't drink the water. A gate and a surrounding fence provide security. Tent campers are welcome. Obtain supplies in San Ignacio.

Reservations, fees: All sites are first come, first served. The fee is very low— $2 per night.

Contact: Drive in and park. Martin will come around to collect the fee.

Directions: From Guerrero Negro, drive south on Highway 1 for about 89 miles to San Ignacio. Heading into town, watch for the handmade sign on the left about three-quarters of a mile from the highway. Open the gate and drive in.

Trip notes: This is a pleasant spot, set in a date palm grove, and we have enjoyed our stays here. Tent campers in particular appreciate it, for they are likely to have the place all to themselves. For things to do in San Ignacio, please see page 166.

⑳ El Padrino Motel, RV Park, and Restaurant

Location: On the outskirts of San Ignacio; Central Peninsula map page 162, grid n4.

Campsites, facilities: There are 70-plus campsites, nine of which have electricity and water while the rest have no hookups. About seven more sites with electricity and water are planned. Trees, one flush toilet, five hot showers, a restaurant, and a bar are on the premises. Don't drink the water. The park is secure, with a gate, a surrounding fence, and a resident caretaker. Tent campers are welcome. Obtain supplies in San Ignacio.

Reservations, fees: All sites are first come, first served. Fees are moderate—$7 per night with no hookups and $9 with hookups.

Contact: El Padrino RV Park, Carretera Peninsular ½ Kilometro, San Ignacio, Baja California Sur, México; phone 011-52-115-4-0089 or fax 011-52-115-4-0300.

Directions: From Guerrero Negro, drive south on Highway 1 for about 89 miles to San Ignacio. The park is approximately 1.25 miles from town. Watch for the prominent sign on the right.

Trip notes: El Padrino is slated to be expanded and will include an extensive date palm grove extending west to the lake. When the plans become reality, this should be a very special place to camp. Guides from El Padrino take small groups out on whale-watching excursions or to view cave paintings. The cost for whale trips is $45 per person, plus $3 for lunch; cave tours run $20 per person.

Central Peninsula's 10 Best Beaches

① Bahía Falsa Beach

Location: On the Pacific Ocean, north of Guerrero Negro; Central Peninsula map page 161, grid g2.

Directions: The beach stretches some four miles between Punta Cono on the north and Punta María on the south. Access is approximately 35 miles up the coast from the Santa Rosalillita road. Leave Highway 1 near Kilometer 38 about 16 miles south of Punta Prieta at the Santa Rosalillita sign. It is about 10 miles on a good dirt road to Santa Rosalillita. A mile and a half short of the village, turn north on a good dirt road, which turns into typical rough country roads with many branches.

Trip notes: Getting to this big beach requires quite a trip, but it's well worth the effort. Fishing for halibut, corvina, perch, and bass can be good. Surfers and sailboarders like to come here. Take only pickups, vans, or four-wheel-drive vehicles. The latter will give you greater peace of mind, for there can be bad stretches and the area is remote. Obtain supplies in El Rosario or Guerrero Negro. Summer is the best time to visit, as winter can be cool.

② Playa María

Location: On the Pacific Ocean, north of Guerrero Negro; Central Peninsula map page 161, grid g2.

Directions: The beach extends some seven miles between Punta María on the north and Punta Lobos on the south. Access is approximately 30 miles up the coast from the Santa Rosalillita road. Leave Highway 1 near Kilometer 38 about 16 miles south of Punta Prieta at the Santa Rosalillita sign. It is about 10 miles on a good dirt road to Santa Rosalillita. A mile and a half short of the village, turn north on a good dirt road, which turns into typical rough country roads with many branches.

Trip notes: Fishing for halibut, corvina, perch, and bass can be good at this big, pretty beach. Clammers won't be disappointed either. It is a very popular destination for surfers and sailboarders. Take only pickups, vans, or four-wheel-drive vehicles, since the road in can get rough. Obtain supplies in El Rosario or Guerrero Negro. Summer is the best season to visit, as winter can be cool.

③ Playa El Marron

Location: On the Pacific Ocean, north of Guerrero Negro; Central Peninsula map page 161, grid g2.

Directions: The beach is on the south side of Punta Negra (or Punta Prieta). Access is approximately 17 miles up the coast from the Santa Rosalillita road. Leave Highway 1 near Kilometer 38 about 16 miles south of Punta Prieta at the Santa Rosalillita sign. It is about 10 miles on a good dirt road to Santa Rosalillita. A mile and a half short of the village, turn north on a good dirt road, which turns into typical rough country roads with many branches.

Trip notes: Surfers and sailboarders love this beautiful crescent-shaped beach that stretches about two miles. Fishing for halibut, corvina, perch, and bass can be good. Take only pickups, vans, or four-wheel-drive vehicles, since the road in can get rough. Obtain supplies in El Rosario or Guerrero Negro. Summer is the best season to visit, as winter can be cool.

④ Rosalillita Beaches

Location: On the Pacific Ocean, north of Guerrero Negro; Central Peninsula map page 161, grids h1–i1.

Directions: Access these beaches by the good side road at the Santa Rosalillita sign near Kilometer 38 on Highway 1, about 16 miles south of Punta Prieta. The drive in is about 10 miles long. Four-wheel-drive roads go south to Highway 1 between Kilometers 62 and 63, about seven miles south of Rosarito. Coming in that way, the dirt road (pickups, vans, and four-wheel-drives only) goes three miles to a shingle beach, then north to the sand beaches around Punta Rosarito and farther north to Santa Rosalillita. You'll find a third access via dirt road from Highway 1 at Kilometer 73, about 10 miles south of Rosarito. It goes three miles to El Tomatal (Miller's Landing), where there is a shingle beach. A fourth access is by paved road from the sign to Morro Santo Domingo at Kilometer 96, Villa Jesús María, on Highway 1. After one mile, turn left on a gravel road and drive another 6.5 miles to Laguna Manuela. To reach the extensive beaches, drive north around Morro Santo Domingo over four-wheel-drive roads in soft sand to harder sand on the beaches.

Trip notes: These beaches extend for about 30 miles south of Punta Santa Rosalillita (Santa Rosalía) to Morro Santo Domingo. All are especially popular with surfers and sailboarders and offer good fishing for halibut, croaker, corbina, bass, and corvina. If you're a digger, you'll find plenty of clams to keep you busy. Large motor homes and trailers are not recommended. Obtain supplies in El Rosario or Guerrero Negro. Summer is the best season to visit, as winter can be cool.

⑤ Bahía de Los Angeles Beaches

Location: On the Sea of Cortéz, around Bahía de Los Angeles; Central Peninsula map page 161, grid g5.

Directions: From Cataviña, drive 65 miles south on Highway 1 to the Bahía de Los Angeles junction. Turn east and head 40 miles to Bahía de Los Angeles.

Trip notes: These beaches extend from Punta La Gringa on the north all the way around the bay more than 10 miles to the south end. Fishing is good for grouper, bass, triggerfish, yellowtail, barracuda, and sierra. Obtain supplies in Bahía de Los Angeles. Winter is the best time to visit, as summer can be very hot.

⑥ Playa de Las Animas

Location: On the Sea of Cortéz, south of Bahía de Los Angeles; Central Peninsula map page 161, grid h5.

Directions: From Bahía de Los Angeles, drive about 28 miles south on a rough dirt road to the marked turnoff, then continue about seven miles to a fork. Take the north branch, go about another four miles to an old rancho on the shore, which is rocky and not good for camping. Drive one-half mile north to a wide sand beach. You can hike about one mile farther north to another wide sand beach.

Trip notes: Your vehicle must have four-wheel drive, due to the soft sand you'll encounter en route. There is about two miles of beach north of the old rancho. Obtain supplies in Bahía de Los Angeles.

⑦ Playa San Rafael

Location: On the Sea of Cortéz, south of Bahía de Los Angeles; Central Peninsula map page 161, grid i5.

Directions: From Bahía de Los Angeles, drive about 45 miles south on a rough dirt road to the marked turnoff, then continue about one-quarter mile to the beach.

Trip notes: There are three miles of white sand beach accessible by road north toward Punta San Rafael and another 15 miles of beach south of that toward Punta San Francisco, which is accessible by foot. Fishing is good for bass, grouper, halibut, and yellowtail. Four-wheel drive is advised from Bahía de Los Angeles, due to the soft sand en route. Obtain supplies in Bahía de Los Angeles. Winter is the best season to visit, as summer can be very hot.

⑧ Playas San Francisquito

Location: On the Sea of Cortéz, south of Bahía de Los Angeles; Central Peninsula map page 161, grid j5.

Directions: From Bahía de Los Angeles, drive about 85 miles south on a rough dirt road, keeping to the left near Rancho El Progreso about 12 miles from the small beach in Caleta San Francisquito and the larger one on Bahía Santa Teresa to the south, on which is the Punta San Francisco Resort. A more difficult route, with a very steep and rocky hill to overcome, is about 80 miles from Highway 1 via El Arco, south of Guerrero Negro.

Trip notes: The *cala* (cove) is small and well protected. Fishing is good for bass, barracuda, and grouper. Santa Teresa Beach, with its fine white sand, is more than a mile long. This is very remote country and it is best to travel in a group for safety. You are completely on your own until you reach San Francisquito with its resort and private residences, where fuel, water, and assistance might be available. Obtain supplies in Bahía de Los Angeles or Guerrero Negro.

9 Malarrimo Beach

Location: Northwest of Guerrero Negro, on the south shore of Bahía de Sebastian Vizcaíno; Central Peninsula map page 162, grid I2.

Directions: From Highway 1 about 43 miles south of Guerrero Negro, turn west at Vizcaíno. The first 22 miles of the approximately 70-mile drive to the turnoff to Malarrimo is paved, and the next 48 miles has been graded in preparation for paving, so you may encounter severe washboarding. If you reach San José del Castro, you have gone a half mile too far. Turn north at the turnoff and continue for another 27 miles on a road best navigated by four-wheel-drive vehicles due to soft sand. Another access suitable for pickups is north and east by dirt road out of Bahía Tortugas, which reaches the north-facing coast about 10 miles west of Malarrimo proper.

Trip notes: If you're a scavenger at heart, you'll love this beach. The peninsula on the south shore of Bahía de Sebastian Vizcaíno sticks out into the ocean like a hook, catching flotsam and jetsam from the North Pacific, burying it in sand, and adding more beach in front of it. Junk of the ages can be picked up on the beach and mined from the dunes well back from the present shore. You'll find anything that has ever floated: Japanese blown-glass net floats, ship wreckage, flotsam and jetsam from ships (including plastic bottles by the thousands, alas), logs from Canada, you name it. Obtain supplies in Guerrero Negro. Summer is the best season to visit, as winter can be cool.

10 Abreojos Beaches

Location: On the Pacific Ocean, south of Guerrero Negro and east of Punta Abreojos; Central Peninsula map page 162, grid n2.

Directions: Access is from Kilometer 98 on Highway 1, 71 miles south of Guerrero Negro. You'll see a sign and a restaurant at the turnoff. Continue on a dirt road for about 50 miles.

Trip notes: These beaches extend about 10 miles from Punta Abreojos south to Estero de Coyote, accessible by road, and for another 14 miles across the entrance to the estero on south to Laguna San Ignacio, accessible by boat. Large motor homes and trailers are not recommended. There is good fishing in the ocean for barracuda, mackerel, bass, bonito, yellowtail, dorado, corvina, and grouper and in the esteros for halibut, grouper, bass, corvina, triggerfish, and sierra. Pismo clams abound. A friend in the Baja Sur state government told us of sending two assistants on business to Abreojos, a small fishing village not geared to tourists. Finding no restaurant, they began knocking on doors to arrange for dinner. After several unsuccessful attempts, one lady tentatively offered to feed them but explained that she had only the simple fare they ate every day, which they might not find appealing. When asked what that simple fare was, she replied, "Just lobster and abalone." Obtain supplies in Guerrero Negro. Summer is the best time to visit, as winter can be cool.

Playa El Requeson's sand spit with the tranquil waters of Bahía Concepción on both sides provides a unique camping experience for RVers and tent campers.

Chapter 4

North Baja Sur

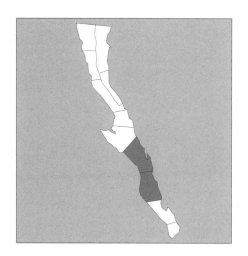

North Baja Sur

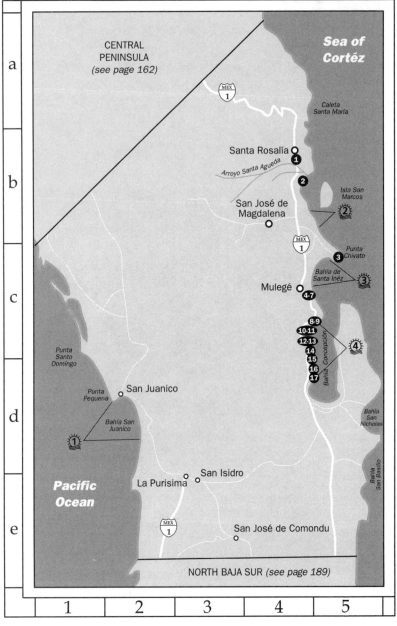

CENTRAL
PENINSULA
(see page 162)

Sea of
Cortéz

*Caleta
Santa María*

Santa Rosalía

Arroyo Santa Agueda

San José de
Magdalena

*Isla San
Marcos*

MEX
1

*Punta
Chivato*

*Bahía de
Santa Inéz*

Mulegé

*Punta
Santo
Domingo*

*Punta
Pequeña*

San Juanico

Bahía Concepción

*Bahía San
Juanico*

*Bahía
San
Nicholas*

*Bahía
San Basilio*

Pacific
Ocean

La Purisima

San Isidro

MEX
1

San José de Comondu

NORTH BAJA SUR *(see page 189)*

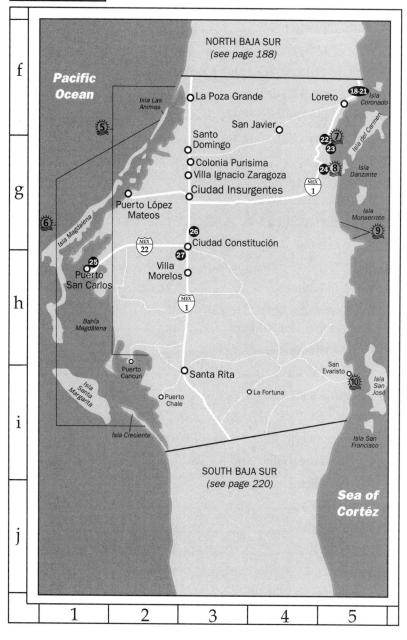

NORTH BAJA SUR
(see page 188)

Pacific Ocean

La Poza Grande

Loreto

Isla Coronado

San Javier

Isla del Carmen

Santo Domingo

Colonia Purisima

Villa Ignacio Zaragoza

Ciudad Insurgentes

Isla Danzante

Puerto López Mateos

Isla Magdalena

Isla Monserrate

Ciudad Constitución

Villa Morelos

Puerto San Carlos

Bahía Magdalena

Isla Santa Margarita

Puerto Cancun

Santa Rita

La Fortuna

San Evaristo

Isla San José

Puerto Chale

Isla Creciente

Isla San Francisco

SOUTH BAJA SUR
(see page 220)

Sea of Cortéz

Isla Las Animas

1 2 3 4 5

f g h i j

North Baja Sur Campgrounds

North Baja Sur's 10 Best Beaches

North Baja Sur

This section of the Baja California Peninsula is very enticing for campers. Excitement builds while travelers descend the Santa Rosalía Grade and reaches a crescendo as the Sea of Cortéz comes into view with Isla San Marcos prominent in the scene. There is an irresistible certainty that the best part of the trip is about to begin—balmy air, warm water, white sand beaches, great fishing, and relaxation.

Numerous RV parks and campsites for both tents and RVs are found on beaches off Highway 1 on the Sea of Cortéz. Punta Chivato and Bahía Concepción offer some of the most stunning scenery in Baja. The Pacific Ocean side of this portion of the peninsula has some outstanding beaches, but access to most of them is a bit difficult. There are persistent rumors of developing a better road from La Purisima north to San Ignacio, which would improve access to a long stretch of coastline.

Santa Rosalía–Mulegé Area
(campgrounds 1–7, pages 199–203)

One of the most popular destinations in Baja, this section of the Sea of Cortéz coast contains two vastly different cities—Santa Rosalía and Mulegé—and some outstanding beaches around Punta Chivato. Campers have a variety of camping areas and activities from which to choose.

A company town without a company, Santa Rosalía has been reorienting its focus toward tourism by preserving the small-town atmosphere and protecting its marina. While not a prime travel destination, it does have narrow, shaded streets that are pleasant for strolling. The town also offers many goods and services.

Mulegé has a lot to offer, which is why so many foreigners have selected it for their winter quarters. Among the many charms are a vast number of date palms and a spring-fed river, the Río Mulegé, which give the town an exotic tropical appearance.

Fishing

Fishing is particularly good around Isla San Marcos, eight miles east of San Lucas Cove and nine miles north of Punta Chivato. Most anglers launch small boats over packed sand at San Lucas Cove RV Park (campground number 2) or Punta Chivato Beach (campground number 3). Others hire a local *panga* fisherman. You can catch grouper, bass, triggerfish, yellowtail, dorado, barracuda, sierra, and skipjack, and the *panga* fishermen know better than anyone else what is biting where at any given time.

Punta Chivato Beach is a popular camping area for people who fish nearby around Islas Santa Inéz, as well as around Isla San Marcos. A good concrete launch ramp west of the Punta Chivato Hotel is available for larger boats.

From Mulegé the waters north to Islas Santa Inéz and south along the shore and off Punta Concepción can be good for grouper, yellowtail, sierra, and bass. There is a good concrete launch ramp near the mouth of the Río Mulegé across the airstrip from the Serenidad Hotel. Commercial *panga* fishermen are always willing to be engaged for a day of fishing, if they are not otherwise occupied.

Boating

Small boats can be launched into the river, which is quite shallow but does give access to the Sea of Cortéz for those who know the channel. Those with large boats can launch at high tide on the ramp, just east of the airstrip in Mulegé. You must thread your way around the Serenidad Hotel to get there, however, taking special care at the sharp right turn on the northwest corner of the hotel to avoid a power pole and cable.

Diving and Snorkeling

Mulegé Divers on General Martínez, the main street through town, offers boats, guides, and rental equipment for scuba diving and snorkeling. A certification card is required for diving. They lead snorkeling excursions outside Punta Concepción or to Islas Santa Inéz. Contact Miguel and Claudia Quintana at General Martínez s/n, Mulegé, Baja California Sur, México; phone or fax their store at 011-52-115-3-0059.

Kayaking

Spend the day paddling a kayak on Bahía Concepción with Baja Tropicales Island Kayak Adventures from Playa Santispac. The fee includes clam digging, refreshments, and a specially prepared clam feast. For reservations, contact Baja Tropicales, Apartado Postal 60, Mulegé, Baja California Sur, México; phone 011-52-115-3-0409 or fax 011-52-115-3-0340. If you're in town and want to just drop in, see Roy and Becky at palapa number 17, Playa Santispac on Bahía Concepción.

Sightseeing

Santa Rosalía was founded in 1885 by Compañia del Boleo to allow the exploitation of rich copper deposits. Remains of the smelter, an old steam engine, and other mining equipment that was used for a hundred years are still present. The unique preconstructed metal Church of Santa Bárbara, designed by Alexandre-Gustave Eiffel, was installed in 1897 on the main street, several blocks west of the waterfront. A few blocks east of it is a renowned bakery, El Boleo, which produces marvelous bread. The French Hotel on the northern mesa above the main street is worth a visit. It is in restored French colonial style and reflects French tastes introduced to Santa Rosalía when the mining company moved in during the last century.

Mulegé is a charming village crammed tightly between the river and steep hills to the north. Don't drive in with a trailer or large motor home. You won't believe how narrow the streets are. They are pleasant to explore on foot, however.

The restored Misión Santa Rosalía de Mulegé, located on a hill west of town, and the old territorial prison on the north side are well worth visiting. You also can arrange excursions out of Mulegé to see Indian rock art.

Dining

Mulegé boasts some very fine restaurants, including Serenidad, El Barril, Las Casitas, and Los Equipales.

Bahía Concepción Area
(campgrounds 8–17, pages 203–208)

Bahía Concepción is one of the most beautiful spots in all of Baja California. Coming from the north, the first view of this gem is absolutely stunning. Many people decide this is just what they have been looking for and park on the first stretch of beach they can find, then luxuriate in the delights of tranquil water and opulent colors: the tans and reds of rocky shores and islands set against the bright blues of sea and sky with fringes of glistening white sand beaches.

One July, some good friends from the San Francisco Bay Area traveled with us on their first trip down Highway l en route to Loreto for the fishing. We stopped to have lunch at Requesón and go for a dip, then had a difficult time tearing them away to continue heading south. After catching *muchos pescados* in Loreto, we returned to Santispac and all had a great time camping and plying the bay in our small inflatable boats. Best of all, we had the place mostly to ourselves because of the time of year.

Fishing

At times you can find sierra, barracuda, bass, and triggerfish, but the netters have pretty much cleaned out the bait fish that the bigger ones need for food. If you want to hire a *panga* fisherman, ask the management at one of the RV parks for assistance.

Boating

Small boats can be launched over the firm sand and anchored close to shore.

Diving and Snorkeling

The water can be quite clear and filled with colorful fish. Try the eastern shore of the bay. You should have no trouble finding butter and chocolate clams, pen shells (the adductor muscle makes great scallops), and big rock scallops. If you have your own tanks, Mulegé Divers can refill them.

Kayaking

Spend an interesting day on Bahía Concepción with Baja Tropicales Island Kayak Adventures from Playa Santispac, which includes clam digging, refreshments, and a clam feast. For reservations, contact Baja Tropicales, Apartado Postal 60, Mulegé, Baja California Sur, México; phone 011-52-115-3-0409 or fax 011-52-115-3-0340. If you're in town and want to drop in, see Roy and Becky at palapa number 17, Playa Santispac on Bahía Concepción.

Other Activities

Windsurfing and waterskiing are popular in these protected waters.

Loreto Area
(campgrounds 18–24, pages 208–211)

This slice of Baja is nearly as attractive as Bahía Concepción. Isla Carmen lies off Loreto and heads a whole string of islands that continue all the way south to La Paz and beyond. The vista from the highway overlook north of Puerto Escondido is every bit as good as that of Bahía Concepción from the high point on the highway north of Santispac.

Fishing can be exceptional around the islands, cruising is great, and the beaches attract many campers. Puerto Escondido, with its excellent harbor, first-class launch ramp, and the Tripui RV Park (see campground number 23), is a focal point of activity.

Fishing

With your own boat in tow, opportunities are unlimited. Anglers will find good fishing offshore for dorado, yellowtail, grouper, bass, barracuda, sierra, jack crevalle, and bonito. Get to know some of the resident experts at Tripui RV Park. If you don't have a boat, you can charter one in Loreto.

Alfredo's Sportfishing Boats has an office on the Malecón (the city waterfront), south of the harbor. Contact Alfredo's at Apartado Postal 39, Loreto, Baja California Sur, México; phone 011-52-113-5-0165 or 0132, or fax 011-52-113-5-0590.

Arturo's Sportfishing Fleet has an office on Miguel Hidalgo, one block from the Malecón. Reach them at Apartado Postal 5, Loreto, Baja California Sur, México; phone 011-52-113-5-0409 or fax 011-52-113-5-0022.

Diving and Snorkeling

Both diving and snorkeling are great activities around the islands. Deportes Blazer on Miguel Hidalgo near the Malecón rents equipment. The owner also fills your tanks upon presentation of a diving certification card. You can reach him at Miguel Hidalgo 23, Colonia Centro, Loreto, Baja California Sur, México; phone 011-52-113-5-0911 or fax 011-52-113-5-0788.

Arturo's Sportfishing also offers guided diving and snorkeling trips and rents equipment.

Golf

There is an 18-hole golf course at Nopoló, south of Loreto. It is open from 6 A.M. to 9 P.M. Contact them at Campo de Golf, Boulevard Misión de San Ignacio, Loreto, Baja California Sur, México.

Tennis

The Centro Turistico de Loreto at Nopoló south of Loreto has tournament facilities and lights.

Other Activities and Excursions

Arturo's Sportfishing also takes people on trips to surrounding islands and mountains, sailing, and waterskiing.

Alfredo's runs whale-watching trips to Puerto López Mateos, as well as trips to Misión San Javier, Primer Agua (an interesting picnic ground in a palm grove with a pool), and boat excursions to Isla Coronado.

Sightseeing

Loreto has improved its downtown area in recent years and the mall is very pleasant for strolling, as is the Malecón (the city waterfront). Misión de Nuestra Señora de Loreto is well worth visiting. Founded in 1697, it was the first mission in the Californias—the mother of them all. Still in operation, it remains lovely.

Nopoló is worth driving around to see the golf course, hotel, wide streets, and the planned subdivisions that never fully materialized. It's a little like a ghost town, with streets in place but almost no buildings. Nearly all the lots are overgrown with weeds, as no one came to buy and build.

If you have a high-clearance vehicle, you will enjoy the 22-mile drive up to San Javier and a visit to the Misión de San Francisco Javier, founded in 1699. It is another well-kept, functioning church with some old vestments carefully preserved from the days of the padres. The road is steep and a bit rough, so only people in pickups, vans, and four-wheel-drive vehicles should attempt the drive.

Dining

A number of very good restaurants are in Loreto—Alfredo's Embarcadero Restaurant, El Nido, and Carmen Restaurant among them.

Pacific Coast Area
(campgrounds 25–27, pages 212–213)

The Pacific Coast area of North Baja Sur is dominated by Bahía Magdalena, a huge mangrove-lined bay that few people know much about. One of those rare experts, Dwight (Chino) Suitter, a fellow Vagabundo who spends winters on the bay, shared some of his hard-won information with us. The two towns—Puerto San Carlos and Puerto López Mateos—are commercial ports and not particularly oriented to tourism. There are few places for people in highway vehicles to camp. Off-roaders, however, have a wide choice of sandy roads to run out and remote beaches on which to camp, both north and south of Bahía Magdalena.

Fishing

Fishing is the main lure in Bahía Magdalena. An unusual opportunity presents itself to people with small boats that can be maneuvered up the small channels, though doing so takes local knowledge. Expect to catch grouper, halibut, bass, snapper, corvina, mackerel, snook, and pompano. Puerto San Carlos is the launching point for adventurous fishing trips 50 miles offshore to Thetis Banks, a target for the long-range boats out of San Diego in search of striped marlin and wahoo. You can find butter and chocolate clams easily at low tide.

Other Activities

Gray whales are in the area from January through April, and Puerto López Mateos and Puerto San Carlos on Bahía Magdalena are developing tourist businesses for whale watching. Once people learn that whales can be approached as closely here as anywhere and that a good paved road leads to both towns, this may turn into as popular a destination as Scammon's Lagoon or Laguna San Ignacio.

❶ Las Palmas RV Park

Location: South of Santa Rosalía; North Baja Sur map page 188, grid b4.

Campsites, facilities: There are 30 full-hookup campsites with palapas, grass, palms, and other trees. Facilities include well-maintained tiled flush toilets, hot showers, laundry, and a restaurant that is open from mid-November through mid-March. The water is good to drink. The park is secured with a gate in a chain-link fence, and the manager lives on the premises. Tent campers are welcome. Obtain supplies in Santa Rosalía.

Reservations, fees: Reservations are accepted. Fees are moderate—$10 per night with full hookups for two people (plus $2 for each additional person), $56 per week, $210 per month, and $1,000 per year for RVs. Tent sites are $6 per night, $35 per week, $120 per month, and $720 per year.

Contact: Las Palmas RV Park, Apartado Postal 123, Santa Rosalía, Baja California Sur, México. There is no phone.

Directions: From Santa Rosalía, drive two miles south on Highway 1 to the park.

Trip notes: This is a good place to spend the night, or to stay longer if you are drawn to Santa Rosalía or are waiting for the ferry to Guaymas. Keep in mind that you cannot depend upon obtaining the Temporary Vehicle Importation Permit required to enter the mainland of México in Santa Rosalía. Plan ahead and get one in Tijuana at the customs office just inside the border. Otherwise, you may have to go on to La Paz for it. (For details, see the Travel Tips chapter—"Licenses and Permits" on page 56 and "Ferries" on page 71.) Winter is the time to visit here, as summer is hot. For things to do in the Santa Rosalía area, please see page 192.

❷ San Lucas Cove RV Park

Location: South of Santa Rosalía; North Baja Sur map page 188, grid b4.

Campsites, facilities: There are 22 campsites on the water and 50 pull-through sites behind them in a large open area, all without hookups. A few palapas and palms are near the water, while a few of the other sites have trees. The concrete and slate rest rooms have flush toilets and hot showers. Don't drink the water. Security is provided by a resident manager. Tent campers are welcome. Obtain supplies in Santa Rosalía.

Reservations, fees: All sites are first come, first served. The fee is low—$6 per night, $35 per week, $120 per month, and $1,000 per year.

Contact: San Lucas Cove RV Park, Apartado Postal 50, Santa Rosalía, Baja California Sur, México. There is no phone.

Directions: Head nine miles south of Santa Rosalía on Highway 1. The access road is at Kilometer 182. Watch for the sign on the left. The exit off Highway 1 is steep a..d sharp at the sign, but there is a gentler exit on a short frontage road just to the north. Go slow as you approach Kilometer 182 so you can get off gently. The park is one-half mile east.

Trip notes: Set on the water in a protected cove with a few palms and mesquite trees, this park is very popular with visitors who come for the pleasant ambience. Swimming in the cove is comfortable. Small boats can be launched over the firm beach and safely anchored just offshore. If you want to fish, Isla San Marcos, six miles away, can be very good for grouper, bass, triggerfish, yellowtail, dorado, barracuda, sierra, and skipjack. Diving is also good. You'll find plenty of other fishing opportunities along the coast, both north and south. Arrange to hire a guide and a *panga* through the park or by asking around. There are clams in the cove. Mostly, this is a good spot for kicking back. On one hot, muggy July night, we were entertained by a marvelous sound-and-light show over the Sea of Cortéz. Sunrise colors seem to be exceptionally intense and varied here. Winter is the time to visit—avoid the summer heat. For other things to do in and around Santa Rosalía, please see page 192.

❸ Punta Chivato Beach

Location: South of Santa Rosalía; North Baja Sur map page 188, grid c5.

Campsites, facilities: You'll find pit toilets, cold showers, and some palapas. Buy drinking water in one-liter plastic jugs at the little store near the Punta Chivato Hotel. There is no security. This is a great spot for tent camping. Obtain major supplies in Santa Rosalía.

Reservations, fees: All sites are first come, first served. The fee is low— $5 per night on the beach east of the hotel. Pay at the hotel.

Contact: Punta Chivato Hotel, Apartado Postal 18, Mulegé, Baja California Sur, México; phone 011-52-115-3-0188.

Directions: From Santa Rosalía, drive 25 miles south on Highway 1 to Kilometer 156. Turn east onto the washboard road and continue about 10 miles to the beach.

Trip notes: The view toward the peninsula is delightful. This is considered by many tourists to be one of the prettiest locations in Baja. A launch ramp west of the hotel is suitable at high tide for large boats. Small boats can be launched across the beach. Fishing can be quite good nearby around Islas Santa Inéz for yellowfin tuna, yellowtail, dorado, skipjack, grouper, sierra, pargo, and barracuda, though a trip north to Isla San Marcos often produces better results. Winter is the time to visit, as summer is hot. For more on things to do in the Mulegé area, please see page 192.

Note: Due to conflicts over the continuing construction of homes adjacent to the beach, there is talk of closing the camping area and opening another at the end of the airport.

❹ Vista Paradiso

Location: In Mulegé; North Baja Sur map page 188, grid c4.

Campsites, facilities: This is a primitive campground with a cleared area that can accommodate a few campers. Water is available, but you should drink bottled water. An outhouse and trees are on the property. Security is provided by a resident family. Tent campers are welcome. Obtain supplies in Mulegé.

Reservations, fees: Camping is first come, first served. The fee is low—$7 per night.

Contact: Drive in and talk to the manager.

Directions: The park is on the north side of the river, four-tenths of a mile east of the end of the pavement at the eastern edge of Mulegé.

Trip notes: The Río Mulegé runs alongside this park and makes for a pleasant setting. Only pickups with campers and smaller vehicles can reach it, for access is through the middle of Mulegé and the streets are too narrow for anything larger. The campground is about as minimal as they come.

❺ Orchard (Huerta Saucedo) RV Park

Location: In Mulegé; North Baja Sur map page 188, grid c4.

Campsites, facilities: There are 43 campsites, of which 25 are pull-through. A few have concrete pads, and all come with full hookups. On the premises are palapas and clean rest rooms with flush toilets and hot showers. The water is safe to drink. A resident guard provides security. Tent campers are welcome. Obtain supplies in Mulegé.

Reservations, fees: Reservations are accepted. Fees are high—$16 per night with full hookups or $6 for tents with two people. Long-term rates are $98 per week and $245 to $265 per month with full hookups, and one free day per week for tents.

Contact: Orchard (Huerta Saucedo) RV Park, Apartado Postal 24, Mulegé, Baja California Sur, México; phone 011-52-115-3-0300.

Directions: The park is on the south side of the river off Highway 1, about one mile south of the turnoff into Mulegé. Watch for the sign.

Trip notes: This is a very pleasant and well-kept park with lots of space, though the riverfront is completely taken up with permanent residences. Many trees provide abundant shade. Winter is the time to visit, as summer is hot. For things to do in the Mulegé area, please see page 192.

❻ Villa María RV Park

Location: In Mulegé; North Baja Sur map page 188, grid c4.

Campsites, facilities: There are 24 pull-through campsites on grass, all with full hookups, plus some tent sites in a separate area with a central palapa. Facilities include clean rest rooms with flush toilets and hot showers, laundry, a dump station, a great swimming pool, and a well-regarded bakery. The water is safe to drink. The owner lives on the premises. Tent camping is encouraged. Obtain supplies in Mulegé.

Reservations, fees: Reservations are accepted. Fees are moderate—$13 per night for two people at sites with full hookups. Lower fees for tent camping can be arranged. Long-term rates are $72 per week and $275 per month.

Contact: Villa María RV Park, Apartado Postal 5, Mulegé, Baja California Sur, México; phone or fax 011-52-115-3-0246.

Directions: The park is on the south side of the river off Highway 1, about 1.5 miles south of the turnoff into Mulegé. Watch for the sign.

Trip notes: The clientele consists primarily of year-round residents, but a designated area is reserved for travelers. There is a common palapa for tent campers to use for cooking, eating, and lounging. Another perk is the bakery, which makes the kinds of treats tourists like—breakfast pastries, rolls, bread. Some of the regulars are standing at the door each morning when it opens. Winter is the time to visit, as summer is hot. For things to do in the Mulegé area, please see page 192.

❼ Serenidad Hotel and RV Park

Location: In Mulegé; North Baja Sur map page 188, grid c4.

Campsites, facilities: There are nine campsites in a concrete-walled compound, all slated to have full hookups. The refurbished rest rooms have flush toilets and hot showers. In the hotel, there is a pool, a restaurant, and a bar. The water is safe to drink. The compound is well secured. Tent campers are welcome. Obtain supplies in Mulegé.

Reservations, fees: Reservations are accepted. Fees are being reset after a closure but have always been moderate—about $10 per night. Pay at the hotel.

Contact: Serenidad Hotel and RV Park, Apartado Postal 9, Mulegé, Baja California Sur, México; phone 011-52-115-3-0530 or fax 011-52-115-3-0311.

Directions: From Highway 1, drive past the turnoff into Mulegé, cross the bridge over the river, and continue south about 2.5 miles. Watch for the sign on the east side marking the turnoff to Serenidad. The dirt access road leads about one-half mile north along the western edge of the airstrip.

Trip notes: The Serenidad was invaded by a group of locals a couple years ago and has only recently been returned to its rightful owners. During the occupation, the establishment was allowed to deteriorate, many things were taken away, and some damage was done. Restoration of the campground and the adjoining hotel is now under way, with plans to install new hookups in the RV spots and rebuild the rest room. Work should be complete by the time this book is out.

For a special treat, head to the hotel's restaurant for the Wednesday night Mexican buffet or the Saturday night pig roast (complete with dancing), two affairs that are renowned among locals. When you arrive, turn into the walled compound on the southern side of the hotel and back your vehicle against the south wall. Winter is the time to visit, as summer is hot. For things to do in the Mulegé area, please see page 192.

❽ Campo Playa Punta Arena

Location: On Bahía Concepción; North Baja Sur map page 188, grid c5.

Campsites, facilities: There's room for an indeterminate number of campers. Marginal toilets and six palapas are provided. Don't drink the water. There is no security. Tent campers are welcome. Obtain supplies in Mulegé.

Reservations, fees: All sites are first come, first served. Fees are low—$3 to park for the night or $5 per night for a palapa on the water.

Contact: Drive in and talk to the manager.

Directions: From Mulegé, drive about 10 miles south on Highway 1. At Kilometer 119, near the north end of the bay, look for the sign and turn left onto a fairly rough dirt road. Continue for about two miles, taking right turns where there are signs. Don't be concerned if you don't see the beach on your approach—it is out of sight to the south.

Trip notes: This is a very pretty beach, a wide sweep of clean white sand stretching several hundred yards and facing south with an expansive view down beautiful Bahía Concepción. Several permanent residences are lined up along the water's edge, but there is plenty of room for transients in RVs or tents. Winter is the favored season to visit here, as summer is hot. For things to do in the Bahía Concepción area, please see page 194.

❾ Playa Santispac

Location: On Bahía Concepción; North Baja Sur map page 188, grid c5.

Campsites, facilities: There are two restaurants, pit toilets, cold showers, and a dump station. Don't drink the water. There is no security. Tent campers are welcome. Obtain supplies in Mulegé.

Reservations, fees: All sites are first come, first served. Fees are low—$4 per night for a small palapa on the water and $5 for a large one. Use of the pit toilets and showers costs $1 each.

Contact: Drive in and talk to the manager.

Directions: From Mulegé, drive about 13 miles south on Highway 1 to the beach, at Kilometer 114.

Trip notes: A great number of people spend the entire winter here, attracted to the well-protected location and the pleasant view. Early birds get their choice of spots. RVers must have a great tolerance for elbow-to-elbow living, but tent campers will find plenty of room. Two more perks: Anna's Restaurant, Bar, and Bakery and Maru Restaurant. Winter is the best time to visit, as summer is hot. For things to do in the Bahía Concepción area, please see page 194.

⑩ Posada Concepción RV Park

Location: On Bahía Concepción; North Baja Sur map page 188, grid c5.

Campsites, facilities: There are eight spaces near the highway for overnighters, all of which have full hookups. Palapas, flush toilets, hot showers, and sulfur hot springs are available on site. Don't drink the water, which is hauled in and not treated. The owner lives on the premises. Tent campers are prohibited. Obtain supplies in Mulegé.

Reservations, fees: All sites are first come, first served. The fee is moderate—$10 per night. A 10 percent discount applies if you stay a month.

Contact: Drive in and talk to the owner.

Directions: From Mulegé, drive about 14 miles south on Highway 1. The park is at Kilometer 112.

Trip notes: Occupied mostly by permanent residents, this RV park will serve in a pinch should you need to get off the highway when overtaken by dark and have nowhere else to go. It's all right, as long as you don't mind camping in the middle of a residential community well back from the one attraction—the beach. For things to do in the Bahía Concepción area, please see page 194.

⑪ Playa Escondida

Location: On Bahía Concepción; North Baja Sur map page 188, grid c5.

Campsites, facilities: Several palapas on the water's edge, pit toilets, and trash barrels are provided. There is no water or security. Obtain supplies in Mulegé.

Reservations, fees: Camping is first come, first served. There is no fee.

Contact: There is no contact person.

Directions: From Mulegé, drive about 14 miles south on Highway 1 to Posada Concepción, then continue south for another half mile. Watch for the sign near Kilometer 112 at a dirt road going three-quarters of a mile east of the highway. Motor homes and trailers are not recommended; there is one steep pitch as the road crosses a rocky ridge that is quite difficult for drivers to negotiate.

Trip notes: Here is a very attractive site. The beach is tucked between hills with islands nearby, affording some protection from the wind. This is an ideal choice for those who want to camp in a tent right on the edge of the placid waters of Bahía Concepción in much less congested conditions than nearby Playa Santispac (see campground number 9). With a kayak or small inflatable boat, campers can enjoy great snorkeling and clamming around the offshore islands and can drift close to roosting seabirds who are not afraid of humans.

⑫ Playa Los Cocos

Location: On Bahía Concepción; North Baja Sur map page 188, grid c5.

Campsites, facilities: Pit toilets and a dump station are provided, but there is no water and no security. Obtain supplies in Mulegé.

Reservations, fees: All sites are first come, first served. Fees are low—$4 per night or a long-term rate of $105 per month.

Contact: Drive in and park. Someone will come around to collect the fee.

Directions: From Mulegé, drive about 15 miles south on Highway 1. The beach access is at Kilometer 111. Go slow and watch for the dirt road to the left, then proceed a few hundred yards east.

Trip notes: Photos of Playa Los Cocos would make a great promo for a South Sea Islands vacation. The glistening, soft-sand beach is lapped by crystal-clear water that rarely displays a ripple and has a gorgeous light green hue from the white sands a few inches beneath the surface. Tent camping is delightful here, with camps pitched inches from the water's edge, enabling one to take a few steps from the shade of a palm tree, cool off with a quick dip, and return to deep contemplation. Small boats can be launched over the sand and anchored just offshore. Many people come early and spend the winter. That makes perfect sense, for summer is just too hot. For things to do in the Bahía Concepción area, please see page 194.

⑬ Playa El Burro

Location: On Bahía Concepción; North Baja Sur map page 188, grid c5.

Campsites, facilities: Palapas, toilets, and a dump site are provided. There is no water and no security. Obtain supplies in Mulegé.

Reservations, fees: All sites are first come, first served. Fees are very low—$3 per night or a long-term rate of $60 per month. The south end is under different management and there is usually no charge.

Contact: Drive in and park. Someone will come around to collect the fee.

Directions: From Mulegé, drive about 16 miles south on Highway 1. The beach is at Kilometer 109.

Trip notes: As you round the hill to the north on the highway, check out the beach below you. It is a popular spot in a protected cove. You can launch small boats over the sand and anchor them in front of your rig. A group of regulars spend their winters at El Burro, and caravaners led by the Vagabundos del Mar uniformly like to stay here. We have heard that years ago a lame burro colt lived near the beach—perhaps this is the source of the name. Tent camping here is delightful. Winter is the favored season to visit, as summer is hot. For things to do in the Bahía Concepción area, please see page 194.

⑭ Playa El Coyote

Location: On Bahía Concepción; North Baja Sur map page 188, grid c5.

Campsites, facilities: A few palapas are set right off the highway. There is an outhouse and a cold shower with water heated from the sun, but no drinkable water and no security. Obtain supplies in Mulegé.

Reservations, fees: All sites are first come, first served. The fee is low— $5 per night with a palapa and $4 without.

Contact: Drive in and park. Someone will come around to collect the fee.

Directions: From Mulegé, drive about 17 miles south on Highway 1. The beach is at Kilometer 108, at the south end of Bahía Coyote. A rough road takes off to the south along the water's edge against a rocky slope and leads to a larger, more open area with some trees.

Trip notes: This protected cove is a good spot for tent campers, especially those looking for a little solitude, since it's not as popular as the other beaches on Bahía Concepción. Winter is the favored season to visit, as summer is hot. For things to do in the Bahía Concepción area, please see page 194.

⑮ Buenaventura Resort Hotel, Restaurant, and RV Park

Location: On Bahía Concepción; North Baja Sur map page 188, grid d5.

Campsites, facilities: There are pit toilets, palapas, hot showers, a restaurant, a bar, a mini-market, and a concrete ramp for launching boats into the surf. Don't drink the water. Security is provided by gates that are closed at night. Tent campers are welcome. Obtain major supplies in Mulegé.

Reservations, fees: All sites are first come, first served. The fee is moderate— $10 per night. Showers cost $1.50 for eight minutes.

Contact: Buenaventura RV Park, Apartado Postal 56, Mulegé, Baja California Sur, México; phone 011-52-115-3-0300.

Directions: From Mulegé, drive about 25 miles south on Highway 1. The beach is at Kilometer 94.

Trip notes: You camp amid a cluster of resort buildings that create a congested atmosphere. The nearby bar and restaurant can be crowded and noisy—not very conducive to tranquillity. Winter is the best season to visit. For things to do in the Bahía Concepción area, please see page 194.

16 Playa El Requesón

Location: On Bahía Concepción; North Baja Sur map page 188, grid d5.

Campsites, facilities: Pit toilets are provided, but there is no water and no security. Obtain supplies in Mulegé.

Reservations, fees: All sites are first come, first served. The fee is very low—$2 per night.

Contact: Drive in and park. Someone will come around to collect the fee.

Directions: From Mulegé, drive about 26 miles south on Highway 1. The beach access is at Kilometer 92. Go slow and watch for the dirt road leading off to the left. Though a little rough, the road is only a few hundred yards long and everyone makes it easily.

Trip notes: If you're a beach lover, what could be better than two beaches together? At Playa El Requesón you camp on a beautiful sand spit flanked on each side by a beach and water. Don't drive out on the really narrow part—it goes under at high tide. This is one of the old-time campsites that is popular with locals as well as tourists. The cove on the north side is great for playing around and clamming. Small vehicles can drive around the hill at the northwest corner of the spit on a portion of the old Baja road to a small cove that's great for tent camping. Winter is the favored season to visit, as summer is hot. For things to do in the Bahía Concepción area, please see page 194.

17 Playa Armenta

Location: On Bahía Concepción; North Baja Sur map page 188, grid d5.

Campsites, facilities: Some small palapas and a pit toilet are provided. There is no water and no security. Obtain supplies in Mulegé.

Reservations, fees: All sites are first come, first served. The fee is very low—$3 per night with a palapa and $2 without.

Contact: Drive in and camp.

Directions: From Mulegé, drive about 27 miles south on Highway 1. The beach access is at Kilometer 91. Turn off the highway at the sign and follow the dirt road around a bluff to a small beach.

Trip notes: Though not one of the better beaches in the area, Playa Armenta will do in a pinch. It's best for tent camping. Winter is the favored season to visit here, as summer is hot. For things to do in the Bahía Concepción area, please see page 194.

⑱ Pelegrino's RV Park

Location: In Loreto; North Baja Sur map page 189, grid f5.

Campsites, facilities: Of the 12 campsites, 10 come with full hookups. On the property are trees, tiled rest rooms with flush toilets and hot showers, and laundry facilities. The water is safe to drink. Security is provided by a resident manager. Tent campers are welcome. Obtain supplies in Loreto.

Reservations, fees: All sites are first come, first served. Fees are high—$14 per night, though weekly or monthly discounts are available.

Contact: Drive in and talk to the manager.

Directions: From Mulegé, drive about 84 miles south on Highway 1 to Loreto. The park is in town, one-half block from the Malecón (waterfront) on Rosendo Robles.

Trip notes: This new RV park right in the town of Loreto is very small, with little room to maneuver.

⑲ El Moro RV Park

Location: In Loreto; North Baja Sur map page 189, grid f5.

Campsites, facilities: Each of the eight campsites has full hookups. Flush toilets and hot showers are provided. The water is safe to drink. The park is secured with a gate and a night watchman. Tent campers are welcome. Obtain supplies in Loreto.

Reservations, fees: Reservations are accepted. Fees are moderate—$10 per night. Long-term rates are one free day per week and $200 per month.

Contact: El Moro RV Park, Rosendo Robles #8, Loreto, Baja California Sur, México; phone 011-52-113-5-0542.

Directions: From Mulegé, drive about 84 miles south on Highway 1 to Loreto. The park is in town, one-half block from the Malecón on Salvatierra. Go through town to the waterfront and turn left at the sign.

Trip notes: Campers have access to a launch ramp five blocks away in the boat harbor. The park is convenient to everything in town. Dogs and chickens making noise next door can disturb your sleep, however. Winter is the favored season to visit here, as summer is hot. For things to do in the Loreto area, please see page 195.

⑳ Villas de Loreto Resort and RV Park

Location: In Loreto; North Baja Sur map page 189, grid f5.

Campsites, facilities: There are 12 campsites with full hookups, three of which are pull-through. Facilities include tiled flush toilets, hot showers, laundry, a pool, a small store, and a dump station. For recreation, you can rent horses, bicycles, kayaks, and sailboards. Rooms are available. The water is safe to drink. The park is in a walled compound with a large wrought iron gate and a resident caretaker. Tent campers are not welcome. Obtain supplies in Loreto.

Reservations, fees: Reservations are not accepted. Fees are moderate—$13 per night for full hookups with a 10 percent discount per week and a 15 percent discount per month.

Contact: Villas de Loreto Resort and RV Park, Apartado Postal 132, Loreto, Baja California Sur, México; phone or fax 011-52-113-5-0586.

Directions: From Mulegé, drive about 84 miles south on Highway 1 to Loreto. The park is on the south side of town on the beach. Go through town on Salvatierra and turn right on Francisco Madero, continuing across the big arroyo until you see the sign.

Trip notes: This RV park is situated in what was once, years ago, the Flying Sportsmen's Lodge. The campsites are against the back wall, away from the water. The compound has many large palms and other trees and an expansive lawn. In case you tire of RV life, there are also motel rooms in front of the campground area facing the Sea of Cortéz. Winter is the favored season to visit here, as summer is hot. For things to do in the Loreto area, please see page 195.

㉑ Loreto Shores Villas and RV Park

Location: In Loreto; North Baja Sur map page 189, grid f5.

Campsites, facilities: There are 38 pull-through campsites with full hookups, trees, and concrete pads and two tent sites with water only. Facilities include clean, tiled rest rooms with flush toilets and hot showers and laundry. The water is safe to drink. Security is provided 24 hours a day by a roving guard inside the gate, which closes at 11 P.M. and opens at 4:30 A.M. Tent campers are welcome. Obtain supplies in Loreto.

Reservations, fees: Reservations are accepted. Fees are moderate—$14 per night for two people, plus $3 for each additional person. Long-term rates are $69 per week, $270 per month, and $3,000 per year.

Contact: Loreto Shores Villas and RV Park, Apartado Postal 219, Loreto, Baja California Sur, México; phone 011-52-113-5-0629 or fax 011-52-113-5-0711.

Directions: From Mulegé, drive about 84 miles south on Highway 1 to Loreto. The park is on the south side of town on the beach. Go through town on Salvatierra and turn right on Francisco Madero, continuing across the big arroyo until you see the sign.

Trip notes: RV spaces, where tenters also are welcome to set up camp, are behind a large multiple-dwelling building that blocks views of the Sea of Cortéz. In years past, visitors could camp right on the beach, but economics, or the building of new homes, have pushed it back to the current location. Winter is the favored season to visit here, as summer is hot. For things to do in the Loreto area, please see page 195.

㉒ Juncalito Beach

Location: South of Loreto; North Baja Sur map page 189, grid g5.

Campsites, facilities: The only facilities are trash barrels. There is no water and no security. Obtain supplies at the store in Tripui RV Park.

Reservations, fees: All sites are first come, first served. There is no fee.

Contact: Drive in and park.

Directions: From Loreto, drive about 14 miles south on Highway 1 (approximately one mile north of the turnoff to Tripui RV Park and Puerto Escondido), then head one-half mile down a rough dirt road to the beach on the southern end of Bahía Juncalito. The village of Juncalito occupies the northern waterfront. Look for the sign on the east side of the highway.

Trip notes: This is a favorite beach with the primitive camping set. Why is it so popular? Because not only is it free, it's located in a very attractive setting. Tripui RV Park—where you'll find a restaurant, a store, and laundry—is just 2.5 miles south of here. The scenery is great, the beach is in a somewhat protected cove, fishing is fantastic around several islands offshore, and boaters can anchor their craft close to the beach. While tent campers will be very pleased, RVers most likely won't. Before going in with a large motor home or trailer, walk it out to see if you'll fit. Odds are this isn't the place for you. Winter is the favored season to visit, as summer is hot. For things to do in the Loreto area, please see page 195.

㉓ Tripui RV Park

Location: South of Loreto at Puerto Escondido; North Baja Sur map page 189, grid g5.

Campsites, facilities: There are 30 campsites with full hookups along a paved road in an area with its own entrance, just before the main entrance to Tripui. Go in the main entrance and register at the office, then return. On the premises are good rest rooms with flush toilets and hot showers, laundry facilities, a pool, a restaurant, a store, and motel rooms. Down at the harbor there's a launch ramp operated by the Marina de Puerto Escondido, which charges a $3 daily fee. The water is safe to drink. The park is secured by a gate and a guard who lives on the grounds. Tent campers are welcome. Obtain supplies in the park store.

Reservations, fees: Reservations are accepted. Fees are high—$14 per night. Long-term rates are $83 per week, $336 per month, and $2,615 per year.

Contact: Tripui RV Park, Apartado Postal 100, Loreto, Baja California Sur, México; phone 011-52-113-3-0818 or fax 011-52-113-3-0828.

Directions: From Loreto, drive 15 miles south on Highway 1. Watch for the signed turnoff. Turn and continue 1.5 miles east on pavement to the park.

Trip notes: We have spent many happy weeks playing at Tripui, one of the better parks in Baja California Sur. The islands offshore are great for cruising, sailing a dinghy to pretty sand beaches, and fishing for dorado and yellowtail. Skipjack are abundant and provide great sport, but are not good to eat. Live mackerel can be caught early in the morning off the entrance to Puerto Escondido. The excellent launch ramp at Puerto Escondido about one mile down the road is one of the best in Baja. Any size boat can be launched on this fine concrete ramp into the protected waters of the harbor. Winter is the favored season to visit here, as summer is hot. For more information on things to do in the Loreto area, please see page 195.

㉔ Playa Ligui

Location: South of Loreto; North Baja Sur map page 189, grid g5.

Campsites, facilities: A pit toilet and trash barrels are provided. There is no water and no security. Obtain supplies from the store at Tripui RV Park.

Reservations, fees: All sites are first come, first served. There is no fee.

Contact: Drive in and park.

Directions: From Loreto, drive about 22 miles south on Highway 1 (six miles south of Tripui RV Park and Puerto Escondido). At the fence, ignore the *Propriedad Privada* (Private Property) sign, but look closely at the small "Trailer Park E. Blanca" sign. It has a rough map showing the turn to take to the low ridge at the south end of the beach and the most accessible camping area. Drive down the dirt road straight east of Highway 1 about three-quarters of a mile to the beach, then take the last right turn and follow the signs marked "Playa" for another three-quarters of a mile. The rest of the beach immediately to the north is used by local fishermen for their *pangas*.

Trip notes: This is not for trailers or larger rigs. There is thorny brush to scratch against, soft sand, and a small beach—but it is pretty. Additional beaches about two miles north and two miles south to Ensenada Blanca can be reached by sand roads suitable only for pickups, vans, or four-wheel-drive vehicles. Inflatable or cartop boats can be carried or dragged across the beach for fun fishing and snorkeling around the many little islands. The small ones that stick straight up are called *Los Candeleros* (the Candles). Some very nice, cozy little coves await exploration down the coast, well within the range of such small boats. Diving and snorkeling around the islands are delightful, with lots of colorful reef fish to look at. We spent a week doing that out of a tent and loved it. Winter is the favored season to visit here, as summer is hot. For things to do in the Loreto area, please see page 195.

㉕ La Curva Beach

Location: North of Puerto San Carlos; North Baja Sur map page 189, grid h1.

Campsites, facilities: No camping facilities are provided. There is no water and no security. Obtain supplies in Ciudad Constitución or Puerto San Carlos.

Reservations, fees: All sites are first come, first served. There is no fee.

Contact: Drive in and park.

Directions: From Puerto San Carlos, drive about 2.5 miles north on Highway 22. When you see an abandoned disco and restaurant on the right, turn and drive to a long beach, which becomes muddy at low tide.

Trip notes: Tent campers especially will enjoy this primitive camping spot. It is heavily used by people from Ciudad Constitución on weekends. You'll find fishing and whale-watching opportunities in Puerto San Carlos. Winter is the season to visit, as summer tends to be scorching hot. For more information on activities in the area, please see page 197.

㉖ Manfred's RV Trailer Park and Restaurant

Location: In Ciudad Constitución; North Baja Sur map page 189, grid g3.

Campsites, facilities: There are 80 campsites, of which 36 are pull-throughs with full hookups and 44 have electricity and water but no sewage lines. On the property are tiled rest rooms with flush toilets and hot showers, a pool, trees, a store, and an authentic Austrian restaurant. The water is suitable for drinking. Gates, which close at 10 P.M., and the resident owners provide security. Tent campers are welcome. Obtain supplies in Ciudad Constitución.

Reservations, fees: Reservations are accepted. Fees are moderate to high— $12 to $14 per night for RVs and $6 to $10 for tents.

Contact: Manfred's RV Trailer Park and Restaurant, Apartado Postal 120, Ciudad Constitución, Baja California Sur, México; phone or fax 011-52-113-2-1103.

Directions: From the center of Ciudad Constitución, drive over half a mile north on Highway 1 to the park on the east side of the road at Kilometer 213.

Trip notes: Manfred's is a good choice for campers who want to become acquainted with the vast Bahía Magdalena area. It is a convenient overnight stopping place with an excellent array of stores and services in Ciudad Constitución that support a large agricultural community. German is spoken, and the Austrian cuisine served at the restaurant here is excellent. Be sure to read the billboard with the rules enumerated. For more on the Pacific Coast area, please see page 197.

㉗ Campestre La Pila

Location: South of Ciudad Constitución; North Baja Sur map page 189, grid h3.

Campsites, facilities: There are 32 pull-through campsites with electricity and water hookups. Flush toilets, hot showers, a pool, and a dump station are available. Don't drink the water. The park is secured with a chain, and the manager lives on the premises. Tent campers are welcome. Obtain supplies in Ciudad Constitución.

Reservations, fees: All sites are first come, first served. The fee is moderate—$8 per night.

Contact: Drive in and go to the office.

Directions: From the northern outskirts of Ciudad Constitución at the junction of Highway 22 (going west to Puerto San Carlos) and Highway 1, drive south through the city on Highway 1 for about 1.5 miles to the big Campestre La Pila sign, then turn west and continue about one-half mile to the campground.

Trip notes: The ground is bare and dusty, and only a few small trees provide landscaping. In other words, there is not a lot to recommend Campestre La Pila, except as a port of refuge if you're on the road when it's getting dark. This is a recreation area for the local people and is not geared to tourism. If you find yourself here, however, Ciudad Constitución is a good place to shop for those hard-to-find items like camera batteries and hardware. It is a farming community and you can purchase many items there that are difficult to obtain south of Ensenada. If you need any major vehicle repairs, this is the place to stop and take care of the problem. Winter is the time to go, as summer is hot. For more on the Pacific Coast area, please see page 197.

North Baja Sur's 10 Best Beaches

① San Juanico Beach

Location: On the Pacific coast, north of Puerto López Mateos; North Baja Sur map page 188, grid d2.

Directions: From Ciudad Insurgentes, drive about 60 miles north on the paved road ending near La Purisima, then continue on the washboard dirt road to San Juanico. People with large motor homes and trailers will have to decide how much shake, rattle, and roll they can handle. You can also come south from San Ignacio on an even worse road, which is suitable only for pickups, vans, and four-wheel drives.

Trip notes: Well known to surfers for years, San Juanico has one of the most beautiful beaches in Baja Sur, running about eight miles south. Most of it is along high sand bluffs and is drivable only at low tide. Fishing is good for halibut, grouper, pargo, snook, sierra, corbina, and corvina. All-terrain vehicles and four-wheel drives can do a loop south and back to San Juanico. You may be able to camp at Scorpion Ranch Preserve at San Juanico, though we have not been able to confirm that it is currently in operation.

② San Bruno Beaches

Location: On the Sea of Cortéz, south of Santa Rosalía; North Baja Sur map page 188, grid b5.

Directions: The beaches extend for five miles south of San Bruno, which is one mile east of Highway 1 at Kilometer 173, about 14 miles south of Santa Rosalía.

Trip notes: These white sand beaches are accessible to people with off-road vehicles. Several rocky areas between the beaches offer good fishing from the shore. Winter is the time to go, as summer is hot. For more on the Santa Rosalía area, please see page 192.

③ Punta Chivato Beaches

Location: On the Sea of Cortéz, south of Santa Rosalía; North Baja Sur map page 188, grid c5.

Directions: The beaches are most easily reached about 12 miles east of Highway 1 at Kilometer 156, approximately 25 miles south of Santa Rosalía, off the washboard road to the Punta Chivato Hotel. Starting with the northernmost beach, Playa La Palmita west of the airstrip, Playas Mapachito and El Chivato extend about 10 miles south along the western shore of Bahía de Santa Inéz. See the listing for campground number 3 in this chapter.

Trip notes: Playa La Palmita is readily accessible by pickups and vans on several dirt roads down small gullies. It takes four-wheel-drive vehicles to work farther south from La Palmita or to access the southern beaches off Highway 1 north of Mulegé. Fishing off the beach might net you a roosterfish. It is a great place for seeking out seashells. We spent four delightful days on Playa La Palmita following the shade around the camper, reading books, enjoying the sweeping view, and heading a hop away from our camp to cool down with a dip in the placid bay waters. Winter is the time to go, as summer is hot. For more on the Santa Rosalía–Mulegé area, please see page 192.

④ Bahía Concepción Beaches

Location: On the Sea of Cortéz, south of Mulegé; North Baja Sur map page 188, grids c5–d5.

Directions: The northernmost beach, at Campo Playa Punta Arena (see campground number 8), is about 10 miles south of Mulegé. It is about 20 miles from there to the southernmost beach, Playa Armenta (see campground number 17). In between are seven other campgrounds.

Trip notes: This is the greatest aggregation of uniformly lovely beaches—all with stunning views and fronting on placid waters—to be found in Baja, the whole of México, or, for that matter, anywhere else in the world we have been, heard of, or read about. In other words, go. If fishing's your thing, you may be disappointed, but the clamming is great. Winter is the best time to visit, as summer gets scorching hot. For more on things to do in the Bahía Concepción area, please see page 194.

⑤ Bahía Magdalena Bay Beaches

Location: On the Pacific coast, in the Bahía Magdalena complex; North Baja Sur map page 189, grids f2–h2.

Directions: These beaches are accessible on sand roads with pickups, vans, or four-wheel drives. Beaches north of Puerto López Mateos include Playa Santa Elenita, which is about four miles north of the Mateos-Insurgentes paved road, and Playas Las Vacas and Los Prados, which are about eight miles north. Others north to La Poza Grande can be reached off the paved road north to La Purisima and the main dirt road north to La Poza Grande. You'll also find beaches south of Puerto López Mateos, such as the one at Curva del Diablo, about 10 miles south of the Mateos-Insurgentes paved road, then about 15 miles west. This is where the tides from north and south meet. La Curva Beach is another (see campground number 25). The beach at Puerto Cancun on Bahía Almeja can be reached from Kilometer 173 on Highway 1 about 25 miles south of Ciudad Constitución, then about 16 miles west on a dirt road. Again, don't try these roads with big rigs.

Trip notes: Shellfish are abundant everywhere along these beaches, and fishing is good for grouper, corvina, bass, snapper, halibut, mackerel, and pompano. It is an all-terrain-vehicle enthusiast's paradise with tidal flats and sand roads. One note of caution: The hard sand turns to mud at low tide. Visit in winter, as summer is hot. For more on the Bahía Magdalena area, please see the following listing.

6 Bahía Magdalena Barrier Island Beaches

Location: On the Pacific coast, in the Bahía Magdalena complex; North Baja Sur map page 189, grids f2–i2.

Directions: The beach on Isla Las Animas can be reached by a small boat from a graded sand road west of La Poza Grande, which is 36 miles north of Ciudad Insurgentes on the paved highway. Small boats can go from both La Banqueta (17 miles north of Ciudad Insurgentes, then 1.5 miles west of the highway through Santo Domingo on good hard sand) and Puerto López Mateos to Isla Santo Domingo. Both Puerto López Mateos and Puerto San Carlos offer small-boat access to Isla Magdalena. Small boats can also go from Puerto Chale (about 15 miles from Highway 1 at Santa Rita, which is about 32 miles south of Ciudad Constitucíon) to Isla Creciente.

Trip notes: Most of the barrier islands of the Bahía Magdalena complex have exciting, pristine beaches, particularly on the ocean side. They are Islas Las Animas, Santo Domingo, Magdalena, and Creciente. In total, the islands extend about 100 miles from north to south. They don't just offer tiny sand coves—Isla Magdalena has two long Pacific beaches, 45 miles from the northern tip of the island at Boca Soledad south to Cabo San Lázaro and 22 miles south of Cabo San Lázaro to Cabo Corso. Isla Santo Domingo has 11 miles of beach. Once you arrive by small boat, you can explore these marvelous ocean beaches by foot, all-terrain vehicle, or motorcycle. Adventurous explorers have a rare opportunity here to go where few have trod.

7 Juncalito Beach

Location: On the Sea of Cortéz, south of Loreto; North Baja Sur map page 189, grid g5.

Trip notes: Please see the listing for campground number 22 in this chapter.

8 Ligui Beaches

Location: On the Sea of Cortéz, south of Loreto; North Baja Sur map page 189, grid g5.

Trip notes: Please see the listing for Playa Ligui (campground number 24) in this chapter.

⑨ Agua Verde Beaches

Location: On the Sea of Cortéz, south of Loreto; North Baja Sur map page 189, grid g5.

Directions: From Kilometer 63 on Highway 1, about 35 miles south of Loreto, head southeast on a dirt road for about 25 miles. The final pitch is steep with sharp switchbacks and is suitable only for pickups, vans, or four-wheel-drive vehicles—not motor homes or trailers.

Trip notes: On the drive in, remember that you have to come back up. Playa San Cosme is at the bottom of the grade. There are low sandy beaches between rock outcrops for about 1.5 miles on the north side of Punta San Cosme. Campsites can also be found elsewhere along the eight miles of road to Agua Verde village. Fishing is fair for grouper and barracuda near the shore. The view of Agua Verde Cove is worth the trip. It has long been a favored anchorage for cruising boats. Now you can enjoy it, too. We anchored there overnight with a group of Vagabundo boaters and were delighted. Winter is when you should visit.

⑩ San Evaristo Beaches

Location: On the Sea of Cortéz, north of La Paz; North Baja Sur map page 189, grid i5.

Directions: The village of San Evaristo is about 45 miles north of San Juan de la Costa on a rough dirt road (about 80 miles north of La Paz). A paved road leads 24 miles into San Juan de la Costa from Kilometer 17 on Highway 1, about 10 miles north of La Paz. Another, but worse, route is approximately 50 miles in from Highway 1 at Las Pocitas, which is about 27 miles south of Santa Rita and 62 miles south of Ciudad Constitución.

Trip notes: You will need a four-wheel-drive vehicle to reach San Evaristo via either route mentioned above. Pickups and vans can get to El Mechudo, about 10 miles south of San Evaristo on the San Juan de la Costa route, but four-wheel drive is necessary from El Mechudo on. We went in some years ago, shortly after this road was completed, with a friend who owns the saltworks at San Evaristo and Isla San José. It was a fascinating trip, but going up and back from La Paz in one day was too much. The cove at San Evaristo is a favored anchorage for cruisers who want to land their dinghies and stretch their legs. It has a very nice little beach that provides a protected place to sunbathe and wade. Other beaches are between San Evaristo and El Mechudo. Fishing can be good for bass, grouper, snapper, pargo, roosterfish, dorado, and sierra, improving the farther north you go.

Cabo San Lucas is on the extreme southern tip of the Baja California Peninsula, with the rocky crags of Land's End disappearing into the junction of the Pacific Ocean and the Sea of Cortéz.

Chapter 5

South Baja Sur

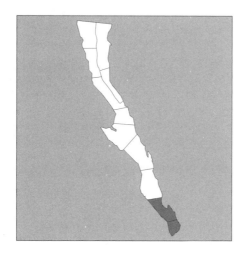

South Baja Sur

Baja Map .... *page* 8

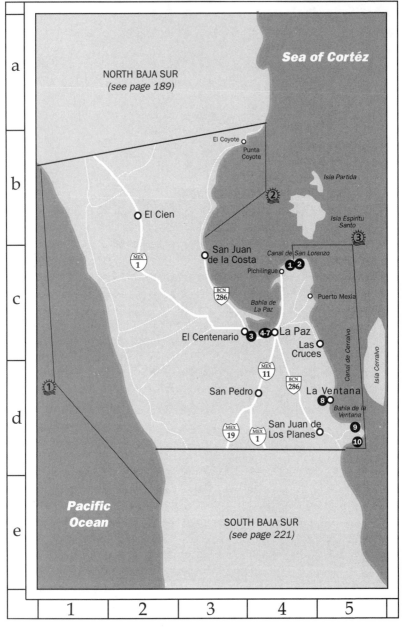

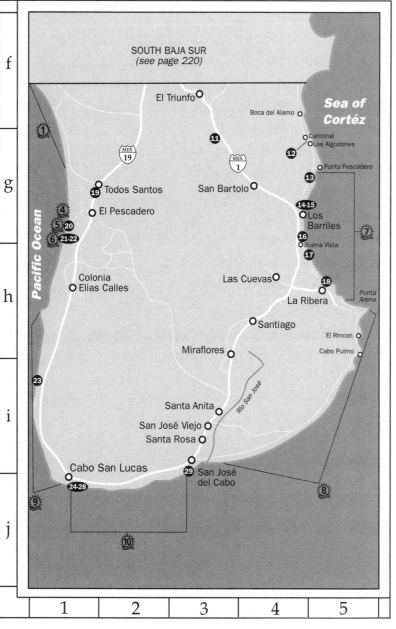

SOUTH BAJA SUR
(see page 220)

El Triunfo

Boca del Alamo

Sea of Cortéz

11

MEX 19

MEX 1

Cardonal
Los Algodones

12

Punta Pescadero

13

19 Todos Santos

San Bartolo

14-15

Los Barriles

4 El Pescadero

5 20

6 21-22

16

Buena Vista

17

7

Pacific Ocean

Colonia
Elias Calles

Las Cuevas

18

La Ribera

Punta Arena

Santiago

El Rincon

Miraflores

Cabo Pulmo

Rio San José

23

Santa Anita

San José Viejo

Santa Rosa

Cabo San Lucas

29 San José del Cabo

24-28

8

9

10

f

g

h

i

j

1   2   3   4   5

South Baja Sur Campgrounds

South Baja Sur's 10 Best Beaches

South Baja Sur

The southern part of the Baja California Peninsula has a special allure. For one thing, the tip of the peninsula is officially in the tropics—south of the Tropic of Cancer. It is a long enough drive (1,000 miles from the border to Land's End) to constitute a major trip with a substantial commitment of time—five days the way we do it. Anything less than a month leaves precious little time for savoring all the delightful experiences that await. We find something of interest wherever we are, and the time just melts away.

La Paz Area
(campgrounds 1–10, pages 235–240)

La Paz enjoys a unique standing in Baja's history, for this is where Hernán Cortéz first landed over 460 years ago. The romantic image of divers endangering their lives searching for riches among beds of pearl oysters, spurred on by legends of black pearls, permeates the atmosphere. This is a cosmopolitan city, the seat of the state government and the commercial center for the nearly 25-year-old state of Baja California Sur. With a mix of antiquity and modernity, the city has a laid-back lifestyle that natives cherish. It will never succumb to the breakneck frenzy of México City or its U.S. counterpart, New York City. Though tourist dollars are important, there is a conscious effort

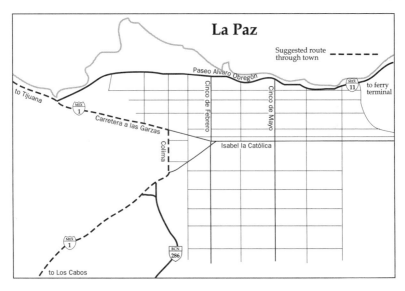

La Paz

Suggested route through town

Paseo Alvaro Obregón

to Tijuana

MEX 1

Carretera a las Garzas

Cinco de Febrero

Colima

Cinco de Mayo

Isabel la Católica

MEX 11

to ferry terminal

MEX 1

BCN 286

to Los Cabos

to avoid turning La Paz into another Cabo San Lucas. As one friend, a young businessman, once observed, "La Paz is a sedate matron, but we would like her to lift her skirts a little." We enjoy being there.

Fishing

While fishing can be good out of La Paz, it is not as consistent as in the Cape or East Cape areas. North toward Isla Espiritu Santo, you'll find pargo, dorado, sierra, barracuda, skipjack, snapper, and grouper. South toward Isla Cerralvo, there are roosterfish, jack crevalle, sailfish, and marlin.

The Mosquito Fleet uses Super Pangas and fishes out of Las Arenas, about 45 miles south of La Paz. Contact them at La Concha Beach Resort about three miles northeast of La Paz on the road to Pichilingue, or call or fax 011-52-112-3-4192. In the United States, contact them at 2361 Veteran Avenue, Los Angeles, CA 90064; phone or fax (818) 541-1465.

The Jack Velez Fleet can be reached at Los Arcos Hotel at Alvaro Obregón 498, facing Bahía de La Paz, or at Apartado Postal 402, La Paz, Baja California Sur, México; phone 011-52-112-2-2744, extension 608; also try 1-5577 or 5-4794; fax 011-52-112-5-5313 or -5-4313.

Boating

Trailered boats may be launched at several places. We prefer the ramp at Marina de La Paz at the foot of Legaspy, though the Palmira Marina on the east side of town is also good and is closer to the Sea of Cortéz. Each charges about $4.

Cruising and camping by boat around Islas Espiritu Santo, Partida, and other islands farther north is a great experience.

Diving and Snorkeling

Baja Diving Service can be reached at Alvaro Obregón 1665-2, La Paz, Baja California Sur, México; 011-52-112-2-1826. This outfitter takes divers on day trips to the famous El Bajo seamount, where huge manta rays and schools of scalloped hammerhead sharks may be seen in summer and fall. Closer day trips are made to Los Islotes, home to a sea lion colony, or the sunken wreck of the *Salvatierra*, a modern-day ferry, south of Isla Espiritu Santo. They provide tanks, weight belts, lunch, and sodas on all trips. Snorkeling excursions include gear, lunch, and refreshments. They offer diving gear rentals and lessons and operate a decompression chamber at Pichilingue. Also available are kayaking tours and bicycle and ATV rentals.

Shopping

La Paz is a free port, and there are numerous shops in the downtown area selling a wide selection of merchandise from around the world at reasonable prices. There are also two large department stores where we tend to restock on clothing: Dorian's, on 16 de Septiembre and 21 de Agosto, and La Perla, a block away on Martínez between Esquerro Mutualismo and Mijares.

The Weaver on Abasolo between Jalisco and Nyarít sells handwoven rugs and native fabrics created by the owner.

Sightseeing

You'll find plenty to see and do in La Paz. An often overlooked spot worth visiting is the Anthropological Museum at Altamirano and Cinco de Mayo. Strolling the Malecón along the waterfront in the evening is very pleasant, as is watching a sunset from Los Pelicanos Bar in Los Arcos Hotel on the Malecón at Rosales. The municipal market at Revolución and Degollado is a browser's delight, with attractive displays of fruits, vegetables, fresh fish and meats, baked goods, clothing, and hardware sold from stalls by vendors who specialize in certain items. And if you don't camp at Playa Balandra (campground number 1) or Playa Tecolote (campground number 2), you should at least drive out to these beautiful spots to have a picnic and drink in the scenery.

Dining

La Paz has a large selection of good restaurants. We like Bismark on Degollado and Altamirano, and El Moro east on the Malecón, the waterfront.

Nightlife

Scorpio's Nightclub is on Boulevard Forjadores and Tabachines. El Taste Restaurant and Nightclub is on the Malecón and Avenida Juarez.

Ferries

Many people take the ferry from La Paz to Topolobampo (Los Mochis) or Mazatlán. For details, see "Licenses and Permits" and "Ferries" in the Travel Tips section of this book.

East Cape Area

(campgrounds 11–18, pages 240–244)

After Cabo San Lucas, this has to be Baja's prime fishing area. Deep water comes into Bahía de Palmas, bringing marlin and other migratory game fish close to shore, earning the Buena Vista fishing resorts a fine reputation among anglers. The East Cape also bills itself as the windsurfing capital of the world—perhaps a little grand, but still reflective of the dependable occurrence of stout winter winds. While conditions are great for sail devices, it is less than ideal for boating. Surfers will discover some great beaches between Los Frailes and San José del Cabo.

Fishing

Just about every type of fish in the Sea of Cortéz can be taken here: marlin (striped, blue, and black), sailfish, roosterfish, wahoo, dorado, yellowfin tuna, amberjack, grouper, pargo, sea bass, jack crevalle, pompano, snapper, sierra, ladyfish, giant needlefish, and others. Deep, deep water comes close to shore in Bahía de Palmas, bringing in the big migratory game fish.

Boaters can launch their craft across the beach in Los Barriles near Playa de Oro RV Park (which no longer accepts travelers) or, if they're guests, by using a tractor or truck at Martín Verdugo's RV Park.

Several hotels have their own fleets of sportfishing boats:

Contact Hotels Playa del Sol and Palmas de Cortéz in Los Barriles at P.O. Box 9016, Calabasas, CA 91372; phone (818) 591-9463 or (800) 368-4334; fax (818) 591-1077.

Contact Hotel Rancho Buena Vista at P.O. Box 1408, Santa Maria, CA 93456; phone (805) 928-1719 or (800) 258-8200; fax (805) 925-2990.

Cabo Pulmo Divers on the beach at Cabo Pulmo rents *pangas* for fishing.

Diving and Snorkeling

Cabo Pulmo has super diving on what is considered to be the only coral reef in the Sea of Cortéz. At least one expert claims that others exist, and coral does appear widely. Perhaps it all depends upon the definition of a reef, which seems to require a great expanse of corals and solid limestone from their consolidation.

Vista Sea Sport conducts dive trips to all the local spots, offers classes, and rents scuba gear. Certification cards are required. Contact them at Apartado Postal 42, Buena Vista, Baja California Sur, México; phone or fax 011-52-114-1-0031.

Windsurfing

This sport has become a mainstay of the local economy. The dependable winter winds attract windsurfers from all over the world. International tournaments are held with high attendance. During the height of the season, Bahía de Palmas is sprinkled with myriad colorful sails whipping back and forth at high speeds.

Sightseeing

The only zoo in Baja Sur is in Santiago, reached by driving about 17 miles west of Los Barriles on Highway 1, then continuing 1.5 miles north of the highway. To find the zoo, drive around the town square, go out the south side, and continue for about one-half mile south, then one-half mile west, and another half mile south. Follow the enamel signs depicting an elephant and an arrow. The zoo houses several Mexican species (coyotes, raccoons, bobcats, deer, etc.) and some domestic animals (including house cats and dogs), as well as a display of fossils discovered in the area. It is worth a visit.

Another eight miles south on Highway 1, the town of Miraflores specializes in leather. A tannery and a shop selling various leather goods is on the left as you enter town.

Pacific Coast Area
(campgrounds 19–23, pages 245–247)

The vast beaches along the Pacific coast south of Todos Santos were unknown to the great majority of Baja travelers until the rough dirt road through here was paved in 1984. Dedicated surfers, though, had staked out their favorite spots long before then—Playa San Pedro, Pescadero Beach, and Playa Los Cerritos. Campers taking the shortest route between La Paz and Cabo San Lucas have discovered these spots, too. The inevitable is now happening: fences have been erected, blocking access to many beaches.

Todos Santos remains a tranquil piece of colonial México, however, with wide shaded streets and restored old buildings. We spent a pleasant hour one afternoon listening to two boys just out of school playing guitars and singing in front of the church across from the town square.

Todos Santos sits on the Tropic of Cancer and is blessed with a dependable water supply. The fortuitous combination of climate and water led to development of a thriving sugarcane industry in the last century. This industry faded when the big spring that fed the crops failed around 1950, then disappeared completely when the price of sugar fell in the mid-1960s. Ruins of several old sugarcane mills still exist. The local spring ultimately recovered and today sustains mango, papaya, and palm trees in the lush arroyo below town.

Fishing

Pangas can be rented out of Punta Lobos (where there's a lighthouse) from individual *pangeros.* The sandy access road is 1.5 miles south of town on Highway 19. At about 2 P.M., the *pangeros* return from fishing and put their boats up on the beach. Check out their catch, which is mostly rock cod but also might include some large sharks. Don't expect any frills, such as lifejackets, VHF radios, tackle, lunch, or drinks, when you ship out with these fellows. It's up to you to be fully equipped.

Surfing

The beaches south of Todos Santos are popular with surfers. There are numerous points that create the right conditions for good runs.

Sightseeing

Walking around Todos Santos is interesting, and there are a few nice shops, including art galleries and clothing boutiques. We enjoy going through the Cultural Museum on the main street.

For a unique experience, go to the oceanfront at Punta Lobos to watch the *pangas* shoot the beach. The technique is to circle behind the breaker line until a big wave is spotted, then straighten out in line with it and open the motor full throttle, timing the approach so as to shoot out of the top of the wave as it breaks, continuing up the abrupt slope of the beach. If they don't make it to the top, a pickup hauls them up with a long rope.

If you want help identifying all the desert plants you have been seeing on your journeys and wondering about, there is a botanical garden three miles south of town on Highway 19.

Dining

We had heard and read about the renowned Santa Fe Restaurant and recently were fortunate enough to be there when they were open and sampled the cuisine for ourselves. They are closed from about August 1 through October. Reservations are a good idea, as people come from all around for a genuine gourmet dining experience; call 112-5-0340. The salads are made fresh from the locally grown varieties of lettuce, herbs, and vegetables. The ravioli in meat sauce and the shrimp fettuccine were simply great.

On the highway south of Todos Santos at Pescadero there's a different sort of restaurant built around a huge old mango tree—Los Arboles. The food, mostly grown on the spot, is delightful, as is the setting.

Cape Area
(campgrounds 24–29, pages 247–250)

San José del Cabo and Cabo San Lucas are rapidly joining together in one long strip of hotels and condominiums. Developers and others in the tourist business have coined the term "Los Cabos" to describe the strip, but this fails to capture the special allure the towns have held since Ray Cannon first began enticing crowds of big game fishermen here with his Baja fishing stories in the early 1960s. The fishing was fantastic then and still is world-class.

Beaches that used to harbor campers through the winter months are now restricted to day use only. They are marked with attractive white lettering on blue highway signs artistically depicting the various activities available—fishing (a fish), beach lounging (a palm tree), snorkeling (a snorkeler), and swimming (a swimmer).

Today, campers must use RV parks. While camping opportunities are diminished, the Cape will always be very popular and high on everyone's must-see list. Even when the last campground has been converted to something else, campers will commute from Todos Santos to experience the beaches—as some are doing now.

Fishing

Whatever the time of year, there are always game fish to seek, including marlin (striped, blue, and black), sailfish, yellowfin tuna, dorado, wahoo, and roosterfish. People with seaworthy boats can venture out on their own. The Cabo Island Marina ramp in town charges a stiff fee of $5 in and $5 out. Parking is available on nearby streets. The public ramp on the south side of the harbor is used to dress out the sportfish catch every afternoon. Parking is a problem around here, but there is no fee. You can catch your own bait in the outer harbor, saving the $2 per piece fee that the local fishermen charge.

Many sportfishing fleets serve the area, some better than others. Here are a few with good reputations according to people we know:

La Playa, just north of San José del Cabo on the coast road, is the place to hire *panga* captains who fish Gordo Banks for wahoo and dorado and whatever else may be around. Boats leave at 6 A.M. and return at noon, and head out again from 6 P.M. to 8 P.M. Reservations can be made on the beach from 11 A.M. to 6 P.M. A tip: Discuss who gets the meat before departing. Captains and crews are accustomed to having it to eat or for additional income. We inadvertently upset them once by walking off with several big wahoo and dorado.

A reservation office for Victor's Aquatics in San José del Cabo is located in the Hotel Stouffer Presidente (011-52-114-2-2250). Contact Jig Stop Tours in Dana Point, California; phone (714) 496-3555 or fax (714) 496-1384.

In Cabo San Lucas there are several fishing fleets we can recommend. Gaviota's Fleet can be contacted at Condo Hotel Bahía, Suite 526, Apartado Postal 144, Cabo San Lucas, Baja California Sur, México; phone 011-52-114-3-0430 or fax 011-52-114-3-0497.

The Pisces Fleet office is located one block from the Giggling Marlin. Contact them at Apartado Postal 137, Cabo San Lucas, Baja California Sur, México; phone 011-52-114-3-1288 or fax 011-52-114-3-0588.

Solmar Sportfishing Fleet is located across from the vendors' stands on the south side of the harbor. Contact them at P.O. Box 383, Pacific Palisades, CA 90272; phone (310) 459-9861, (800) 344-3349, or fax (310) 454-1686.

Diving and Snorkeling

You'll find sandfalls off *El Arco* (the Arch, a hole eroded in a rock) at Land's End and several other interesting dive sites, including Santa María Cove, Japanese Shipwreck, Cabeza Ballena, Pelican Rock, Lover's Beach, and Sunken Ship at the tip of the cape. There are many dive shops and a state-of-the-art hyperbaric medical facility in Cabo San Lucas. We list those facilities with which we and our friends are familiar.

Amigos del Mar is located across from the vendors' stands on the south side of the harbor in Cabo San Lucas. They rent all gear by the piece, fill tanks for those who show a certification card, and offer instruction. They also offer a variety of boat cruises that don't involve diving or snorkeling. Contact them at Apartado Postal 43, Cabo San Lucas, Baja California Sur, México; phone 011-52-114-3-0505 or fax 011-52-114-3-0887 in Cabo; phone (800) 344-3349 or fax (310) 454-1686 in the United States.

Club Acuadeportes is located at Chileno Beach at Kilometer 14 on Highway 1 and Hacienda Beach, in front of the Hacienda Hotel in Cabo. They rent dive gear by the piece, fill tanks if you show a certification card, and offer instruction. They also rent Sunfish, catamarans, pedal boats, canoes, kayaks, wave runners, and other beach and water sports equipment, and offer boat cruises that don't involve diving. Contact them at Apartado Postal 136, Cabo San Lucas, Baja California Sur, México; phone or fax 011-52-114-3-0117.

Beach Bumming

Heading to the beach for the day isn't always as easy as it sounds. There are so many here you can spend a lot of time deciding just which one to hit. Here are the beaches between San José del Cabo and Cabo San Lucas. All are dedicated for day use only and allow no camping:

- La Playa: just north of San José del Cabo, where the *pangas* leave for fishing trips
- Playa Hotelera: in front of the hotels in San José del Cabo
- Playa Costa Azul: access off Highway 1 between Kilometers 28 and 29
- Playa Palmilla: at the Hotel Palmilla
- Playa Costa Brava: access off Highway 1 between Kilometers 18 and 19
- Playa El Tule: access off Highway 1 between Kilometers 16 and 17
- Playa Chileno: access off Highway 1 between Kilometers 14 and 15
- Bahía Santa María: access off Highway 1 between Kilometers 12 and 13
- Playa Médano: the big beach in Cabo San Lucas, between Las Cascadas and the Hotel Hacienda

- Playa del Amor: access by water taxi, heading toward the Arch
- Playa Solmar: in front of the Hotel Solmar

Golf

Several highly touted courses give golfers plenty of playing options. Working westward from San José del Cabo, you can start at the nine-hole public Fonatur course in San José, the first golf facility in the Cabo area. After that is the high-cost Palmilla housing complex with 18 holes on its Jack Nicklaus Signature Course.

Continuing west is the Cabo Real Robert Trent Jones Jr. Course with 18 holes. Next is Cabo del Sol with its 18-hole Jack Nicklaus Course.

Just east of Cabo is the Cabo San Lucas Country Club, with 18 holes designed by Roy Dye.

Other Activities

There are all sorts of other things to do, including glass-bottomed boat trips, catamaran cruises, parasailing, horseback riding, zipping around in all-terrain vehicles or scooters, and whale watching. The Cape area is designed to keep visitors occupied.

Shopping

The many enticing shops in town offer good prices and wide selections for anything you might expect to find in México. On the south side of the harbor, there's an open-air vendor area, the Handicrafts Plaza, where launches from the cruise ships dock. Here the prices are higher, quality is questionable, and shoppers find themselves in a pressure-cooker environment because the cruise ship passengers have little time to compare, think, and come to a reasoned decision.

The municipal market in San José del Cabo is special. It is on Mauricio Castro one block south of Doblada, the one-way street that gets you back to Highway 1 from Boulevard Mijares in the middle of town. Wandering around in here makes shopping for veggies, meat, and fish enjoyable.

Dining

You'll have plenty of restaurants from which to choose. At the simple end of the spectrum, Asadero Fiesta Grill, a barbecue place next door to Squid Roe, serves the best ribs and chicken you can hope to find anywhere. Eat there or take it out.

At the other end of the spectrum is Da Giorgio's, on Highway 1 three miles north of Cabo. Diners feast in such a truly beautiful setting with a spectacular view of Land's End and Cabo San Lucas that lunch or dinner is always a special treat. The open-air restaurant features a series of pools and waterfalls cascading down a cliff. Be there at sunset for the grandest view.

In the middle is El Faro Viejo Trailer Park Restaurant, one block west of Morelos (Highway 19) between Mijares and Felix Ortega. They serve twice as much food as you can eat, so share a plate with someone.

Also in the middle is the improbable Señor Sushi's at Marina and Guerrero.

Nightlife

If you're looking for a night of carousing in Cabo and can't find satisfaction at the Giggling Marlin, Cabo Wabo, Studio 94, or Squid Roe, you aren't really trying. For a two-handed margarita and a block and tackle that hoists you into the air feet first, go for the Giggling Marlin. Gloria tried both and survived, but the second marg' got her. All of the clubs have big crowds and loud music.

❶ Playa Balandra

Location: Northeast of La Paz; South Baja Sur map page 220, grid c4.

Campsites, facilities: About 12 vehicles can park overnight in a small paved lot. Tenters can set up camp off to the side on packed desert soil. Beach palapas, trash barrels, and pit toilets are provided. There is no water or security. Obtain supplies in La Paz.

Reservations, fees: All sites are first come, first served. There is no fee.

Contact: Drive in and park.

Directions: From Ciudad Constitución, drive 133 miles south on Highway 1 to La Paz. The beach is on the paved road 4.2 miles east of Pichilingue, the La Paz ferry terminal north of town on the east side of Bahía de La Paz.

Trip notes: This secluded cove cradles a pretty beach with glistening white sand and azure waters. It's great for swimming and lounging about. However, because the cove is sheltered by a ridge from cooling sea breezes it can get hot. While overnighting is acceptable, the beach is not suitable for longer stays, nor can it accommodate many rigs or tents. Local people come here for picnics and use can be heavy, especially on weekends. The beach once had a much-photographed balancing rock, but it fell over some years ago. There has been talk of putting the landmark back up somehow, but that hasn't happened yet. Winter is the preferred season, as summer is hot. For things to do in the La Paz area, please see page 224.

❷ Playa Tecolote

Location: Northeast of La Paz; South Baja Sur map page 220, grid c4.

Campsites, facilities: There are two restaurant palapas. The small one on the west end of this long beach is not always open. The larger restaurant has rest rooms, available only to diners. Trash barrels are provided, but there is no water or security. Obtain supplies in La Paz.

Reservations, fees: Camping is first come, first served. There is no fee.

Contact: Drive in and park.

Directions: From Ciudad Constitución, drive 133 miles south on Highway 1 to La Paz. The beach is on a paved road 4.8 miles east of Pichilingue, the La Paz ferry terminal north of town on the east side of Bahía de La Paz. Go past the turnoff to Balandra.

Trip notes: The beach here is about 1.5 miles long, facing north to Isla Espiritu Santo across the four-mile-wide Canal de San Lorenzo. This wide swath of soft sand is backed with dunes and, behind that, a broad, level plain. It is exposed to northerly winds, which can make for heavy surf; otherwise surf is minimal. Camp away from the restaurants in either direction behind the dunes in RVs or tents. The hill on the west end provides afternoon shade and an unobstructed view of Isla Espiritu Santo. The larger restaurant rents boats, Jet Skis, and other watercraft and can arrange fishing trips. Winter is the preferred season, as summer is hot. For things to do in the La Paz area, please see page 224.

❸ Oasis RV Park

Location: North of La Paz; South Baja Sur map page 220, grid c4.

Campsites, facilities: There are 24 campsites with full hookups. Clean rest rooms with flush toilets and hot showers, laundry facilities, a pool, and a restaurant are on the premises. Don't drink the water. A gate provides security. Tent campers are welcome. Obtain supplies in La Paz.

Reservations, fees: Reservations are accepted. Fees are moderate—$12 per night for two people and $2 for each additional person, $60 per week, and $240 per month.

Contact: Oasis RV Park, Kilometro 15 Carretera al Norte, El Centenario, La Paz, Baja California Sur, México; phone 011-52-112-4-6090.

Directions: The park is on Highway 1 as it meets Bahía de La Paz at El Centenario, nine miles north of La Paz.

Trip notes: This end of Bahía de La Paz is so shallow that mudflats are exposed at low tide. Another drawback: It is far from the city, which somewhat hinders campers who want easy access to sightseeing, shopping, dining, nightlife, and the La Paz ambience. Winter is the preferred season, as summer is hot. For things to do in the La Paz area, please see page 224.

❹ Casa Blanca RV Park

Location: In La Paz; South Baja Sur map page 220, grid c4.

Campsites, facilities: There are 43 campsites with full hookups. Facilities include clean rest rooms with flush toilets and hot showers, laundry, a pool, a tennis court, and a store. Don't drink the water. For security, there is a gate in the walled compound and a guard. It's not suitable for tents. Obtain supplies in La Paz.

Reservations, fees: Reservations are accepted. Fees are high—$15 per night for two people, plus $2 for each additional person. Long-term rates are $250 per month, $1,350 for six months, and $2,500 per year.

Contact: Casa Blanca RV Park, Apartado Postal 681, La Paz, Baja California Sur, México; phone 011-52-112-4-0009 or fax 011-52-112-5-1142.

Directions: From Ciudad Constitución, drive 133 miles south on Highway 1 to La Paz. The park is on the west side of town near the Fidepaz development, at Avenida Delfines. The sign on the right is prominent.

Trip notes: Young trees grace this very pleasant, somewhat new park. However, the high walls of the facility are made of concrete blocks painted white, and the reflected glare and heat struck us as too strong for comfort. Winter is the best season to visit, as summer is hot. For things to do in the La Paz area, please see page 224.

⑤ El Cardón Trailer Park

Location: In La Paz; South Baja Sur map page 220, grid c4.

Campsites, facilities: There are 80 RV sites (36 pull-through) with full hookups, palapas, and concrete pads. Ten additional tent sites have palapas. Several tiled rest rooms—each with a sink, flush toilet, and hot shower—are in a common building. Other facilities include laundry and a pool. Don't drink the water at the campsites; it is brackish well water. Three spigots provide good city water. Security is good, as the park is in a walled compound with a gate and a 24-hour guard. Obtain supplies in La Paz.

Reservations, fees: Reservations are accepted. Fees are moderate—$8 per night for tents and $10 for RVs for two people, plus $2 for each additional person. Stay a week and get one day free. Fees for monthly stays are $7 per day. There is an extra charge for use of air conditioners.

Contact: El Cardón Trailer Park, Apartado Postal 104, La Paz, Baja California Sur, México; phone 011-52-112-4-0078.

Directions: From Ciudad Constitución, drive 133 miles south on Highway 1 to La Paz. The park is on the west side of town on the highway into La Paz. The sign on the right is prominent.

Trip notes: The oldest park in La Paz, this family-run operation has served campers well for decades. Within the park, you'll find many old shade trees. Winter is the preferred season, as summer is hot. For things to do in the La Paz area, please see page 224.

⑥ La Paz RV Park

Location: In La Paz; South Baja Sur map page 220, grid c4.

Campsites, facilities: There are 47 campsites (nine pull-through) with full hookups, concrete pads, palapas, trees, and barbecues. Facilities include flush toilets, hot showers, laundry, satellite TV access, a pool, and a spa. The water is safe to drink. Security is good, as the park is in a walled compound with a gate and a guard. Obtain supplies in La Paz.

Reservations, fees: Reservations are accepted. Fees are high—$15 per night. Long-term rates are $90 per week, $300 per month, and $3,000 per year for RVs and $10 per day, $60 per week, $200 per month, and $2,000 per year for tents.

Contact: La Paz RV Park, Apartado Postal 482, La Paz, Baja California Sur, México; phone 011-52-112-2-8787 or fax 011-52-112-2-9798.

Directions: From Ciudad Constitución, drive 133 miles south on Highway 1 to La Paz. Just past El Cardón, watch for a trailer park sign. Turn left toward the waterfront, then right on the last street and enter the park.

Trip notes: The palm trees, gravel driveways, and concrete pads in this clean park prevent the place from getting too dusty or dirty. Though the park is not directly on the beachfront, you only have to walk a couple blocks to get there. Winter is the preferred season, as summer is hot. For things to do in the La Paz area, please see page 224.

⑦ Aquamarina RV Park

Location: In La Paz; South Baja Sur map page 220, grid c4.

Campsites, facilities: There are 24 RV campsites with full hookups, trees, and asphalt or concrete pads. Facilities include clean, tiled rest rooms with flush toilets and hot showers, laundry, a pool, a concrete launch ramp, and berthing for boats. The water is safe to drink. Security is good; the park is in a walled compound with gates, a 24-hour guard, and a dog. Tent campers are not welcome. Obtain supplies in La Paz.

Reservations, fees: Reservations are accepted. Fees are high—$15 per night.

Contact: Aquamarina RV Park, Apartado Postal 133, La Paz, Baja California Sur, México; phone 011-52-112-2-3761 or fax 011-52-112-5-6228.

Directions: From Ciudad Constitución, drive 133 miles south on Highway 1 to La Paz. At El Cardón, turn east toward the center of La Paz on Abasolo three blocks past the CCC Supermarket and proceed to Nyarít. Turn left and continue to the waterfront.

Trip notes: Lush palms and flowering shrubs give this park a more tropical appearance than any other in Baja. Aquamarina has been a labor of love for owners and La Paz pioneers Richard and Maria Luisa Adcock. (Maria is México's first and only female licensed ship captain.) They also operate La Paz Diving Service for charter groups on the ship *Marisla,* which is docked in front of Aquamarina. The park is now open from mid-October through mid-March. It is locked to new arrivals from noon until the following morning on weekends and holidays, but if you make some noise or bang on one or both of the gates, the watchman will let you in. Winter is the preferred season, as summer is hot. For things to do in the La Paz area, please see page 224.

❽ La Ventana Campground

Location: Southeast of La Paz; South Baja Sur map page 220, grid d5.

Campsites, facilities: Between 50 and 70 vehicles can park here. Several water spigots, flush toilets, and cold showers are provided. Don't drink the water. There is no security. Tent campers are welcome. Obtain main supplies in La Paz; limited supplies can be purchased in San Juan de Los Planes.

Reservations, fees: All sites are first come, first served. The fee is very low—$3 per night.

Contact: Drive in and park.

Directions: From Highway 1 on the southern outskirts of La Paz, take State Highway 286 south for 24 miles until you reach a gravel road leading north. Turn left and head five miles to La Ventana. The campground is on the north side of the village.

Trip notes: Campsites are set among sparse palms and mesquite trees, providing limited shade. The campground is on a sheltered sand beach with a view of Isla Cerralvo 10 miles away across Canal de Cerralvo. Small, lightweight boats can be launched over the sand. Windsurfers frequent the beach during the winter, when winds are strong and dependable. Nearby fishing is fair. Motor homes up to 34 feet long can make it here, though the gravel road in may be rough. Winter is the preferred season, as summer is hot. For more on fishing in and around La Paz, please see page 224.

❾ Punta Arena de la Ventana Beach

Location: Southeast of La Paz; South Baja Sur map page 220, grid d5.

Campsites, facilities: The beach is ideal for tent camping. There are no facilities or security. Obtain main supplies in La Paz; limited supplies can be purchased in San Juan de Los Planes.

Reservations, fees: Camping is first come, first served. There is no fee.

Contact: Drive in and park.

Directions: From Highway 1 on the southern outskirts of La Paz, take State Highway 286 south for about 29 miles to San Juan de Los Planes, then continue three miles on pavement and eight miles on a washboard dirt road to the Punta Arena access road, which bears left. Follow this road about four miles to the beach. The lighthouse is in view to the east.

Trip notes: With Isla Cerralvo in sight directly across the channel, this is a delightful spot for RVers and tenters alike. As it is remote, you may feel more comfortable having others along for company. The beach extends about 10 miles north toward La Ventana and offers good fishing. At daybreak, schools of jack crevalle (toro) often work the surf in feeding frenzies. Try casting into them for great sport. Roosterfish may be in the area as well. Fishermen put their *pangas* in here and can be helpful in dispensing fishing information. Sometimes they're even willing to hire themselves out as guides. For a pleasant hike, stroll a couple miles to the west and you'll find a beached modern, rusty steel ship, the *Cedros,* broadsided right at the surf line. Winter is the preferred season, as summer is hot. For things to do in the La Paz area, please see page 224.

⑩ Bahía de los Muertos Beach

Location: Southeast of La Paz; South Baja Sur map page 220, grid d5.

Campsites, facilities: The beach is ideal for tent camping. There are no facilities or security. Obtain main supplies in La Paz; limited supplies can be purchased in San Juan de Los Planes.

Reservations, fees: Camping is first come, first served. There is no fee.

Contact: Drive in and park.

Directions: From Highway 1 on the southern outskirts of La Paz, take State Highway 286 south for about 29 miles to San Juan de Los Planes, then continue three miles on pavement and another 10 miles on a washboard dirt road to the beach.

Trip notes: Tenters and RVers may set up camp at the extreme north end of the bay, where fishing is good. Head to the fish camp here to ask the commercial fishermen about what's biting or if they will hire themselves out as guides. Some of the La Paz sportfishing operators drive their clients to this beach to partake of the great fishing for pargo and roosterfish off Isla Cerralvo. Small boats can be launched across the firm beach. Winter is the preferred season, as summer is hot. For more on fishing in the La Paz area, please see page 224.

⑪ Rancho Verde RV Park

Location: North of San Bartolo; South Baja Sur map page 221, grid g3.

Campsites, facilities: There are 29 campsites with water and sewer hookups, tables, barbecues, and trees. Also available are flush toilets, hot showers, nature trails, bicycle and off-road-vehicle trails, horseback rides, and a citrus orchard with a variety of fresh fruit. A pool is planned. The water is good to drink. The park is totally fenced, and security is provided by resident owners. Tent campers are welcome. Obtain supplies in La Paz.

Reservations, fees: Reservations are accepted. Fees are moderate—$11 per night for RVs and $7 for tents, with one free day per week. Horses rent for $10 per hour.

Contact: Rancho Verde RV Park, P.O. Box 1050, Eureka, MT 59917; phone (406) 889-3030 or fax (406) 889-3033 in the United States, or 011-52-112-5-7570 in México.

Directions: From San Bartolo, drive about eight miles north on Highway 1 to the park at Kilometer 143.

Trip notes: Part of a 3,000-acre ranch, this RV park is in a hilly inland area with brush and trees that provide a different kind of landscape than that found at the more common beach campgrounds. Winter is the preferred season, as summer is hot. For information on the East Cape area, please see page 227.

⑫ El Cardonal Resort

Location: North of Los Barriles; South Baja Sur map page 221, grid g4.

Campsites, facilities: Each of the four full-hookup RV campsites and the 10 tent sites with no hookups have concrete pads, trees, tables, and barbecues. Facilities include tiled rest rooms with flush toilets and hot showers, laundry service, a restaurant, a store, and a boat ramp. For recreation, there's badminton, volleyball, horseshoes, snorkeling, bow and arrow equipment, rental horses, and tours. Motel rooms are available. The water is good to drink. Resident owners provide security. Obtain supplies in Los Barriles.

Reservations, fees: Reservations are accepted. Fees are moderate—$8 per night, $50 per week, $200 per month, and $1,500 per year for RVs with full hookups; $5 per night, $30 per week, $120 per month, and $1,200 per year for tents.

Contact: El Cardonal Resort, Los Barriles, Baja California Sur, México; phone or fax 011-52-114-1-0040.

Directions: From La Paz, drive about 65 miles south on Highway 1 to Los Barriles. Then proceed north along the coast for 14 miles on a sometimes rocky dirt road.

Trip notes: Here is an off-the-beaten-path find on a remote stretch of beautiful coastline. It's a lovely location for tent camping on the shore of the Sea of Cortéz, with a sandy beach and great recreational potential. You can explore the rocky shore north and south of El Cardonal, swim, snorkel, fish from shore, or join a tour to examine cave paintings. Winter is the preferred season, as summer is hot. For information on the East Cape area, please see page 227.

Note: Large motor homes or trailers should not attempt the trip, as rock overhangs impinge on clearance and steep, rocky stretches are difficult to negotiate.

⑬ Los Barriles Beach

Location: North of Los Barriles; South Baja Sur map page 221, grid g5.

Campsites, facilities: There are three camping areas with no facilities or security. The beach is ideal for tent camping. Obtain supplies in Los Barriles.

Reservations, fees: Camping is first come, first served. There is no fee.

Contact: Drive in and park.

Directions: From La Paz, drive about 65 miles south on Highway 1 to Los Barriles, then head north along the coast. Two miles upcoast from the center of town, follow a well-used set of wheel tracks one-quarter mile to the Sea of Cortéz, then turn left and proceed 200 yards along a beach with numerous campsites.

Trip notes: Free access to beachfront makes this a good place to camp in a tent or RV. For small, maneuverable vehicles, there's a tiny campsite 2.1 more miles along the road to the east and a larger site two-tenths of a mile farther; both are primitive and have no developed facilities. Several hotels in Los Barriles charter *pangas* and cruisers to fish the deep waters of the Sea of Cortéz. Winter is the preferred season, as summer is hot. For information on the East Cape area, please see page 227.

⑭ Juanito's Garden RV Park

Location: In Los Barriles; South Baja Sur map page 221, grid g5.

Campsites, facilities: There are 20 RV campsites, all with full hookups and some with palapas and trees. Six additional tent sites have palapas, trees, electricity, and good drinking water. Facilities include tiled rest rooms with flush toilets and hot showers, a laundry, store, and restaurant. Long-term storage is available. The water is safe to drink. The park is fenced with a gate and has a resident manager. Obtain supplies in Los Barriles.

Reservations, fees: Reservations are accepted. Fees are moderate—$10 per night, $242 per month, and $2,640 per year without a palapa or $3,000 with a palapa.

Contact: Juanito's Garden RV Park, Apartado Postal 50, Los Barriles, Baja California Sur, México; phone or fax 011-52-114-1-0024.

Directions: From La Paz, drive about 65 miles south on Highway 1 to Los Barriles. The park is on the north end of town, on the inland side of the road.

Trip notes: Though not right on the beach, this RV park is within walking distance, just a quarter mile away. In the park, which is set on a slight slope, dust is kept down by a layer of imported beach sand. Features include clean, private rest rooms with locking doors, a coin-operated washing machine ($1), and well-kept landscaping. Winter is the favored season, as summer is hot. For things to do in the East Cape area, please see page 227.

⑮ Martín Verdugo's RV Park and Motel

Location: In Los Barriles; South Baja Sur map page 221, grid g5.

Campsites, facilities: There are 72 RV campsites with full hookups (two pull-through) and 25 sites for tents, a few of which have electricity and water. On the premises are trees, clean tiled rest rooms with flush toilets and hot showers, a laundry, a pool, motel rooms, and steel mats for launching boats over the sand. The water is safe to drink. The park is secured with a guard and a perimeter fence. Obtain supplies in Los Barriles.

Reservations, fees: Reservations are accepted. Fees are moderate—$12 per night for RVs in front, $11 in back, and $10 for tents. Long-term rates are $80 per week for RVs in front, $74 in back, and $66 for tents; $260 per month for RVs in front, $245 in back, and $225 for tents.

Contact: Martín Verdugo's RV Park and Motel, Apartado Postal 17, Los Barriles, Baja California Sur, México; phone or fax 011-52-114-1-0054.

Directions: From La Paz, drive about 65 miles south on Highway 1 to Los Barriles. The park is on the north side of town on the beach.

Trip notes: Martín is always busy around the park, working hard to make sure everything is clean and functioning properly. Rock and mortar walls define the exterior boundaries of the property and contain grading where there is a slight slope. This is a very popular place, and long-term reservations for winter stays in front near the water must be made a year or more in advance. Winter is the favored season, as summer is hot. For things to do in the East Cape area, please see page 227.

⑯ Spa RV Park

Location: South of Los Barriles; South Baja Sur map page 221, grid g5.

Campsites, facilities: There are eight campsites with full hookups. You'll find trees, hot showers, a toilet in a trailer, laundry facilities, a pool, Jacuzzi, party palapa, store, restaurant, and an area for launching light boats across the sand. The water is safe to drink. Security is provided by resident owners. Tent campers and children are forbidden. Obtain supplies in Los Barriles.

Reservations, fees: All sites are first come, first served. The fee is high—$15 per night, $39 for three nights, $85 per week, and $290 per month.

Contact: Drive in and talk to the owner.

Directions: From La Paz, drive about 65 miles south on Highway 1 to Los Barriles. Continue three miles south, then turn left at the Hotel Buena Vista entrance.

Trip notes: The campsites are small with limited room to maneuver rigs. Winter is the favored season, as summer is hot. For more information on things to do in the East Cape area, please see page 227.

⑰ La Capilla RV Park

Location: South of Los Barriles; South Baja Sur map page 221, grid h5.

Campsites, facilities: There are 20 campsites with full hookups and palapas. Flush toilets and hot showers are provided. The water is safe to drink. There is no security on the premises, but the owners live nearby. Tent campers are welcome. Obtain supplies in Los Barriles.

Reservations, fees: All sites are first come, first served. The fee is low—$7 per night.

Contact: Drive in and talk to the manager.

Directions: From La Paz, drive about 65 miles south on Highway 1 to the Los Barriles turnoff. Continue 3.6 miles south, then turn left at the signed road to Rancho Leonero and drive 1.7 miles to the park (one-half mile beyond the sign indicating the turnoff to Rancho Leonero).

Trip notes: You could say the facilities are rustic, but this is a pretty good choice for tent campers—no asphalt or concrete to contend with, just desert soil to pound in tent stakes on a beach with an ocean view. The campsites are open to cooling breezes in a somewhat remote area with no other development around. The beach is clean white sand with normally mild surf, great for strolling and shelling. It's also fine for putting in cartop boats and inflatables. Winter is the favored season, as summer is hot. For more information on things to do in the East Cape area, please see page 227.

🔞 La Ribera RV Park

Location: In La Ribera; South Baja Sur map page 221, grid h5.

Campsites, facilities: There are 13 pull-through campsites with full hookups and some palapas. Flush toilets, hot showers, and laundry facilities are available. The water is safe to drink. A gate secures the park. Tent campers are welcome. Obtain supplies in La Ribera.

Reservations, fees: Reservations are accepted. Fees are moderate—$9 per night with full hookups and $6 for tents.

Contact: La Ribera RV Park, c/o Lee Bray, Apartado Postal 27, Buena Vista, Baja California Sur, México. There is no phone.

Directions: From Highway 1 at Las Cuevas, turn onto the paved road to La Ribera. Go about 6.5 miles, through La Ribera, then turn left at the sign for the park and continue another half mile.

Trip notes: Old mango trees provide generous shade for RVers at this park. Guests with tents or pickups may set up camp on the fenced and gated beach a quarter mile away. Ask park management to open the beach gate for you. Winter is the favored season, as summer is hot. For things to do in the East Cape area, please see page 227.

⑲ El Litro Trailer Park

Location: On the south side of Todos Santos; South Baja Sur map page 221, grid g1.

Campsites, facilities: There are eight campsites with full hookups and space for about 30 RVs, in addition to a tenting area with lots of trees. A flush toilet and one cold shower are available. Don't drink the water. Guards provide security 24 hours daily. Obtain supplies in Todos Santos.

Reservations, fees: Camping is first come, first served. The fee is moderate—$10 per night or $63 per week. Monthly rates are $8 per night for RVs and $4 per night for tents.

Contact: Drive in and talk to the manager.

Directions: In Todos Santos, drive two blocks south of the Pemex station. Look for the sign, turn, and go four blocks west.

Trip notes: This new park provides ready access to Todos Santos, an interesting town to explore on foot. Currently there are eight campsites, but the plan is to expand to 25. Winter is the best time to come, as summer is hot. For things to do in the Pacific Coast area, please see page 228.

⑳ San Pedrito RV Park

Location: South of Todos Santos; South Baja Sur map page 221, grid g1.

Campsites, facilities: There are 72 pull-through campsites with full hookups. Tent campers are welcome in a designated area on the beach with 18 palapas. Facilities include modest rest rooms with flush toilets and hot showers, laundry, a pool, a restaurant, a bar, and beachfront motel rooms. The water is safe to drink. For security, there is a gate and the owner lives on the premises. Obtain supplies in Todos Santos.

Reservations, fees: Reservations are accepted. Fees are high—$15 per night for a full-hookup site, $3 per person for no hookups, and $2 per day for parking. Long-term rates are $91 per week and $330 per month for sites with hookups.

Contact: San Pedrito RV Park, Apartado Postal 15, Todos Santos, Baja California Sur, México. There is no phone.

Directions: From Todos Santos, drive 4.5 miles south on Highway 19. A large sign marks the turnoff to the park. Follow the road two miles to the beach.

Trip notes: A longtime favorite among surfers, this is also one of our favorite camping spots. We spend a few nights here on every trip. Each site has an ocean view and a small palm tree. Other palms are scattered around. The beach in front of the RV spaces is treacherous, containing a huge pile of round boulders, which were chipped off of the rocky point to the north by the action of the water over the millennia. They are constantly rocking and rolling as waves bombard them, posing dangers to bare feet out for a casual stroll. A safer sand beach begins a few hundred yards south. There is ample parking on firm ground behind the sand beach suitable for tents and self-contained RVs. Winter is the best time to come, as summer is hot. For things to do in the Pacific Coast area, please see page 228.

㉑ Los Cerritos RV Park (ejido)

Location: South of Todos Santos; South Baja Sur map page 221, grid h1.

Campsites, facilities: There are 50 pull-through campsites, all with sewer hookups but no electricity or water. Flush toilets are available. There are a couple of taps with nonpotable water. Security is not provided. Tent campers are welcome. Obtain supplies in Todos Santos.

Reservations, fees: All sites are first come, first served. The fee is low—$4 per night, or $3 nightly for monthly stays.

Contact: Drive in and park.

Directions: From Todos Santos, drive 7.2 miles south on Highway 19. The turnoff for the park at Kilometer 64, one-quarter mile south of El Pescadero, is marked with a sign. Follow the road two miles west to the beach.

Trip notes: One of the most magnificent beaches in Baja is situated about a quarter mile from here, and the full six-mile sweep of this gem is within view of the park. Surfers have come here for years and it's no wonder why. Most people prefer to camp closer to the beach, particularly if they have self-contained RVs or tents. Drive around to the ocean side of the park to enter. Planned improvements include a meeting palapa and hurricane-damage cleanup. Also, fees will be increased. Winter is the best time to come, as summer is hot. For things to do in the Pacific Coast area, please see page 228.

㉒ Playa Los Cerritos

Location: South of Todos Santos; South Baja Sur map page 221, grid h1.

Campsites, facilities: The beach is ideal for tent camping. There are no facilities or security, though campers may use the trash barrels and rest rooms at the RV park. Don't drink the water in the RV park. Obtain supplies in Todos Santos.

Reservations, fees: Camping is first come, first served. The fee is very low—$3 per night.

Contact: Drive in and park. Someone will come around to collect the fee.

Directions: From Todos Santos, drive 7.2 miles south on Highway 19. Take the marked turnoff for Los Cerritos RV Park and go two miles to the beach.

Trip notes: Here it is—one of the most spectacular beaches in all of Baja. Of course, surfers have known this for years. There is ample space to park or pitch tents in front of the RV park or to the north up against the rocky ridge. Payment is collected by the same people as at the adjoining RV park, the local *ejido*. Consider it an access fee to the beach. Winter is the best time to come, as summer is hot. For things to do in the Pacific Coast area, please see page 228.

㉓ Playa Las Cabrillas

Location: South of Todos Santos; South Baja Sur map page 221, grid i1.

Campsites, facilities: The beach is ideal for tent camping. There are no facilities and no security. Obtain supplies in Todos Santos.

Reservations, fees: Camping is first come, first served. There is no fee.

Contact: Drive in and park.

Directions: From Todos Santos, drive 17.4 miles south on Highway 19 to the beach access sign at Kilometer 81.

Trip notes: There's limited room for camping at this long, steep, very wide beach, and it can get pretty crowded. The beach is composed of fine, soft white sand that is perfect for lounging or strolling. Note, however, that the undertow is strong. There are caves in a hill to the north where the surf enters. You'll find hard-sand space for a few medium-sized rigs or tents just off the highway. Trailers could have a hard time maneuvering their way in. Winter is the best time to come, as summer is hot. For things to do in the Pacific Coast area, please see page 228.

㉔ El Arco RV Park

Location: East of Cabo San Lucas; South Baja Sur map page 221, grid j1.

Campsites, facilities: There are 40 pull-through campsites, of which 24 have full hookups. Some come with concrete pads. Modest rest rooms with flush toilets and hot showers, laundry facilities, a pool, and a restaurant are available. Don't drink the water. The park is secured with a chain and by the presence of numerous people. Tent campers are welcome. Obtain supplies in Cabo San Lucas.

Reservations, fees: Reservations are accepted. Fees are high—$15 per night for RVs with full hookups and $8 for tents. Long-term rates are $250 per month and $2,484 per year.

Contact: El Arco RV Park, Apartado Postal 114, Cabo San Lucas, Baja California Sur, México; phone 011-52-114-3-1686.

Directions: From Cabo San Lucas, drive 3.3 miles east on Highway 1. The park is on a hill overlooking the ocean and Land's End.

Trip notes: "Stunning" is just one word to describe the view of the harbor, *El Arco* (the Arch), and the rugged rocks of Land's End—and it's all yours when you set up camp here. There is a downside, though: the park is crowded and dedicated mainly to permanents, so it's rather unattractive for overnighters. Winter is the best time to come, as summer is hot. For things to do in the Cape area, please see page 230.

25 Cabo Cielo RV Park

Location: East of Cabo San Lucas; South Baja Sur map page 221, grid j1.

Campsites, facilities: There are 24 campsites with full hookups. A store and tiled rest rooms with flush toilets and hot showers are on the property. Don't drink the water. The park is secured with a chain and the manager lives on the premises. Tent campers are welcome. Obtain supplies in Cabo San Lucas.

Reservations, fees: All sites are first come, first served. Fees are moderate—$9 per night. Long-term rates are $210 per month.

Contact: Drive in and talk to the manager.

Directions: From Cabo San Lucas, head 2.3 miles east on Highway 1 to the park.

Trip notes: Campers have a palm tree at each site and a view of Land's End. The park is situated in an open field, not a very interesting place to camp. As the trees mature and improvements continue to be made, however, we trust it will become more attractive. Winter is the best time to come, as summer is hot. For things to do in the Cape area, please see page 230.

26 Club Cabo Motel and RV Park

Location: East of Cabo San Lucas; South Baja Sur map page 221, grid j1.

Campsites, facilities: There are 15 campsites, most of which have full hookups. Facilities include tiled rest rooms with flush toilets and hot showers, palapas, trees, tables, barbecues, laundry, a trampoline, a pool, a Jacuzzi, and motel rooms. Don't drink the water. The park is secured with a chain and motion-sensing floodlights, and the owner lives on the premises. Tent campers are welcome. Obtain supplies in Cabo San Lucas.

Reservations, fees: Reservations are encouraged, with a 10 percent discount. Fees are moderate—$6 per night per person.

Contact: Club Cabo Motel and RV Park, Apartado Postal 463, Cabo San Lucas, Baja California Sur, México; phone 011-52-114-3-3348.

Directions: From the junction of Highway 1 and the Highway 19 bypass around Cabo San Lucas, drive south on the unmarked street in the big arroyo going toward Club Cascadas, following the signs to Club Cabo. Turn left on the sandy road to the east paralleling the beach and go past the back end of the Vagabundos del Mar RV Park. The park adjoins the Vagabundos park on its east side.

Trip notes: The quiet, pleasant park is in a secluded setting away from town. Best of all, it offers beach access. The owners can tip you off to where the great surfing spots are, and will even rent you a surfboard in case you didn't bring one along. Winter is the best time to come, as summer is hot. For things to do in the Cape area, please see page 230.

㉗ Vagabundos del Mar RV Park

Location: East of Cabo San Lucas; South Baja Sur map page 221, grid j1.

Campsites, facilities: There are 95 campsites (38 pull-through), all with full hook-ups, concrete pads, trees, and tables. Tent campers may use 38 of the sites. Facilities include clean tiled rest rooms with flush toilets and hot showers, laundry, a pool, a restaurant/bar, and a meeting palapa. Don't drink the water. The park is secured with a gate and 24-hour guard service, and the manager lives on the premises. Obtain supplies in Cabo San Lucas.

Reservations, fees: Reservations are encouraged. Fees are high—$16 per night, $100 per week, $400 per month, and $3,000 per year for RVs or tents.

Contact: Vagabundos del Mar RV Park, Apartado Postal 197, Cabo San Lucas, Baja California Sur, México; phone 011-52-114-3-0290 in México or for reservations (800) 474-2252 in the United States; fax 011-52-114-3-0511 in México or for reservations (707) 374-6843 in the United States.

Directions: From Cabo San Lucas, head one mile east on Highway 1 to the park on the south side of the highway.

Trip notes: This one's a winner—one of the most attractive and well-maintained parks in Baja. For landscaping there are lots of native mesquite trees and introduced palms. If you're boating or fishing, an added bonus is that this is the closest park to the launch ramps in Cabo. Winter is the best time to come, as summer is hot. For more on things to do in the Cape area, please see page 230.

㉘ El Faro Viejo RV Park

Location: In Cabo San Lucas; South Baja Sur map page 221, grid j1.

Campsites, facilities: There are 24 large pull-through, full-hookup campsites for RVs and 12 sites for tents with concrete pads and trees. Clean tiled rest rooms with flush toilets and hot showers, a store, and one of the best restaurants in Cabo San Lucas—known simply as The Trailer Park Restaurant—also are on the property. Don't drink the water. Security is good, as the park is inside a walled compound with a locked gate and a watchman. Obtain supplies in Cabo San Lucas.

Reservations, fees: Reservations are accepted. Fees are moderate—$12 per night for two people, plus $3 for each additional person.

Contact: El Faro Viejo RV Park, Apartado Postal 64, Cabo San Lucas, Baja California Sur, México; phone 011-52-114-3-1927.

Directions: The park is on the north end of town, one block west of Morelos (Highway 19) between Mijares and Felix Ortega.

Trip notes: The grounds of this recently spruced-up park with landscaped RV sites are very well maintained. Each site has trees and plants. This is not the ideal place for tent campers, being right in the city. It gets very crowded every night when the restaurant/bar patrons flock in. Winter is the preferred season, as summer is hot. For more on things to do in the Cape area, please see page 230.

29 Brisa del Mar RV Resort

Location: West of San José del Cabo; South Baja Sur map page 221, grid j3.

Campsites, facilities: There are 80 full-hookup, pull-through campsites set back from the beach and 34 campsites on the beach with electricity and water only. Facilities include tiled rest rooms with flush toilets and hot showers, laundry, a pool, a store, a seasonal bar and restaurant, Ping-Pong and pool tables, a volleyball court, and a horseshoe pit. Don't drink the water. Security is with a night watchman. Tent campers are welcome at all sites. Obtain supplies in San José del Cabo.

Reservations, fees: Camping is first come, first served. Fees are high—for RVs, it's $16.50 to $25 per night with full hookups, $90 per week, $330 per month, and $3,200 per year. Tents are $9 per night, $63 per week, and $270 per month.

Contact: Brisa del Mar RV Resort, Apartado Postal 45, San José del Cabo, Baja California Sur, México; phone or fax 011-52-114-2-3999.

Directions: From San José del Cabo, take Highway 1 west about two miles to Kilometer 28. Brisa del Mar is on the beach.

Trip notes: This park is very popular with snowbirds who flock here for the winter. It is on a lovely beach close to San José del Cabo and, in fact, is the only RV park on a beach in the Los Cabos area. Winter is the best time to come, as summer is hot. For things to do in the Cape area, please see page 230.

South Baja Sur's 10 Best Beaches

① Loma María to Todos Santos Beaches

Location: On the Pacific Ocean, south of the Bahía Magdalena complex and north of Todos Santos; South Baja Sur map pages 220 and 221, grids b1–g1.

Directions: A rough dirt road approaches the coast from about 17 miles south of Santa Rita on Highway 1 (about 51 miles south of Ciudad Constitución), then runs south along the coast to Todos Santos. The beaches extend for some 110 miles. Punta Conejo can be reached more directly via a 12-mile, fair dirt road that exits Highway 1 at Kilometer 80 (about 13 miles south of El Cien and 68 miles south of Ciudad Constitución). Other rough dirt roads leave Highway 1 for coastal ranches 29, 40, and 41 miles south of El Cien.

Trip notes: This is as straight as a coastline can get, with very few projections or points and no shelter for boats—just one long stretch of beach. The beaches here are generally not frequented by tourists. Punta Conejo is favored by surfers and windsurfers. Adventurers in four-wheel-drive vehicles might find the pristine beaches exciting to explore. Of course, it's always wise for four-wheelers to travel in groups in remote areas in case of mechanical breakdown.

② San Juan de la Costa Beaches

Location: On the Sea of Cortéz, north of La Paz; South Baja Sur map page 220, grids a4–b3.

Directions: Access is by the 24-mile paved road to San Juan de la Costa, which leaves Highway 1 at Kilometer 17 about 10 miles north of La Paz, and the dirt road that continues another 35 miles to El Mechudo.

Trip notes: There are a number of sand, pebble, and mixed beaches along the western shore of Bahía de La Paz. The dirt road north of San Juan de la Costa has soft, sandy stretches that can easily bog down larger vehicles, as is the case with side roads to the shore. Trailers are difficult to manage here. Pickups, vans, and four-wheel-drive vehicles will fare better. Fishing for roosterfish, grouper, snapper, pargo, sierra, and dorado improves the farther north you go.

③ La Paz Beaches

Location: On the Sea of Cortéz, northeast and east of La Paz; South Baja Sur map page 220, grids c4–d5.

Directions: These beaches extend from Playa Balandra (campground number 1) and Playa Tecolote (campground number 2), around Punta Coyote and south to Bahía de los Muertos Beach (campground number 10). There are dirt roads east of Tecolote, and a network of rough, sandy four-wheel-drive roads fans out from the southeast edge of La Paz to the northern area. Other dirt roads that leave the pavement out of San Juan de Los Planes lead to the southern section. (For directions, see campgrounds 8 through 10.)

Trip notes: Long beaches such as Tecolote, Cachimba, La Sorpresa, and Arena de la Ventana are interspersed with sandy coves and rocky cliffs. This is a great area for exploring with groups of four-wheel-drive vehicles. The fishing can be exceptional as well. For types of fish found in the area and the names of companies leading sportfishing cruises out of La Paz, see page 224.

④ Playa San Pedro

Location: On the Pacific Ocean, south of Todos Santos; South Baja Sur map page 221, grid g1.

Directions: The turnoff from Highway 19 is 4.4 miles south of the southern outskirts of Todos Santos, just before the signs and entrance road to San Pedrito RV Park. However, the road is currently closed to vehicular traffic, though motorcycles and ATVs can make it. After the turnoff, it's 1.5 miles to the beach.

Trip notes: A popular surfing spot, this beautiful sand beach extends about three-tenths of a mile between two rocky points and is backed by a large palm grove. It is perfect for tent campers who can haul in their gear on motorcycles or ATVs. Note: Many guidebooks and maps list this as Playa San Pedrito, though we quizzed locals who stoutly maintained it was Playa San Pedro. Winter is the best time to come, as summer is hot. For things to do in the Pacific Coast area, please see page 228.

⑤ Pescadero Beach

Location: On the Pacific Ocean, south of Todos Santos; South Baja Sur map page 221, grid g1.

Directions: The beach extends about four miles between Punta San Pedro south to Punta Pescadero. San Pedrito RV Park (campground number 20) is at the north end. It's best to ask for directions in Pescadero on how to get through the fields.

Trip notes: We haven't found this one listed in other guidebooks or on maps. The wide beach is covered with a blanket of soft sand and is a favorite destination for surfers. Except for the northern reaches, it is remote, offering seclusion to those who make the effort to attain it. The beach slopes rather steeply, creating an undertow that can be dangerous to inexperienced swimmers. Winter is the best time to come, as summer is hot. For things to do in the Pacific Coast area, please see page 228.

⑥ Playa Los Cerritos

Location: On the Pacific Ocean, south of Todos Santos; South Baja Sur map page 221, grid g1.

Directions: The beach extends about five miles between Puntas Pescadero and Gaspareño.

Trip notes: This wide beach curves westward, exposing an unbroken five-mile sweep to clear view from Los Cerritos RV Park (campground number 21) and Playa Los Cerritos (campground number 22) at the north end. Walking on the soft white sand is pure joy.

⑦ East Cape Beaches

Location: On the Sea of Cortéz, from north of Los Barriles to south of La Ribera; South Baja Sur map page 221, grids g5–h5.

Directions: The beaches extend from four miles north of Los Barriles south to Punta Arena. The campgrounds from Los Barriles Beach (number 13) to La Ribera RV Park (number 18) afford public access to this stretch of coastline. A sandy road parallels the coast in both directions from La Ribera, with numerous four-wheel-drive roads branching off it toward the beaches.

Trip notes: These beaches form an almost continuous 25-mile strip. Blanketed with soft white sand, they become wider the farther south you go. There is ample opportunity to find solitude, as many stretches between public access points are remote. The wide, sweeping beach at the southern end between Punta Colorada and Punta Arena invites long walks and is great for shelling. Private lands block many access points, but adventurous souls can find ways in. For information on the numerous fishing, diving, snorkeling, and windsurfing opportunities in the East Cape area, see page 227.

⑧ Punta Arena to San José del Cabo Beaches

Location: On the Sea of Cortéz, south of La Ribera and north of San José del Cabo; South Baja Sur map page 221, grids h5–i3.

Directions: To get to La Ribera, exit Highway 1 on a paved road that begins approximately 12 miles south of Los Barriles and drive about seven miles east. Los Frailes is about 22 miles south of La Ribera. The beaches extend for some 33 miles south of Los Frailes. Below is a log of accessible beaches, with mile marks starting from Los Frailes:

Mile 8: Rancho El Tule—Follow the wide arroyo to the beach. The people at the rancho seem somewhat hostile to travelers and have placed big speed bumps in front of the headquarters. They may not welcome campers, so be nice.

Mile 10.9: An access road leads to the beach.

Mile 14.4: Rancho San Luis is on the beach.

Mile 14.9: A short access road leads to the beach.

Mile 17.0: Rancho Boca de Las Palmas. A wide arroyo accesses the beach.

Mile 18.8: Rancho La Fortuna. A wide arroyo accesses the beach.

Mile 19.3: There's an access road to a big beach.

Mile 20.3: An access road leads to the beach.

Mile 20.8: Shipwreck Beach is a favorite of surfers. A good, short road accesses this big beach.

Mile 22.6: A big, sandy arroyo accesses the nearby beach.

Mile 23.9: An access road goes to Playa Tortuga.

Mile 24.6: An access road leads to the beach, between brush-covered dunes.

Mile 25.5–25.7: Several small parking areas are off the coast road, just above the beach.

Mile 32.0: A big beach is at the end of the access road.

Mile 33.4: Just outside San José del Cabo is an access road to the beach at La Playa.

Trip notes: Surfing is the main activity along this stretch of coast, and there are plenty of places to go. However, only small, maneuverable vehicles can make the drive safely. Choice campsites on this long string of magnificent beaches are inaccessible to larger highway vehicles because of dangerous road conditions. Side roads leading to beaches are packed wheel tracks in sand. A paved road on a new alignment is being built south of La Ribera. Ultimately, it is supposed to go down the coast to San José del Cabo. Coming into La Ribera from Highway 1, this road veers south before town. Obviously, whatever realignment the new paved road takes will alter the log given above, but at least you will have something to go by as this remote coast opens up.

🌞 Beaches between Punta Gaspareño and Land's End

Location: On the Pacific Ocean, south of Todos Santos and north of Cabo San Lucas; South Baja Sur map page 221, grids h1–j1.

Directions: Access the beaches at Playa Las Cabrillas (campground number 23) or from several four-wheel-drive roads off Highway 19. To reach Migriño Beach, drive 27 miles south of Todos Santos or 16 miles north of Cabo San Lucas on Highway 19 to Kilometer 97, then follow the rough road in (suitable for small vehicles).

Trip notes: The long, 33-mile stretch between Punta Gaspareño and Land's End is essentially one immense, unbroken beach. It's wide and backed by dunes, with soft white sand offering great opportunities for seclusion to those who are willing to hike. The slope is rather steep and the surf pounds here, creating undertows that pose serious threat to inexperienced swimmers. Still, surfers like riding the waves off the points on this coastline.

Note: Development by private landowners along Highway 19 is forcing the closure of some access roads. There probably will always be some way in, though, since the *Zona Federale* (up to the high tide mark all around México) is dedicated to the public.

🔟 Cape Area Day-Use Beaches

Location: Between San José del Cabo and Cabo San Lucas; South Baja Sur map page 221, grids j1–j3.

Directions: You can access several beaches off Highway 1. Routes are designated by road signs.

Trip notes: One of the best things about coming to the Cape is being able to loll about on these beaches soaking up the sun's rays and splashing around in the surf. People camping in this region find these day-use beaches are delightful to visit, though they can become quite congested. Sadly, they are falling prey to development one by one, so you may find access to certain beaches restricted. Enjoy them while you can.

Playa Tecolote north of La Paz is a broad expanse of white sand beach that is perfect for strolling.

Resources

Resources

Road Signs

Encountering Mexican road signs for the first time can be confusing, especially if you don't speak Spanish. Since a few signs pertain to driving conditions that may be dangerous, it is wise to get acquainted with them before crossing the border:

Acceso a playa—
beach access

Camino sinuoso—
winding road

Alto—*stop*

Ceda el paso—*yield*

Circulación—*traffic*

Cruce ferrocarril—
railroad crossing

Conserve su derecha—
keep to the right

Curva peligrosa—
dangerous curve

Concida cambio de luces—
dim your lights

Despacio—*slow*

Desviación—*detour*

Estacionamiento—*parking*

Doble circulación—
two way

Estacionamiento para casas
rodantes—*trailer park*

Escuela—*school*

Hombres trabajando—
men working

Ganado—*livestock*

Inspección—*inspection*

Gasolinera—*gas station*

Maxima—*speed limit in kilometers per hour*

Grava suelta—
loose gravel

No estacionarse—
no parking

No hay paso—*road closed*

Peatones—*pedestrians*

No rebase—*no passing*

Peligro—*danger*

No tire basura—*no littering*

Pendiente peligrosa—
dangerous downgrade

Puente angosto—
narrow bridge

Sanitarios—*toilets*

Precaución—*precaution*

Telephono—*telephone*

Restaurante—*restaurant*

Tope—*speed bump*

Semaforo—*stoplight*

Vado—*dip*

Solo izq (izquierdo)—
left turn only

Zona de derrumbes—
falling rock

*When you say this with the proper
rolling of the double "r," it sounds
like rocks tumbling down a hill.*

Metric Conversions

Length

Kilometer	0.62 mile	multiply by 0.6 to find miles
Meter	39.37 inches	multiply by 1.1 to find yards
Centimeter	0.39 inch	multiply by 0.4 to find inches
Millimeter	0.039 inch	multiply by 0.04 to find inches

Area

Hectare	2.47 acres	multiply by 2.5 to find acres

Weight

Kilogram	2.2046 pounds	multiply by 2.2 to find pounds
Gram	0.035 ounce	multiply by 0.035 to find ounces

Capacity

Liter	1.057 quarts	multiply by 0.26 to find gallons

Speed

Kilometers per hour	0.6 miles per hour
Miles per hour	1.6 kilometers per hour

Temperature

Celsius temperature = Fahrenheit temperature − 32° x 5/9

Fahrenheit temperature = 9/5 x Celsius temperature + 32°

Special Days in México

January 6—*Día de Reyes.* Gifts are exchanged.

February 2—*Día de la Candelaria.*

February 5—*Día de la Constitución.*

Late February to early March, three days before Ash Wednesday—*Carnaval.* Ensenada and La Paz are worth visiting at this time.

April, from Palm Sunday to Easter Sunday—*Semana Santa.*

May 5—*Cinco de Mayo.*

November 1 and 2—*Día de los Muertos* (Day of the Dead). People visit cemeteries and bake special bread.

December 12—*Día de la Virgen de Guadalupe.*

December 24 and 25—*Día de la Navidad.*

December 31—*Fin de Año.*

Information Sources

Tourism

United States

Mexican Office of Surface Tourism, 2707 North Loop West, Suite 450, Houston, TX 77008; (713) 892-5353 or (800) 662-6394.

Mexican Office of Tourism, 405 Park Avenue, Suite 1401, New York, NY 10022; (212) 838-2949 or fax (212) 753-2874.

Mexican Office of Tourism, 70 East Lake Street, Suite 1413, Chicago, IL 60601; (312) 606-9252 or fax (312) 606-9012.

Canada

Mexican Office of Tourism, 2 Bloor Street West, Suite 1801, Toronto, Ontario M4W 3E2; (416) 925-0704 or fax (416) 925-6061.

Mexican Office of Tourism, 1 Place Villa Marie, Suite 1526, Montreal, Quebec H3B 2B5; (514) 871-1052 or fax (514) 871-3825.

Fishing

Mexican Department of Fisheries, 2550 Fifth Avenue, Suite 101, San Diego, CA 92103; (619) 233-4324.

General Information

Vagabundos del Mar Boat and Travel Club, 190 Main Street, Rio Vista, CA 94571; (707) 374-5511, (800) 474-BAJA, or fax (707) 374-6843. E-mail: VAGS@compuserve.com.

Mexican Consulates

United States

Consular Representative, 480 North Grand Avenue, Nogales, AZ 85621; (520) 287-2521 or fax (520) 287-3175.

Consular Representative, 1990 West Camelback Road #110, Phoenix, AZ 85015; (602) 433-2294 or fax (602) 242-2957.

Consular Representative, 553 South Stone Avenue, Tucson, AZ 85701; (520) 882-5595.

Consulate, 382 Camacho Road, Calexico, CA 92231; (760) 357-3863.

Consulate, 905 North Fulton Street, Fresno, CA 93728; (209) 233-3065 or fax (209) 233-5638.

Consulate, 2401 West Sixth Street, Los Angeles, CA 90057; (213) 351-6800 or fax (213) 389-9186.

Consulate, 201 East Fourth Street, Oxnard, CA 93030; (805) 483-4684.

Consulate, 1010 Eighth Street, Sacramento, CA 95814; (916) 441-3287.

Consular Representative, 588 Sixth Street, San Bernardino, CA 92401, (909) 889-9836 or fax (909) 889-8285.

Consulate General, 1549 India Street, San Diego, CA 92101; (619) 231-8414 or fax (619) 231-4802.

Consulate General, 870 Market Street #528, San Francisco, CA 94102; (415) 392-5554 or fax (415) 392-3233.

Consulate, 380 North First Street #102, San Jose, CA 95112; (408) 294-3414 or fax (408) 294-4506.

Consulate, 828 North Broadway, Santa Ana, CA 92701; (714) 835-3069.

Consular Representative, 48 Steele Street, Denver, CO 80206; (303) 331-1110 or fax (303) 331-1872.

Consulate, 400 O Street Southwest #100, Albuquerque, NM 87102; (505) 247-2139 or fax (505) 842-9490.

Consular Representative, 458 East 200 South, Salt Lake City, UT 84111; (801) 521-8502 or fax (801) 521-0534.

Consular Representative, 2132 Third Avenue, Seattle, WA 98121; (206) 448-3526.

Canada

Consular Representative, 1130 West Pender Street #810, Vancouver, British Columbia V6E 4A4; (604) 684-3547 or fax (604) 684-2485.

Tourist Assistance

Baja California Norte Tourist Assistance Offices

Ensenada: phone 011-52-61-72-3022 from the United States, 91-61-72-3022 within México, or 72-3022 locally.

Mexicali: phone 011-52-65-52-5877 from the United States, 91-65-52-5877 within México, or 52-5877 locally.

Rosarito: phone 011-52-661-2-0200 from the United States, 91-661-2-0200 within México, or 2-0200 locally.

San Felipe: phone 011-52-657-7-1155 or 7-1865 from the United States, 91-657-7-1155 or 7-1865 within México, or 7-1155 or 7-1865 locally.

Tecate: phone 011-52-665-4-1095 from the United States, 91-665-4-1095 within México, or 4-1095 locally.

Tijuana: phone 011-52-66-88-0555 from the United States, 91-66-88-0555 within México, or 88-0555 locally.

Baja California Sur Tourism Office

La Paz: phone 011-52-112-4-0424 from the United States, 91-112-4-0424 within Mexico, or 4-0424 locally; fax 011-52-112-4-0768 from the United States, 91-112-4-0768 within México, or 4-0768 locally.

American Consulates

Consulate General, Tapachula 96, Tijuana, Baja California, México; 011-52-66-81-7400 or fax 011-52-66-81-8016. Write to: P.O. Box 439039, San Diego, CA 92143.

Consular Agent, Boulevard Marina de Pedregal, Local #3, Cabo San Lucas, Baja California Sur, México; 011-52-114-3-3566.

Kayaking excursions are a great way to get a new perspective of the coast—and have fun while you're at it.

Index

About the Authors

Fred and **Gloria Jones** have traveled extensively throughout Baja for many years. They have driven their camper from one end of the peninsula to the other innumerable times, explored off-highway in a four-wheel-drive truck, cruised both coasts in their boat, hiked and ridden horseback in remote mountain terrain, and scrutinized it all from the air. They have slept out in the open on the ground, in tents, truck campers, and boats. They have camped in the highest mountains and the deepest canyons, on beaches on Sea of Cortéz islands and along both coasts, and at campgrounds across the region.

Explorers, scuba divers, big-game fishermen, and naturalists, the couple has a deep and abiding interest in the history, archaeology, people, and culture of Baja California. Both have been active in the Commission of the Californias, a former coordinating body between the governments of California, Baja California Norte, and Baja California Sur, contributing their expertise on tourism and natural resources.

The Joneses currently manage a nonprofit travel club with 10,000-plus members that has specialized in Baja travel for more than 30 years—Vagabundos del Mar. Fred is vice president and general manager, and Gloria is on the board of directors. He has had substantial experience managing campgrounds as director of the California Department of Parks and Recreation, which is responsible for the State Park System. Gloria shared that experience as assistant to the director.

Between them, these award-winning freelance writers and photographers have coauthored two books besides this one (*A Climber's Guide to the High Sierra* and *The Desert Bighorn—Its Life History, Ecology and Management*); contributed to a compilation of hair-raising outdoor experiences in the book *No S— There I Was*; served as field editors for *Western Boatman Magazine* and conservation editors for *Baja Explorer Magazine*; authored numerous professional publications on wildlife, natural resources, parks, and recreation; and contributed many outdoor features and columns to newspapers and national and regional magazines. Both are members of the Outdoor Writers Associations of America and California. Gloria is currently president of the latter organization.

FOGHORN ⌒ OUTDOORS

Founded in 1985, Foghorn Press has quickly become one of the country's premier publishers of outdoor recreation guidebooks. Through its unique Books Building Community program, Foghorn Press supports community environmental issues, such as park, trail, and water ecosystem preservation.

Foghorn Press books are available throughout the United States in bookstores and some outdoor retailers. If you cannot find the title you are looking for, visit Foghorn's Web site at http://www.foghorn.com or call 1-800-FOGHORN.

The Complete Guide Series

- *California Camping* (848 pp) $20.95—New 10th edition
- *California Hiking* (688 pp) $20.95—New 3rd edition
- *California Waterfalls* (408 pp) $17.95
- *California Fishing* (768 pp) $20.95—New 4th edition
- *California Golf* (864 pp) $20.95—New 7th edition
- *California Beaches* (640 pp) $19.95
- *California Boating and Water Sports* (608 pp) $19.95
- *California In-Line Skating* (480 pp) $19.95
- *Tahoe* (678 pp) $20.95—New 2nd edition
- *Pacific Northwest Camping* (720 pp) $19.95
- *Pacific Northwest Hiking* (648 pp) $20.95—New 2nd edition
- *Washington Fishing* (528 pp) $19.95
- *Alaska Fishing* (448 pp) $20.95—New 2nd edition
- *New England Hiking* (416 pp) $18.95
- *New England Camping* (520 pp) $19.95
- *Utah and Nevada Camping* (384 pp) $18.95
- *Southwest Camping* (544 pp) $17.95

The National Outdoors Series

- *America's Secret Recreation Areas—Your Recreation Guide to the Bureau of Land Management's Wild Lands of the West* (640 pp) $17.95
- *America's Wilderness—The Complete Guide to More Than 600 National Wilderness Areas* (592 pp) $19.95
- *The Camper's Companion—The Pack-Along Guide for Better Outdoor Trips* (464 pp) $15.95
- *Wild Places: 20 Journeys Into the North American Outdoors* (305 pp) $15.95

A book's page length and availability are subject to change.

For more information, call 1-800-FOGHORN,
e-mail: foghorn@well.com, or write to:
Foghorn Press
340 Bodega Avenue
Petaluma, CA 94952

Baja Chapter Reference Map

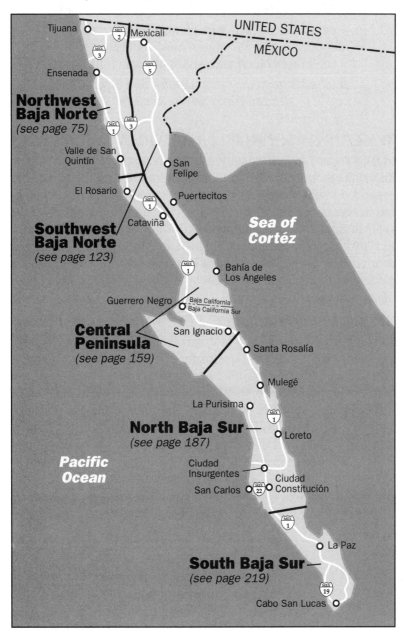

Tijuana
Mexicali
MEX 2
MEX 3
UNITED STATES
MÉXICO
Ensenada
MEX 5

Northwest Baja Norte
(see page 75)
MEX 1
MEX 3

Valle de San Quintín
San Felipe
El Rosario
Puertecitos
Cataviña

Southwest Baja Norte
(see page 123)
MEX 1

Sea of Cortéz

MEX 1
Bahía de Los Angeles
Guerrero Negro
Baja California
Baja California Sur

Central Peninsula
(see page 159)
San Ignacio
Santa Rosalía
Mulegé
La Purisima
MEX 1

North Baja Sur
(see page 187)
Loreto

Pacific Ocean

Ciudad Insurgentes
San Carlos
MEX 22
Ciudad Constitución
MEX 1

La Paz

South Baja Sur
(see page 219)
MEX 19
Cabo San Lucas